The Nondramatic Works of
BEN JONSON

a reference guide

A
Reference
Guide
to
Literature

Everett Emerson
Editor

The Nondramatic Works of
BEN JONSON
a reference guide

DAVID C. JUDKINS

G.K. HALL & CO.

70 LINCOLN STREET, BOSTON, MASS.

Library of Congress Cataloging in Publication Data

Judkins, David C., 1938-
   The nondramatic works of Ben Jonson.

   Bibliography.
   Includes index.
   1.   Jonson, Ben, 1573?-1637—Bibliography.
I.   Title.
Z8456.6.J83   [PR2631]   016.822'3   81-7257
ISBN 0-8161-8036-9   AACR2

This publication is printed on permanent/durable acid-free paper
MANUFACTURED IN THE UNITED STATES OF AMERICA

Contents

The Author

David Judkins received his Ph.D. from Michigan State University. A former Fulbright Fellow, he has written a number of articles including "Recent Studies in the Cavalier Poets," which appeared in English Literary Renaissance. Professor Judkins is currently Associate Professor of English at the University of Houston.

Preface

The Reference Guide is arranged in chronological order according
to the year of publication, or in the case of some earlier items, the
year a manuscript is dated. Within the year of publication all items
are alphabetized by the author or editor's last name. There are no
subdivisions by books, articles, etc. The Reference Guide lists crit-
ical/biographical/bibliographical books or portions of books, articles,
notes, reviews, theses, and dissertations. I have not systematically
listed editions of Jonson's prose and poetry; however, many are included because of their critical introductions.

Reprints of the latest and/or most reliable editions or reissues
of items are listed. Every reissue or reprint of every item is not
included. For instance, Robert Herrick's three poems on Jonson are
first listed in 1648 when Hesperidies was published. Although the
poems have probably been reprinted over one hundred times, only L. C.
Martin's 1956 edition of The Complete Works of Robert Herrick is noted.
Except in special cases page numbers are not included in reprint information. An asterisk preceding the entry number designates an item
that was not available for examination.

Since generic divisions within the discipline of English literature have traditionally been accepted, I make no apology for separating
Jonson's nondramatic from his dramatic work in the Reference Guide.
However, Jonson himself certainly did not in his own mind always keep
the two areas separate. Some of his most famous lyrics are from his
plays, and portions of his criticism are embedded in his dramas.
Studies of his prose style almost always include his dramatic prose
as well as Discoveries, and although his connection with Shakespeare
is largely of interest to students of drama, his most complete statement on Shakespeare is in his poem, "To the Memory of My Beloved,
The Author, Mr. William Shakespeare." With these qualifications in
mind I have tried to take a common sense, nonpedantic approach to the
question of what to include or not include. I have tried to keep the
reader's interest in mind by listing all items that I believe will be
useful to the student of Jonson's nondramatic work. By the same to-
ken the annotations should not be read as mini abstracts. Rather
they are included for guidance to help the reader decide whether or
not the book or article would be useful to him.

Introduction

In 1889 Alfred Waites argued that Jonson had written Bacon's
Essays and other prose works. Pointing out parallelisms between
Jonson's prose and Bacon's, he speculated that Bacon had been instru-
mental in securing Jonson's release from prison after he had killed
Gabriel Spencer in a duel. To repay the debt Jonson agreed to become
Bacon's ghost writer. But perhaps most important, Waites reasoned
that a man of Jonson's recognized genius must have written more prose
than the slender volume, Timber or Discoveries, printed posthumously.
While Waites argued for this change of authorship, others maintained
that Bacon, Marlow, or someone else had written all or most of Shakespeare's plays for almost exactly the opposite reason. A man with
only a basic education from a small provincial town was simply incapable of turning into a literary, creative genius. Shakespeare of
Stratford was pictured as an illiterate yokel at worst, a competent
actor at best. Jonson, on the other hand, was an imposing, some would
even say intimidating, figure, for his time. His admirers regard him
as the father of English criticism and the founder of the neoclassic
mode of poetry. He attempted to define the poet's role in society,
and more important to him, he attempted to define society itself
through an idealistic neoconservatism. We are captivated by his
strength, his aggressiveness, and his willingness to wade into any
kind of scrap or quarrel. Though he also lacked the benefit of a
university education, the depth and breadth of his learning was vast.
Yet his own work, his poetry, drama, masques, and prose, give many
readers, including T. S. Eliot and Edmund Wilson, the picture of only
a potentially great writer, who for one reason or another never quite
broke through, who never produced what a man of his level of genius
should be capable of producing. There are the recognized flashes of
brilliance, but there is no sustained great work much less body of
work. Waites believed he had solved the problem. Bacon plus Jonson
equaled undisputed greatness of the highest order. Unfortunately, if
one is an admirer of Jonson, Waites' arguments seem at least naive if
not actually preposterous. More recently scholars and critics have
taken a different approach. Instead of enlarging Jonson's canon, they
have been reassessing and reinterpreting his acknowledged work--par-
ticularly his poetry and prose. It is not, they suggest, that Jonson
did not live up to his potential, but that we fail for a variety of

reasons to recognize his true greatness. Cultural differences are
cited. We do not understand the poetry of praise. The plain style
is less in tune with modern taste. And then there is the question of
imitation.

Jonson practiced the Renaissance art of imitation more than most
other writers. Timber or Discoveries is a collection of free prose
translations of excerpts from classical and a few contemporary sources,
in a commonplace book found among his papers after his death and first
published in the Workes (1640). Some critics over the years have
accused Jonson of plagiarism, but most scholars maintain that from a
variety of sources Jonson borrowed material that he shaped according
to his own unique English manner. All the ideas incapsulated in the
carefully wrought paragraphs in Discoveries originated elsewhere, and
in many cases the phrasing itself is largely borrowed. This knowledge
may reduce some readers' enjoyment of the book and lower Jonson in
their estimation. Others, recognizing that what Jonson did was accepted practice for his time, will thank him for gathering, loosely
translating and organizing these memorable passages. Comparing it to
Bacon's Essays, some critics, notably Swinburne, have found Discoveries
the finest thing Jonson did.

Besides this prose, Jonson wrote plays and masques (not my concern
here) and a body of remarkable poetry. Epigrammes and The Forrest
were published in 1616. Under-wood was published in 1640 after his
death. A fairly large quantity of poetry was not collected until
later. Jonson's poetry is capable of carrying readers on flights of
lyric beauty and dragging them through sewers of gross scatology. To
say that his style, versification, and subject matter are varied is
a monumental understatement. He is most often a social and occasional poet, but he can be very private; and not very well hidden within
all his lines lies his massive ego. His moral didacticism is exasper-
ating, particularly when we remember that he was an alcoholic, poet
laureate to one of the most viciously corrupt courts in British history, and author of two masques and an epithlamion for the scandalous
marriage of Lady Francis Howard and Sir Robert Carr, Earl of Somerset.
Yet he wrote stinging, haughty epigrams on those whom he considered
fools, imposters, flatterers, and corrupters. It might even be suggested that Jonson cultivated the pedantic, heavily classical aspect
of his writing, to ingratiate himself to James I, who, of course, took
great pride in his own scholarship.

On occasions Jonson could be warm, gracious, and generous in his
praise. "To Penhurst" begins the development of a new type of poem
that constitutes one of the most interesting subgenres in seventeenth
century poetry and is a frequent topic of comment by critics. His
epitaphs on his son and daughter are deeply moving tributes to his
children. "Inviting a Friend to Supper," "An Epistle Answering to
One that Asked to be Sealed of the Tribe of Ben," and "To the Immortal
Memory and Friendship of that Noble Pair, Sir Lucius Cary and Sir H.
Morison" may well be the finest celebrations of friendship in Renais-

sance English poetry. But, and this may seem a complete paradox, the overriding impression of Jonson is that he was a man of contention and controversy.

A self-styled literary dictator, he held forth with his "tribe" or his "sons" in the Apollo room of the Old Devil Tavern or at numerous other watering holes in London. Although there is no record of these meetings, we do get a sense of Jonson's contentious and opinionated nature from William Drummond's Conversations, the notes made by Drummond of Hawthornden in 1619 when Jonson visited him in Scotland. Jonson says, among other things, that "Sidney did not keep decorum. . . . Spenser's stanzas pleased him not. . . . Samuel Daniel was a good and honest man, had no children, but not a Poet." His remark on Donne is more famous: "Donne for not keeping of accent deserved hanging." His comment on Shakespeare, that "he wanted art," is even more famous. The interpretations of these Conversations have themselves given rise to considerable dispute. Is Jonson irascible, egotistical, not to mention gluttonous and drunken; or is Drummond excessively reserved, snobbish, perhaps effete? In other words, are the Conversations the frustrated outpourings of a host whose home has been invaded by a famous but boring free-loading ego-maniac? Or does Drummond simply not appreciate the spirit of Jonson?

Jonson's contentious nature can also be seen in his response to the unfavorable reactions to some of his plays. In 1629 when The New Inn was literally booed off the boards, Jonson wrote an "Ode to Himself," in which he vowed to "leave the loathed stage." The poem spawned seven poetic responses which have come down to us today. Some are friendly, comforting, and reassuring. Others ask why Jonson cannot take a measure of the criticism he has so generously served to others. Later in 1633 after the production of The Magnetic Lady another poetic exchange occurred. A minor poet and playwright, Alexander Gill, wrote:

> And yet thou crazy wretch art confident
> Belching out full-mouth'd oather with foule intent
> Calling us fools and rogues unlettered men
> Poor narrow souls that cannot judge of Ben.

And Jonson answered in kind:

> Thinking to stir me, thou hast lost thy End,
> I'll laugh at thee poor wretched Tike, go send
> Thy blatant Muse abroad, and teach it rather
> A Tune to drown the Ballads of thy Father:
> For thou hast nought (in thee) to cure his Fame,
> But Tune and Noise the Eccho of thy Shame.

The most memorable and certainly the longest conflict was Jonson's well-known dispute with Inigo Jones, architect for James and Charles and designer of the court entertainments and masques. Although Jonson could not have been an easy man to work with on any kind of cooperative venture, their argument seems to have taken on the character of a classic conflict over the relative merits of content and form. Jonson insisted on the sovereignty of the script, the poetry, the content. Jones argued for the primacy of the pageant, the production, the form. In the end Jones won, and Tomas Carew, Jonson's young friend, was given the job of writing masques.

Jonson died when he was sixty-five. He was bedridden, partially paralyzed, alcoholic. By many accounts he had become a miserable, cantankerous, stubborn, stroke-infeebled old man. Yet there followed his death an outpouring of poetic tributes reserved normally for royalty. The incongruities he nourished during his life followed him to the grave, and continue to surface periodically as critics comment on his work, and both foster and reinforce our sense of the contentious spirit of the man and the spirit of contention and dispute on which he believed that criticism must rest. Nevertheless, in the seventeenth century Jonson was so venerated that when Dryden raised a question about his work, he was forced publicly to defend his right to challenge Jonson's authority.

Thus the picture that begins to emerge is that of a very complex man. Assertive and self-assured, he seems to have attracted the loyalty and devotion of poets and scholars not only his own age, but in many cases men much younger. Yet his work is, to say the least, imitative. It lacks the emotion and excitement which filled his own life. He is often regarded as a highly competent craftsman, though not a great writer. And we expect more from a man who demanded so much of others. If we must submit to this extraordinary ego, we expect some benefits--more than a mere dozen lyrics or some translated homilies from the ancients. Many critics say there is more. Jonson has done his part; we are just not doing ours. And Alfred Waites says there was much more; Jonson just signed his friend's name to it. Would that it were so. Then we would be spared introductions to his work in which it is argued that modern readers do not understand his genius, and we would no longer see yet another call for reevaluation of his work.

Jonson has received his due. He has been given the benefit of perhaps the finest editorial work on an English writer in the twentieth century. The eleven-volume edition of Jonson by C. H. Herford and Percy and Evelyn Simpson required some fifty years of concentrated effort. His straightforward, rather plain poems have received the full benefit of contemporary explicative criticism, and his classical sources have been exhaustively retraced. But this is not to say that there is no further reason to study Jonson or that there is nothing more to say about him. As students come to his verse and prose they will find a writer of limited genius but nonetheless worth reading both for his own sake and for gaining a sense of the continuity of English verse. And there will always be critics who, following the Jonsonian tradition, are willing to take an unpopular, perhaps not thoroughly defensible position, to give us a new reading of an established author.

Acknowledgments

More and more often bibliographies, even annotated bibliographies, are being compiled by computers. This volume was put together by a person with the help of others whom I wish to acknowledge. First, I should recognize other bibliographers whose work I have drawn on. S. A. Tannenbaum did the pioneer work in Jonsonian bibliography with Ben Jonson: A Concise Bibliography (1938). This work was updated and supplemented with the help of Dorothy R. Tannenbaum in Supplement to a Concise Bibliography of Ben Jonson (1947). Professor George Guffey updated their work in 1968 with "Ben Jonson," in Supplements to Elizabethan Bibliographies. In addition D. Heyward Brock and James M. Welsh's Ben Jonson: A Quadricentennial Bibliography, 1947-1972 has been very helpful. I would also like to thank three graduate students who have assisted me in this project. Mary Walker helped me organize and plan the research. Later Judy Wenzel did much of the work on the index. Gary Myers deserves special thanks for his help and support during the major part of my work.

Abbreviations

AN&Q	American Notes and Queries
Archiv	Archiv für das Studium der neueren Sprachen
ArQ	Arizona Quarterly
BC	Book Collector
BYUS	Brigham Young University Studies
CCC	College Composition and Communication
CE	College English
CEA	College English Association Critic
CJ	Classical Journal
CL	Comparative Literature
CLAJ	College Language Association Journal (Morgan State College)
CP	Concerning Poetry
CQ	Cambridge Quarterly
CR	The Critical Review
CritQ	Critical Quarterly
DalR	Dalhousie Review
EA	Etudes Anglaises
E&S	Essays and Studies by Members of the English Association

Abbreviations

EIC	Essays in Criticism (Oxford)
ELH	English Literary History
ELN	English Language Notes (University of Colorado)
ELR	English Literary Renaissance
ELWIU	Essays in Literature (Western Ill. Univ.)
EM	English Miscellany
ES	English Studies
EWR	East-West Review (Doshisha Univ., Kyoto, Japan)
Expl	Explicator
FP	Filoloski Pregled (Belgrade)
GHJ	George Herbert Journal
HLQ	Huntington Library Quarterly
JEGP	Journal of English and Germanic Philology
JWCI	Journal of the Warburg and Courtauld Institute
LCUT	Library Chronicle University of Texas
LGRP	Literaturblatt Fuer Germanische und Romanische Philologie
MLN	Modern Language Notes
MLQ	Modern Language Quarterly
MLR	Modern Language Review
ModA	Modern Age
MP	Modern Philology
N&Q	Notes and Queries
NDEJ	Notre Dame English Journal

Abbreviations

Neophil	Neophilologus (Groningen)
NEQ	New England Quarterly
NLauR	New Laurel Review
NM	Neuphilologische Mitteilungen
NMQ	New Mexico Quarterly
NY	New Yorker
PBSA	Papers of the Bibliographic Society of America
PLL	Papers in Language and Literature
PMLA	Publications of the Modern Language Association
PQ	Philological Quarterly
QJS	Quarterly Journal of Speech
QQ	Queen's Quarterly
ReAL	RE/Antes Liberales
REL	Review of English Literature (Leeds)
Ren&R	Renaissance and Reformation
RenP	Renaissance Papers
RES	Review of English Studies
RLC	Revue de Littérature Comparée
RLST	Rackham Literary Studies
RMS	Renaissance and Modern Studies
RN	Renaissance News
RORD	Research Opportunities in Renaissance Drama
RQ	Renaissance Quarterly
SAQ	South Atlantic Quarterly

Abbreviations

SatR	Saturday Review (Eng. indicates English publication but is used only during those years both English and American periodicals were published under this title.)
SB	Studies in Bibliography
SCN	Seventeenth-Century News
SEL	Studies in English Literature, 1500–1900
SELit	Studies in English Literature (English Literary Society of Japan)
ShakS	Shakespeare Studies
ShN	Shakespeare Newsletter
ShS	Shakespeare Survey
SJH	Shakespeare-Jahrbuch (Heidelbert)
SLI	Studies in Literary Imagination
SMS	Studier i Modern Sprakvetenskap
SP	Studies in Philology
SQ	Shakespeare Quarterly
SR	Sewanee Review
SRen	Studies in the Renaissance
TLS	Times Literary Supplement
TSLL	Texas Studies in Language and Literature
UCSLL	University of Colorado Studies in Language and Literature
UES	Unisa English Studies
UTQ	University of Toronto Quarterly
VQR	Virginia Quarterly Review
YCGL	Yearbook Comparative and General Literature

Abbreviations

YES   Yearbook of English Studies

YR   Yale Review

Writings about Ben Jonson, 1615-1978

1615

1   C., R. "Scribimus indocti doctique epigrammata passim." In
    "The Times' Whistle." Canterbury: Library of Canterbury.
    MS y. 8. 3.
        In this short epigram the author, who had apparently
    seen Jonson's Epigrams in manuscript, since they were not
    printed until 1616, is highly critical of Jonson: he
    should abandon the writing of epigrams and go back to the
    stage. "Peruse his book, thou shalt not find a dram/Of
    wit befitting a true epigram." Published in 1871.1;
    1922.4, 1969.4.

1616

1   ANTON, ROBERT. The Philosophers Satyrs. London: printed by
    T. C. Reed and B. A. Isop for R. Jackson, sig. L4v.
        An early, short reference to Jonson noting his labored
    though beautiful lyric style. Reprinted in 1952.7.

2   D., I. "Amicissimo, & Meritissimo Ben: Jonson." In The
    Works of Benjamin Jonson. London: printed by Will
    Stansby, sig.¶ 6r.
        A Latin commendatory poem at the beginning of Jonson's
    Works, it praises Jonson for his morality and versification.
    Reprinted in 1952.7.

3   HEYWARD, EDWARD. "To Ben Jonson, on His Works." In The Works
    of Benjamin Jonson. London: printed by Will Stansby,
    sig.¶ 4v.
        Praises Jonson for, among other things, his grace and
    art. Reprinted in 1952.7

1617

1   BOLTON, EDMUND. "Hypercritica." In Rawlinson Misc. MS 1.
      Oxford: Bodleian Library.
         An early, perceptive comment on Jonson's poetry. Bolton
      does not develop his point or support his argument, but
      like many other seventeenth-century critics, just makes a
      statement. "I never tasted English more to my liking, nor
      more smart, and put to the height of use in poetry, than
      in the vital, judicious, and most practicable language
      of Ben Jonson's poems." Published in 1815.1.

2   DAVIES, JOHN of Hereford. "To my learnedly witty friend,
      Mr. Benjamin Jonson." In Wits Bedlam. London: G. Eld.,
      sig. K2.
         A short epigram which praises Jonson for his witty
      though thoughtful prose and verse. Reprinted in 1878.2.

1620

1   JONES, INIGO. "To his false friend Mr. Ben Jonson." In
      Harleian MS 6057 fol. 30. London: British Museum.
         The date of this item is uncertain, but it was written
      sometime after Jonson returned from his trip to Scotland in
      1619. In this forty-two-line poem Jones complains of the
      way in which Jonson has treated him and then attacks his
      writing.

>   ". . . I confess with like for thou has writ
>   of good and bad things, not with equal wit.
>   The reason is, or may be quickly showne
>   the good's translation, but the ill's thine own."

      Published in 1952.7.

1627

1   DRAYTON, MICHAEL. "To My Most Dearley-Loved Friend Henry
      Reynolds Esquire, of Poets and Poesie." In The Battaile
      of Agincourt. London: printed for William Lee, p. 207.
         Complimentary lines making note of Jonson's learning
      and knowledge. Reprinted in 1932.4.

1629

1   ANON. "The Cuntry's Censure on Ben Jonson's New Inn." In
      Ashmole MS 38. Oxford: Bodleian Library, pp. 79-80.

Jonson wrote "Ode to Himself" following the poor recep-
tion of his play The New Inn. In the poem Jonson blames
the public's vulgar taste and dullness for the play's fail-
ure. Seven poets responded to Jonson's poem. Their responses are listed under the years in which they were published or dated except for those which were only recently
published. These are listed under 1629, when they were
most likely written. See also 1631.1; 1638.3; 1640.2-3;
1661.1.

The above is a vicious satire and parody on Jonson's
poem. It is indicative of the violent reactions Jonson
could inspire.

> "Thy Pegasus can stirr, yet thy best care
> Makes her but shuffle; like the parson's mare
> Who from his own side wit says thus by me:
> He hath bequeath'd his belly unto thee
> To hold that little learning which is fled
> Into thy gut from out thy empty head."

Published in 1952.7.

2 GOODWIN, R. "Vindiciae Jonsonianae." In Harleian MS 4955.
   London: British Museum.
      A poem of general praise for Jonson and his work. Pub-
   lished in 1912.3.

1631

1 POLWEHELE, JOHN. "To the admired Ben Jonson to encourage him
   to write after his farewel to the stage. 1631. alludinge
   to Horace ode 26. Lib. I. Musis amicus &c." In MS
   "Poems of John Polwehle." Privately owned by Mr. Percy J.
   Dobell (as of 1952).
      Reassurance for Jonson that his poetic powers have not
   left him. Published in 1952.7.

1632

1 CARY, LUCIUS, VISCOUNT FALKLAND. "An Epistle to his Noble
   father, Mr. Jonson," and "An Anniversary Epistle on Sir
   Henry Morison, with an Apostrophe to My Father. Jonson."
   In Harleian MS 4955. London: British Museum.
      Falkland was probably the noblest member of the informal
   group known as Jonson's "sons." The first poem above is
   full of general praise with allusions to specific works.
   The second poem refers to Jonson's poem, "To the immortall
   memorie, and friendship of that noble paire, Sir Lucius
   Cary and Sir H. Morison." Published in 1912.4.

1633

1   GILL, ALEXANDER. "To B. Jonson on his Magnetic Lady." In
       Ashmole MS 38, p. 15. Oxford: Ashmolean Museum.
           Although this poem is specifically directed toward Jon-
       son's play, it contains bitter criticism of Jonson himself
       and his other writings.

> "And yet thou crazy wretch art confident
> Belching out full-mouth'd oather with foule intent
> Calling us fools and rogues unlettered men
> Poor narrow souls that cannot judge of Ben."

       Zouch Townley and Jonson himself wrote responses.
       Published in 1912.1; 1952.7.

2   TOWNLEY, ZOUCH. "To Mr. Ben Jonson against Mr. Alexander
       Gills verses Wrighten by hym against the play called
       Magnettick Ladye." In Ashmole MS 38 (6907), p. 58. Oxford:
       Ashmolean Museum.
           Townley does not deal with any of the issues raised by
       Gill, but rather he casts disparagement upon Gill for having
       written such a poem. Published in 1912.1; 1952.7.

1634

1   ANON. "To Mr. Jonson." In Harleian MS 6917, fol. 100b. Lon-
       don: British Museum.
           This obscure poem refers to the problems Jonson had
       collecting his pension. Generally the writer seems to
       praise Jonson for his poetic abilities and urges him to
       rise above the petty people and petty concerns. Published
       in 1952.7.

2   ANON. Untitled. In Harleian MS 4955, fol. 84. London: Brit-
       ish Museum.
           A short poem which notes Jonson's heavy drinking, ill
       health, and difficulties in collecting his pension. Pub-
       lished in 1842.1

3   CHAPMAN, GEORGE. "An Invective of Mr. George Chapman against
       Mr. Ben: Jonson." In Ashmole MS 38, pp. 16-18. Oxford:
       Bodleian Library.
           A bitter though unfinished poem written as if were dic-
       tated from Chapman's death bed. Though Jonson and Chapman
       had been friends, they quarreled when Jonson and Inigo
       Jones had their disagreements.
           For a full discussion of the importance and dating of
       his poem see 1941.2, pp. 374-78. Published in 1941.2

1635

1   HEYWOOD, THOMAS. "A Panegerick to the worthy Mr. Robert Dover."
    In Annalia Dubrensia, by Michael Drayton et al. London:
    printed by Robert Raworth, for Mathew Walbancke, sig. Kr.
        Jonson and Drayton are linked as the two most notable
    poets in England. Reprinted in 1973.16.

1638

1   DAVENANT, WILLIAM. "To Doctor Duppa, Deane of Christ Church,
    and Tutor to the Prince. An acknowledgement for his col-
    lection on honour of Ben. Jonson's memory." In Madagascar;
    with Other Poems. London: John Haviland for Thomas
    Walkley, pp. 138-41.
        A tribute to Duppa for his work in compiling the poems
    for Jonsonus Virbius cited below.

2   DUPPA, BRYAN, comp. Jonsonus virbius; or the Memoire of B. J.
    Revived. London: printed by E. P. for Henry Seile, 74 pp.
        Commemorative poems on the death of Jonson by the follow-
    ing poets: Lucius Cary, Viscount Falkland; Richard Sack-
    ville, Lord Buckhurst; Sir John Beaumont; Sir Thomas Haw-
    kins; Henry King; Henry Coventry; Thomas May; Dudley Diggs;
    George Fortescue; William Habington; Edmund Waller; James
    Howell; John Vernon; John Cleveland; Jasper Mayne; William
    Cartwright; Joseph Rutter; Owen Feltham; George Donne;
    Shackerley Marmion; John Ford; Ralph Brideoake; Richard
    West; Robert Meade; H. Ramsay; Sir Francis Wortley;
    Thomas Tereent; Robert Waring; William Bew; and Samuel
    Evans. Two poems are unsigned. Interesting though largely
    predictable in their veneration of Jonson. Henry King's is
    perhaps the least ceremonial and most personal. Reprinted
    in 1952.7.

3   RANDOLPH, THOMAS. "A gratulatory to Mr. Ben Jonson for his
    adopting of him to be his Son;" "An answer to Mr. Ben Jon-
    son's Ode to persuade him not to leave the stage"; and "An
    eglogue to Mr. Jonson." In Poems with the Muses Looking-
    glasse: and Amyntas. Oxford: printed by L. Lichfield for
    F. Bowman, pp. 22-23, 71-73, 97-102.
        Published after Randolph died at the age of thirty in
    1634. A devoted follower of Jonson, he could apparently
    see no faults in his mentor. Though the poems are full of
    praise, they do not reach the heights of effusion of lesser
    poets. Reprinted in 1929.10.

1639

1   BANCROFT, THOMAS. "To Ben Jonson," and "To the Same." In
     Two Books of Epigrams and Epitaphs. London: printed by
     J. Oakes for M. Wlabancke, sig. Blr.
         Poems combine a degree of personal introspection with
     the style of the public epigram. After showing some envy
     for Jonson in the first poem, Bancroft writes in the
     second:

         "Let ignorance with envy chat,
         In spite of both, thou fame dost win,
         Whose messe of Learning seems like that,
         Which Joseph gave to Benjamin.

     Reprinted in 1922.4.

1640

1   ANON. "To Mr. Benjamin Jonson"; "B. J. approbation of a copy
     of verses"; "To Mr. Ben Jonson demanding the reason why he
     call'd his plays works"; "B. J. answer to a Thief bidding
     him stand"; "Thiefs reply"; "On Ben: Jonson"; "Another on
     Ben: J"; and "The Virtue of Sack." In Wits Recreations,
     with a thousand outlandish proverbs. Compiled by G. H[er-
     bert]. London: printed by R. H[odgkinson].
         These epigrams and epitaphs make references to Jonson's
     personal and literary reputation. They are gently humor-
     ous and show respect but not reverence for Jonson.
     Reprinted in 1663.1; 1874.1

2   CAREW, THOMAS. "To Ben Jonson. Upon occasion of his Ode of
     defiance annext to his Play of the new Inne." In Poems.
     London: printed by J. D. for T. Walkley, pp. 108-10.
         Supports Jonson's view of public taste and attempts to
     console the poet but questions why Jonson should be sur-
     prised at the response which he received considering the
     source of that response. Reprinted in 1949.2.

3   C., I. "Ode. To Ben Jonson Upon his Ode to himself." In
     Q Horatius Flaccus: His Art of Poetry Englished by Ben
     Jonson. London: printed by J. Oakes, sigs. A10v-A12v.
         Although this poem has been attributed to John Cleveland,
     his most recent editors, Morris and Withington, do not
     accept the attribution. The poet supports Jonson and joins
     in the satirical tone attacking public taste. He ends with
     fulsome praise for Jonson. Reprinted in 1952.7.

4 DODDRIDGE, RICHARD. Untitled poem prefixed to <u>Sicily and</u>
   <u>Naples, or the Fatall Union</u>, by Samuel Harding. Oxford:
   W. Turner, sig. Av.
      Addressed to Samuel Harding, who is favorably compared
   to Jonson and Thomas Randolph. Reprinted in 1922.4

5 DOWNEY, NICHOLAS. Untitled poem prefixed to <u>Sicily and Naples,</u>
   <u>or the Fatall Union</u>, by Samuel Harding. Oxford: W. Turner, sig. A2v.
      Compares and contrasts Jonson to Samuel Harding.
   Reprinted in 1922.4.

6 HERBERT, EDWARD, Lord HERBERT of CHERBURY. "Upon his friend
   Mr. Ben: Jonson, and his Translation." In <u>Q Horatius</u>
   <u>Flaccus: His Art of Poetry Englished by Ben Jonson</u>.
   London: printed by J. Oakes, sig. A7r.

      A commemorative epigram on Jonson's translation.
      "Twas not enough, Ben: Jonson to be thought
         Of English Poets best, but to have brought
      In greater state, to their acquaintance, one
         Made equal to himself and thee; that none
      Might be thy second: while thy glory is
         To be the Horace of our times and his."

   Reprinted in 1923.7.

7 HODGSON, WILLIAM. "On the Author, The Poet Laureat, Ben Jonson." In <u>The Workes of Benjamin Jonson</u>. Vol. 1. London:
   printed by Richard Bishop for Andrew Crooke, sig. A4r.
      A dedicatory poem of unbridled praise for Jonson. "For
   lyric sweetness in an ode, or sonnet,/To Ben the best of
   all wits might veil their bonnet." Reprinted in 1952.7.

8 HOLYDAY, BARTON. "To Ben Jonson." In <u>Q Horatius Flaccus:</u>
   <u>His Art of Poetry Englished by Ben Jonson</u>. London: printed
   by J. Oakes, sigs. A7v-A9v.
      Extended praise for Jonson's translation suggesting that
   he has actually improved upon Horace.

9 TOWNLEY, ZOUCH. "To Mr. Jonson." In <u>Q Horatius Flaccus: His</u>
   <u>Art of Poetry Englished by Ben Jonson</u>. London: printed
   by J. Oakes, sig. A10r.
      Praises Jonson for, among other things, "his learned
   sweat that makes a language clean."

<u>1643</u>

1 GLAPTHORNE, HENRY. White-Hall. A Poem Written 1642. London:
   printed for Francis Constable, sig. B2v.

1643

> In a vision the poet sees Jonson
> "Up to the chin in the Pierian flood
> Quaffing crowned bowls of Nectar with his bays
> Growing about his temples. . . ."

Reprinted in 1874.3

2   HOWELL, JAMES. "To My Father Mr. Ben: Jonson," and "To my honoured friend and fa. Mr. B. Jonson," In Epistolae Ho-Elainae. London: printed for Humphrey Moseley, pp. 22-23, 34-36.
    In the first letter Howell speaks mainly about Jonson's plays, but he recognizes in him a creative spirit, a kind of "madness" or "true Enthusiasm." In the second letter Howell relates some court gossip touching on the quarrel between Jonson and Jones. Reprinted in 1892.3.

1646

1   DANIEL, GEORGE. "Jonson and his peers"; "To the Memorie of the Best Dramaticke English Poet Ben: Jonson"; and "Upon Ben Jonsons Booke," In "Poems Written upon Severall Occasions." Additional MS 19255, fol. 12, fols. 24-25. London: British Museum.
    Daniel was not one of Jonson's "sons" nor does it appear that he was even acquainted with the poet; nevertheless, he obviously admired Jonson very much. Selected reprints in 1878.1; 1952.7; 1959.6.

2   SUCKLING, Sir John. "A Sessions of the Poets." In Fragmenta Aurea. London: printed for Humphrey Moseley, p. 13.
    Suckling's famous satirical jab at what he considered Jonson's pretentiousness.

> "The first that broke the silence was good old Ben,
> Prepared before with canary wine,
> And he told them plainly he deserved the bays,
> For his were called works, where others were but plays."

Reprinted 1971.19.

1647

1   BEAUMONT, FRANCIS. "Mr. Francis Beaumont's Letter to Ben Jonson. . . ." In Comedies and Tragedies. London: printed for Humphrey Robinson and Humphrey Moseley, sigs. Xxx3r-Xxx4r.

In this letter, which may have been written as early as 1608, Beaumont laments his separation from Jonson's circle; he particularly misses the witty exchanges which made up their conversations. Reprinted in 1912.2.

2 _____, and FLETCHER, JOHN. Comedies and Tragedies.
London: printed for Humphrey Robinson and Humphrey Moseley, sigs. ar-gr.
Numerous dedicatory verses by contemporaries such as Denham, Howell, and Cartwright mention Jonson's contributions to English poetry and compare him to Beaumont and Fletcher.

3 HOWELL, JAMES. "To Mr. B. J.," and "To Sir Tho. Hawk, Knight." In A New Volume of Familiar Letters. London: printed by T. W. for Humphrey Moseley, pp. 2-3, 49-50.
The first letter dated Westminster 3 July, 1635, cautions Jonson to temper his writing, and reconsider his attack on Inigo Jones. The second, dated 5 April, 1636, notes Jonson's bragging and self-commendation which nearly spoiled a dinner party both Howell and Jonson attended. Reprinted 1892.3.

1648

1 FANE, MILDMAY, Earl of WESTMORLAND. "In Obitum Ben Jons. Poetae Eximii." In Otia Sacra. n.p.: privately printed, p. 169.
An epitaph for Jonson with the perhaps weak compliment, "His craft exceeded far a Dawbers way." Reprinted 1879.3; 1952.7.

2 HERRICK, ROBERT. "Upon M. Ben Jonson. Epit."; "His Prayer to Ben. Jonson"; "Upon Ben Jonson"; and "An Ode for him." In Hesperidies. London: printed for John Williams and Francis Eglesfield, pp. 173-70 [sic], 249-343.
Four poems on Jonson and his influence on English literature. Herrick, the most famous of Jonson's "sons," venerates Jonson and laments his absence. Reprinted in 1956.11.

1650

1 ANON. Untitled. In Ashmole MS vol. 38, p. 181. Oxford: Ashmolean Museum.
Famous epitaph on Jonson, the first line of which he gave: "Here lies Ben Jonson that once was one," followed

1650

by Shakespeare's "Who while he liv'd was a sloe thing/and
now being dead is Nothing." This is of dubious authenticity. Published 1922.4.

2   HEATH, ROBERT. "To one that asked me why I would write an
English Epigram after B. Jonson." In Clarastella. London:
for H[umphrey] Moseley, p. 30.
    Suggests Jonson is the greatest of English epigramma-
tists.

3   TUBBE, HENRY. "To B. Jonson." In "Poems of Henry Tubbe,"
Harleian MS 4126, fol. 113. London: British Museum.
    Laments Jonson's absence through death and further
laments his inability to lament with the poetic skill
Jonson deserved. The date of this item should be regarded
only as an estimate. Published in 1952.7

1651

1   CARTWRIGHT, WILLIAM. Comedies, Tragi-comedies with other
poems. London: printed for Humphrey Moseley, sig. ***3r.
    Many dedicatory poems mention Jonson. See particularly
Francis Vaughan's. He writes:

"Thus Jonson is decry'd by some who fleece
His Works, as much as he did Rome or Greece:
They judge it lawfull Prize, doing no more
To him, than he to those that dy'd before.

2   SHEPPARD, SAMUEL. "The Poets invitation to Ben Jonson's Ghost
to appear again," and "Ben Jonson's due Ecomium," In
Epigrams theological, philosophical, and romantick. London:
by C. D. for Thomas Bucknell, pp. 88-89, 138.
    General praise particularly for the epigrams. Reprinted
in 1952.7.

1652

1   SHIRLEY, JAMES. "Prologue at the Black-Fryers." In The
Sisters. London: printed for Humphrey Robinson and Humphrey Moseley, sig. A3r-A3v.
    Jonson rivals Apollo in poetic harmony. Reprinted in
1933.2.

1656

1   ANON. "Verses written over the Chair of Ben: Jonson, now
      remaining at Robert Wilsons, at the signe of Jonson's head
      in the Strand." In Wit and Drollery. London: F. or Nath:
      Brook, p. 79.
         An invocation to Jonson that wine might inspire the
      reader as it did Jonson. Reprinted in 1952.7.

1658

1   COKAYNE, Sir ASTON. "To my noble Friend, Mr. Marmaduke Wivel."
      In A Chain of Golden Poems. London: printed by W. G., p.
      166.
         Poet humbles himself before Jonson's learning and poetic
      ability.

2   ELIOT, JOHN. "To his Noblest Friend Mr. Endimion Porter upon
      Verses writ by Ben. Johnson"; "An Epigram, To his Friend Ben
      Johnson, upon his Libellous Verses against the Lords of the
      Green-Cloath concerning his Sack"; and "To Ben Johnson again,
      upon his verses dedicated to the Earl of Portland, Lord
      Treasurer." In Poems consisting of epistles & Epigrams,
      Satyrs, Epitaphs and Elogies, Songs and Sonnets. . . . Lon-
      don: for Henry Brome, pp. 26, 27, 34.
         These poems are mildly critical of Jonson and poke fun
      at him in a gently humorous fashion. The epigram is a re-
      mark on Jonson's "An Epigram, To the House-hold," Underwood
      68. Jonson responded to the third poem, which he had appar-
      ently seen in manuscript, in "To my Detractor" in his un-
      gathered verse.

3   M[ENNES], J[OHN]. "A letter to Ben Jonson." In Wit Restor'd
      in Severall Select Poems not formerly Publish't. London:
      printed for R. Pollard, N. Brooks, and T. Dring, pp. 79-81.
         This poem appears to have been written a short time be-
      fore Jonson's death. Basically complimentary, the poet says
      Jonson's works will make him immortal. Reprinted in 1922.4.

1661

1   FELTHAM, OWEN. "An answer to the Ode, 'Come leave the loath-
      ed Stage and c.'" In Lusoria; or Occasional Pieces, in
      Feltham's Resolves. 8th ed. London: Ann Seile, pp. 17-18.
         The reception of Jonson's play, The New Inn, was nothing
      less than what the poet deserved. Moreover, for one who had

1661

been such a stinging critic, he should not protest when some comes back his way. Reprinted in 1952.7.

1662

1 FULLER, THOMAS. "Ben Jonson." In The History of the Worthies of England. London: printed by J. G., W. L., and W. G., p. 243.

The first biographical sketch of Jonson. Notes Jonson's humble origin, his early schooling, and the high place he achieved as a dramatic poet. Provides a somewhat different picture of Jonson in the company of others than one usually visualizes. "He would sit silent in learned company, and suck in (besides wine) their several humors into his observation. What was ore in others, he was able to refine to himself." Reprinted in 1952.5.

1663

1 ANON. Wits Recreations, with a thousand outlandish proverbs. Compiled by G. H[erbert]. London: printed by M. Symmons and S. Symmons. Reprint of 1640.1.

1664

1 BROME, ALEXANDER. "Ben Jonson's sociable rules for the Apollo." In Songs and other Poems. 2d ed. London: for Henry Brome, pp. 325-26.

Brome, who wrote numerous drinking songs, recreates the tavern atmosphere that must have been so familiar to Jonson. Reprinted in 1952.7.

1667

1 WINSTALEY, WILLIAM. "An Anecdote about Ben Jonson and Thomas Randolph." In Poor Robin. London: printed for the Company of Stationers, p. 78.

This anecdote, which Randolph's modern editor, G. Thorn-Drury, regards as most likely spurious, describes how Jonson and Randolph became acquainted. Although Randolph is not a highly regarded poet today, he was considered by his contemporaries as an excellent disciple of Jonson's.

1668

1   DRYDEN, JOHN. Of Dramatick Poesie, An Essay. London: for
Henry Herringman, passim.
Dryden was the first critic to attempt a balanced judgment
of Jonson. Earlier criticism had taken the form of either
unbridled praise or ugly, unjustified ridicule. Dryden
attempts to show both the strengths and weaknesses of Jonson. For instance, he notes that Jonson "was not only a
professed Imitator of Horace, but a learned Plagiary of all
the others. . . ." Nevertheless he also says that Jonson
"has done his Robberies so openly, that one may see he
fears not to be taxed by any Law. He invades Authors like
a Monarch, and what would be theft in other poets, is only
victory in him." Dryden's view were and still are themselves the subject of critical review. Reprinted in
1978.10.

1670

1   HYDE, EDWARD, Earl of CLARENDON. "Life of Edward, Earle of
Clarendon." In Bodleian MS Clarendon 123, p. 48. Oxford:
Bodleian Library.
Prudent though strong recognition for Jonson's contribution to drama, poetry, and criticism. "He did exceeding-
ly exalt the english language, in eloquence, propriety,
and masculine expressions." Published in 1857.4.

1671

1   DRYDEN, JOHN. Preface to An Evenings Love, or The Mock Astrol-
oger. London: printed by T. N. for Henry Herringman, sig.
14-a2r.
Defends self for earlier critical remarks made about Jonson. Dryden believed one should be able to criticize hon-
estly some of Jonson's work without being accused of trying to destroy a literary hero. Reprinted in 1978.9.

2   HOWARD, EDWARD. "The Second Prologue personated like Ben
Jonson rising from below." In The Womens Conquest. London:
by J. M. for H. Herringman, sig. C3v.
After rising from the underworld Jonson gives his views
on the present state of poetry in general and the theater
in particular. Reprinted in 1952.7.

1671

3   SHADWELL, THOMAS. Epilogue to <u>The Humorists, A Comedy</u>. London: printed for Henry Herringman, sigs. A5v-A6r.
      See both "The Preface" and "The Epilogue." In the latter Shadwell writes:

> "The Mighty Prince of poets, learned BEN,
> Who alone div'd into the Minds of Men,
> Saw all their Wandrings, all their Follies knew,
> And all their vain fantastick Passions drew."

Reprinted in 1927.11.

1672

1   DRYDEN, JOHN. "Epilogue," and "Defense of the Epilogue, or an Essay on the Dramatique Poetry of the last Age." In <u>The Conquest of Granada: The Second Part</u>. London: printed by T. N. for Henry Herringman, pp. 159-70.
      In the "Epilogue," maintains that wit has risen to a higher level than it was in Jonson's day and that if Jonson were writing in Dryden's time he would receive some very severe criticism. In the "Defense," tries to explain his position by stating that he was not criticizing Jonson as much as he was defining a change of taste that had occurred over the years. For example, he admits that he finds Jonson's diction pretentious, though his own audience might not have found it so. Reprinted in 1978.11.

1675

1   PHILLIPS, EDWARD. "Benjamin Jonson." In <u>Theatrum Poetarum Anglicanorum</u>. London: printed for Charles Smith, sec. 2, pp. 19-20.
      A biographical sketch with critical comments. Says of the poetry: "He is sometimes bold and strenuous, sometimes magesternal, sometimes limpid and full enough of conceit, and sometimes a Man as other Men are." Reprinted in 1800.1.

1676

1   DUPORT, JAMES. "In Benjamin Jonsonum Poetam Laureatum, and Dramaticorum sue Seculi facile Principem." In <u>Musae Subsecivae</u>. Cambridge: ex officina Joann Hayes, pp. 8-9.
      Poem looks upon Jonson's contribution to English letters. Reprinted in 1952.7.

2   [GOULD, ROBERT.] "Upon Ben Jonson's Picture." In <u>Ludus</u>
    <u>Scacchiae: A Satyr against Unjust Wars</u>. London: for
    Robert Clavel, pp. 22-23.
        Gould picks a familiar theme in Jonson criticism.

        "Jonson: in whom, those distant Parts (ne'r great
        But when divided) Judgment and Fancy met.
        All was not Rapture; Nor (to shun that) Supine,
        Like their dull works who put their Prose in Rime)
        But a just, Equal Heat, Each part inform'd
        Which, both at once, Beauty and strength adornd."

        Reprinted in 1941.3.

1680

1   AUBREY, JOHN. "Mr. Benjamin Jonson Poet Laureat." In Aubrey
    MS 6 fol. 108. Oxford: Bodleian Library.
        A biographical sketch which is another early source of
    information on Jonson. Aubrey's claim that Jonson killed
    Marlow in a duel is inaccurate. Reprinted in 1949.1.

2   _____. "Mr. William Shakespeare." In Aubrey MS 4, pp. 27, 78.
    Oxford: Bodleian Library.
        Has nearly as much to say about Jonson as Shakespeare.
    Jonson was not as good an actor but a good instructor.
    Shakespeare and Jonson met daily for witty exchanges.
        Also considers Jonson's criticism of Shakespeare.
    Reprinted in 1949.1.

3   WALTON, ISAAC. Untitled notes on Ben Jonson. In Aubrey MS 6,
    pp. 11, 12, 17. Oxford: Bodleian Library.
        These notes appear as a letter to John Aubrey. Much of
    the information is inaccurate except for the remarks on
    Jonson's drinking wine "too much before he went to bed, if
    not oftener and sooner." Published in 1925.17.

1682

1   ANON. "Did but Ben. Jonson know how Follies rise." In <u>The</u>
    <u>Tory-Poets: a Satyr</u>. London: by R. Johnson, p. 9.
        If Jonson knew how bad writing is today, he would return
    "And lash the idiots into Sence."

1683

1 OLDHAM, JOHN. "Ode Upon the Works of Ben Jonson. Written in
1678." In Poems, and translations. London: for Jos.
Hindmarsh, pp. 69-68.
A long commentary poem on Jonson which speaks of his
"manag'd rage," "fancy," "restraint," "discipline," and
"milder judgment." Reprinted in 1960.15.

1684

1 SANDYS, GEORGE. Anglorum Speculum: or The Worthies of England in Church and State. London: printed for John Wright,
Thomas Passinger, and William Thackary, pp. 512-13.
Brief capsule account of Jonson's life and the enduring
quality of his works.

2 WINSTANLEY, WILLIAM. "Ben Jonson." In England's Worthies.
London: printed by J. C. and F. C. for Obadiah Blagrave,
pp. 242-44.
Winstanley relies on earlier biographers, particularly
Fuller and Phillips.

1687

1 WINSTANELY, WILLIAM. "Mr. Benjamin Jonson." In The Lives of
the most Famous English Poets. London: printed by H.
Clark for Samuel Manship, pp. 123-28.
Standard biographical information again heavily depen-
dent on Fuller and Phillips. Winstanley does note Jonson's role in helping Thomas Coryant with his book of
Crudities. Reprinted in 1963.24.

1691

1 LANGBAINE, GERARD. "Benjamin Jonson." In An Account of the
English Dramatic Poets. Oxford: printed by L. L. for
George West and Henry Clements, pp. 281-306.
A catalog of Jonson's plays and masques along with production information. Relies heavily on Fuller for his
biographical information. Offers no original criticism but
refers to noted writers who praised Jonson. Reprinted in
1971.11.

1691-92

1 WOOD, ANTHONY. "Benjamin Johnson." In <u>Athenae Oxonienses</u>.
   London: printed for Thomas Bennet, pp. 518-19.
      Wood notes that Jonson may have spent a few weeks at
   Cambridge University as a young man, but points out that
   in 1619 at the invitation of Dr. Richard Corbet, Jonson
   went to Oxford where he was given an honorary M. A. Wood
   also gives a brief list of Jonson's plays and masques.
   Reprinted in 1868.4.

1694

1 BLOUNT, Sir THOMAS POPE. "Ben Jonson." In <u>De Re Poetica</u>,
   <u>Part 2</u>. London: printed by Rich Everingham for R.
   Bently, pp. 104-12.
      Largely extracts from other critics and biographers
   regarding Jonson's life and works. Reprinted in 1974.7.

2 WOTTON, WILLIAM. <u>Reflections upon Ancient and Modern Learn-</u>
   <u>ing</u>. London: printed by J. Leake for Peter Buck, passim.
      Remarks on Jonson's <u>The English Grammar</u>.

1696

1 DENNIS, JOHN. "To Mr. Congreve." In <u>Letters upon several</u>
   <u>Occasions</u>. London: for Sam. Briscoe, pp. 405-12.
      Dennis is the first critic to strike a theme which will
   often be sounded in Jonsonian criticism. The poet lacked
   passion, "I mean that fine and that delicate Passion by
   which the Soul shows its Politeness, ev'n in the midst of
   its trouble. Now to touch a Passion is the surest way to
   Delight. For nothing agitates like it." Reprinted in
   1952.7.

1698

1 CONGREVE, WILLIAM. <u>Amendments of Mr. Collier's False and</u>
   <u>Imperfect Citations</u>. London: printed for J. Tonson,
   pp. 97-98.
      Discusses a difference of interpretation in some lines
   from <u>Discoveries</u>. Reprinted in 1972.5.

1699

1   LANGBAINE, GERARD. The Lives and Characters of the English
     Dramatic Poets. Edited and abridged by Charles Gildon.
     London: printed for Tho Leigh and William Turner, pp. 77-
     81.
         Brief, one-paragraph biographical sketch followed by a
     listing of Jonson's works. Reprinted in 1973.21.

1704

1   ANON. "Ben Jonson. and Mr. Baker." In Visits from the Shades.
     London: n.p., pp. 38-48.
         A ficitious dialogue in which Jonson's critical views
     are discussed in general and in particular how they might
     apply to the contemporary stage. Reprinted in 1972.1.

1711

1   DRUMMOND, WILLIAM. "Heads of a Conversation betwixt the
     famous Poet Ben Jonson, and William Drummond of Hawthornden,
     January, 1619." In The Works of William Drummond of Haw-
     thornden. Edinburgh: printed by James Watson, pp. 224-26.
         When Jonson visited Drummond in 1619, Drummond took
     notes on their conversations. Not published in Jonson's
     or Drummond's lifetimes, they appear only in an abridged
     form in The Works. For a complete modern text see 1925.17.
     The Conversations provide insights on Jonson's views on a
     wide range of subjects. In particular comments on Shake-
     speare and other playwrights and poets of his time have
     provided later critics with a picture of Jonson's thoughts
     on writings. Ends with a brief sketch of Jonson's charac-
     ter.

1717

1   THEOBALD, LEWIS. "Memorandums." In The Censor. Vol. 1.
     London: printed for Jonas Brown, pp. 102-4.
         Printed here are the Jonson "Memorandums" which describe
     the type of wine Jonson drank to inspire his writing. The
     poorer the wine the poorer the play. The author surely
     meant that the "Memorandums" be regarded as humorous and
     fictitious. However, this original source was forgotten,
     and when the "Memorandums" were discovered in the early
     19th century, written in an 18th century hand on the fly
     leaf of a quarto of Catiline, they were accepted as

authentic. <u>The Censor</u> originally appeared as a serial.
This article appears in issue number 14 (11 May): 171.
   For further information on the "Memorandums" see 1906.3,
1925.17, and 1936.13.

1719

1   JACOB, GILES. "Ben Jonson." In <u>The Poetical Register</u>. London:
      printed for E. Curell, pp. 146-52.
         A very short account of Jonson's early life followed by
      a listing of his plays and masques. Reprinted in 1970.25.

1720

1   JACOB, GILES. "Ben Jonson." In <u>An Historical Account of the
   Lives and Writings of Our Most Considerable English Poets</u>.
   London: printed for E. Curell, pp. 272-75.
         Acknowledgment of Jonson as a poet with quotations
      from epigrams and a listing of other poems. Reprinted in
      1970.24.

1725

1   POPE, ALEXANDER. Preface to <u>The Works of Shakespeare</u>. Lon-
      don: Jacob Tonson, pp. i-xxiv.
         Pope holds that there was no lasting ill-feeling between
      Jonson and Shakespeare, that they were friends as long as
      they knew each other. The animosity between the two is
      imagined by partisans for each side when in fact there
      were no sides. Both men were great writers and Jonson
      was a perceptive critic.

1726

*1   MURALT, BEAT LOUIS. "Ben Jonson." In <u>Letters Describing the
   Character and Customs of the English and French Nations</u>.
   2d ed. London: printed by T. Edline, pp. 19-24.
         Cited in Tannenbaum 1938.13.

1730

1   HURLOTHUMBO [pseud]. "A Poem by Ben Jonson?" In <u>The Merry
   Thought Or, The Glass-Window & Bog-house Miscellany</u>. 2d
   ed. London: J. Roberts, p. 10.

1730

A collection of poems scratched on glasses and windows
in taverns and other places. Notes one poem which may
have been by Jonson.

1734

*1   CASLEY, D., ed. "Two Documents of Jonsonian Interest." In
     A Catalogue of the MMS. of the King's Library. London:
     printed for David Casley.
       Cited in Tannenbaum 1938.13.

1747-1766

*1   ANON. Biographia Britannica, 6 vols. London: printed for W.
     Innys, passim.
       Cited in Tannenbaum 1938.13.

1747

1   JOHNSON, SAMUEL. Prologue and Epilogue (by David Garrick)
     spoken at the opening of the Theatre in Drury-Lane. Lon-
     don: printed by E. Cave, 12 pp.
       In the history of the theater Jonson is known for his
     "studious patience and laborious art." Reprinted in
     1964.12.

2   WINCOP, THOMAS, ed. Scanderbeg; of Love and Liberty, A
     Tragedy. London: W. Reeve, pp. 119-24.
       A brief life of Jonson with reprints of three epitaphs
     by Jonson, a list of plays and information on when the
     plays were produced and printed.

1748

1   WHALLEY, PETER. An Inquiry into the Learning of Shakespeare.
     London: T. Waller, passim.
       Compares Jonson unfavorably to Shakespeare by criticiz-
     ing Jonson's obscurity. Calls for an edition of Jonson
     with proper explanatory and textual notes. (Whalley's
     edition of Jonson appeared in 1756.)

1753

1   ANON. "The Life of Ben Jonson." London Magazine 22 (July):
     303-4.

A short sketch of the major events in Jonson's life. Brief remarks on his reputation and influence.

2   CIBBER, THEOPHILUS, comp. "Ben Jonson." In <u>The Lives of the Poets of Great Britain and Ireland</u>. Vol. 1. London: printed for R. Griffiths, pp. 235-49.
    Covers the standard facts of Jonson's life. Author has a low opinion of Jonson's poetry. "Ben had certainly no great talent for versification, nor does he seem to have had an extraordinary ear; his verses are often wanting in syllables and sometimes have too many." Reprinted in 1968.3.

*3   [HURD, RICHARD.] "On the Provinces of Several Species of Dramatic Poetry." In <u>Q Horatii Flaci Epistolae ad Pisones et Augustum</u> [Epist. II. 1] <u>with an English commentary and notes. To which are added two dissertations: the one, on the provinces of the several species of dramatic poetry: the other on poetical imitation. . . .</u> 2 vols. 2d ed. London: W. Thurlbourne.
    See 1811.1.

1756

1   CHETWOOD, WILLIAM RUFUS. <u>Memoirs of the Life and Writings of Ben. Jonson, Esq.</u> Dublin: n.p., 136 pp.
    A comprehensive life interspersed with dates of plays, some poems, and letters about Jonson. Also contains the text of <u>Eastward Ho</u>. Reprinted in 1970.9.

2   WHALLEY, PETER, ed. Preface, and "The Life of Benjamin Jonson," In <u>The Works of Ben. Jonson</u>. Vol. 1. London: Midwinter, et al., pp. i-lxiii.
    The major eighteenth-century edition of Jonson's <u>Works</u>. Biographical essay summarizes current information on Jonson's literary career and his personal life. Whalley summarizes his general critical assessment as follows: "With respect to Jonson's character as a writer, he is universally allowed to have been the most learned and judicious poet of his age. His learning indeed is to be seen in almost everything he wrote; and sometimes perhaps it may appears, where we could wish it might not be seen, although he seldom transgresseth in this point; for a just decorum and preservation of character, with propriety of circumstance and of language, are his striking excellencies, and eminently distinguish his correctness and art."

1757

1 HURD, RICHARD. <u>A Letter to Mr. Mason on the Marks of Imita-</u>
<u>tion</u>. Cambridge: printed by W. Thurlbourn & J. Woodyer,
80 pp.
Jonson is mentioned throughout this essay along with
other writers. Hurd believes that no other writer suc-
ceeded as well as Jonson in the art of imitation.

1761

1 CHURCHILL, CHARLES. <u>The Rosciad</u>. London: printed for the
Author, pp. 8-9.
The poem describes a trial or contest held to determine
which actor will take the place of the deceased Rosicus.
Jonson is one of the judges, and in describing him the poet
assesses his style and influence. These fairly standard
remarks mention Jonson's restrained fancy but deep understanding of man. Reprinted in 1956.7.

1766

1 [Capell, Edward.] <u>Reflections on Originality in Authors . . .</u>
<u>with a word or two on the Character of Ben Jonson. . . .</u>
London: R. Horsfield, pp. 63-65.
A short discussion of Jonson's propensity for borrowing,
which the author calls pure plagarism.

1766

1 FARMER, RICHARD. <u>An Essay on the Learning of Shakespeare</u>.
Cambridge: printed by J. Archdeacon for J. Woodyer, pp.
2-5.
To prove his thesis that Shakespeare was in fact a
learned man, Farmer must first "litigate" Jonson's reference to Shakespeare's "small Latin and less Greek."
Reprinted in 1821.1.

1782

1 AYSCOUGH, SAMUEL, comp. "Manuscripts of Jonsonian Interest in
the British Museum." In <u>A Catalogue of the Manuscripts</u>
<u>Preserved in the British Museum</u>. . . . London: printed
for Samuel Ayscough by J. Rivington.

1786

1 CUMBERLAND, RICHARD. "B.J.'s Imitations of Philostratus; his
satirical glances at Shakespeare; his hag compared with
witches in Macbeth." Observer 4:136-47.
Notes that "Drink to me only with thine eyes" is a
loose translation from Philostratus, Letter xxiv. Reprinted in 1803.1.

1789

1 [NEVE, PHILIP.] "Ben Jonson." In Cursory Remarks on . . .
Ancient English Poets. London: privately printed, pp. 39-
43.
Provides a general assessment: there are few of Jonson's
works that can be recommended "to a reader of taste, for
his amusement or approbation." Reprinted in 1801.2.

1793

1 ANDERSON, ROBERT. "The Life of Jonson." In The Poetical Works
of Benjamin Jonson. Edinburgh: printed by Mundell & Son,
pp. 523-30. (In A Complete Edition of the Poets of Great
Britain, Vol. 4. Edited by Robert Anderson. London:
Printed for John & Arthur Arch; and for Bell & Bradfute
and I. Mundell & Co. Edinburg.)
A comprehensive life with more complete critical commentary than normally was customary in the eighteenth
century. Of Jonson's poetry Anderson writes: "His
Epigrams are sometimes happily turned; but more frequently
pointless. His Epitaphs are universally admired, and just-
ly entitled to the highest praise. His Songs are sprightly
and elegant, and deservedly popular. The merit of his
Lyric pieces is much greater than has been allowed. . . ."

2 D'ISRAELI, ISAAC. "Ben Jonson." In Curiosities of Literature.
London: J. Murray, pp. 114-24.
Jonson had "a great share of arrogance, and was desirous
of ruling the realms of Parnassus with a despotic septre."
Prints "Ode to Himself" and two replies to illustrate Jon-
son's quarrelsome nature. Reprinted in 1972.8.

1797

1 WOODHOUSELEE, ALEXANDER FRASER TYTLER, Lord. Essay on the
Principles of Translation. 2d ed. London: T. Cadell &
W. Davies, pp. 64-67.

1797

A short discussion of Jonson's translation of Horace's
Art of Poetry. Mildly critical of Jonson for being too
literal and not sufficiently poetical in his translation.
Reprint of 1675.1.

1799

1   CHALMERS, GEORGE. A Supplemental Apology for the Believers
     in the Shakespeare Papers. London: Thomas Egerton, pp.
     235-37.
          Argues that Jonson's Epigram LVI "On Poet-Ape" is ad-
     dressed to Shakespeare. Reprinted in 1971.6.

*2   SEWARD, WILLIAM. "Ben Jonson." In Biographiana. Vol. 2.
     London: J. Johnson, pp. 411-12.
          Cited in Tannenbaum 1947.10.

1800

1   PHILLIPS, EDWARD. "Ben Jonson." In Theatrum Poetarum Anglic-
     anorum. Vol. 1. Edited by S. E. Brydges. London: J.
     White, pp. 241-50.
          Reprint of 1675.1.

1801

1   ANON. "Parallel Passages--Plagiary Considered: Pope--Ben Jon-
     son--Prior--Lewis--Lord Oxford." Monthly Mirror 11
     (March):229-35.
          In reading Jonson the author is astonished by "whole
     sections translated into his works word for word" from
     Horace and Cicero.

2   NEVE, PHILIP. "Remarks on Ancient English Poets: Jonson."
     Monthly Mirror 11 (January):22-24.
          Reprint of 1789.1.

1802

1   [RITSON, JOSEPH.] Bibliographia Poetica, a Catalog of Eng-
     lish Poets. London: C. Roworth, p. 259.
          A note on the editions of Ben Jonson's Works.

2   WALDRON, FRANCIS GODOLPHIN. "The English State." In The Shake-
     spearean Miscellany. London: printed by Knight & Compton,
     pp. 16-23.

1807

Reprints an abridged and edited version of Whalley's
"Life of Jonson."

1803

1   CUMBERLAND, RICHARD. Untitled. In British Essayists. Vol.
     42. Edited by Alexander Chambers. London: printed for
     J. Johnson, et al., pp. 205-13.
        Reprint of 1786.1.

1805

1   [BRYDGES, Sir SAMUEL EGERTON, bart.]. "Ben Jonson." In
     Censura Literataria. Vol. 1. London: Longman, Hurst,
     Rees, & Orme, pp. 94-99.
        A transcription of some manuscript notes by William
     Oldys, Sir Walter Raleigh's eighteenth-century biographer.
     Oldys gives a slightly different account of Jonson being
     the tutor of Raleigh's son. He also suggests that the
     fire that destroyed Jonson's house occurred about 1629,
     a later date than usually given. Other miscellaneous bits
     of information are printed. Reprinted in 1966.5.

1806

1   IRELAND, WILLIAM-HENRY. "Ben Jonson." In The Confessions of
     W. H. Ireland. London: printed by Ellerton and Byworth,
     pp. 193-94.
        This famous forger wrote Jonson's name after some lines
     of poetry which he had blotted out under a picture of
     Shakespeare he had drawn and attributed to Cowley, the
     actor. Reprinted in 1874.9.

2   LANDON, CHARLES PAUL, ed. Galerie Historique des hommes les
     plus célèbris de tous les siècles et de tontes les nations.
     Vol. 1. Paris: printed for C. P. Landon, n.p.
        Biographical sketch of Jonson describing his traditional
     place in the development of English literature.

1807

1   ANON. "The Life of Ben Jonson [with a Portrait]." Monthly
     Mirror, n.s., 2 (July):5-10.
        A brief account of Jonson's life.

25

1808

1 ANON. Review of An Examination of Charges . . . , by Octavius
   Graham Gilchrist. British Critic 32 (September):289-92.
      Strong support for Gilchrist's views, cited in 1808.2.
   "Jonson was rough and bold, proud of conscious talents,
   and severely indignant when attacked, but of mean and con-
   cealed envy he seems to have been totally incapable."
   See 1808.2.

2 GILCHRIST, OCTAVIUS GRAHAM. An Examination of the Charges
   maintained by Messrs. Malone and Chalmers, and others, of
   Ben Jonson's Enmity &c. towards Shakespeare. London:
   printed for Taylor & Hessey by J. Moyes, 62 pp.
      Attempts to refute earlier charges that Shakespeare and
   Jonson were rivals, perhaps even enemies. Gilchrist does
   not believe that Jonson should be regarded as an embittered
   curmudgeon who was jealous of Shakespeare's success.

1810

1 CHALMERS, ALEXANDER, and JOHNSON, DR. SAMUEL, eds. "The Life
   of Ben Jonson." In The Works of the English Poets, from
   Chaucer to Cowper. Vol. 5. London: J. Johnson, pp.
   443-57.
      Johnson wrote no life of Jonson. Chalmer's introduction
   to his edition of Jonson's poetry consists of a fairly
   complete biographical sketch and some brief critical remarks. He sees spontaneity in Jonson's best work and
   frequent, striking epigrammatic turns.

1811

1 HURD, RICHARD. "On the Provinces of Dramatic Poetry." In
   The Works of Richard Hurd. Vol. 2. Edited by Joseph
   Addison. London: printed for T. Dadell & W. Davies, pp.
   96-105.
      Finds Jonson rigid, intemperant, and indelicate. "It is
   not to be wondered that his wit is too frequently caustic;
   his raillery coarse, and his humor excessive." Reprinted
   in 1967.9.

1814

1 D'ISRAELI, ISAAC. "Ben Jonson and Thomas Decker." In Quarrels
   of Authors. Vol. 3. New York: John Murray, pp. 123-70.

26

A discussion of the famous poets' quarrel. "The genius of Jonson was rough, hardy, and invincible, of which the frequent excess degenerated into ferocity. . . ."

1815

1   BOLTON, EDMUND. "Hypercritica" In <u>Ancient Critical Essays upon English Poets and Poesy</u>. Vol. 2. Edited by Joseph Haslewood. London: Harding & Wright.
     Reprint of 1617.1.

1816

1   GIFFORD, WILLIAM, ed. <u>The Works of Ben Jonson. With Notes, Critical and Explanatory, and a Biographical Memoir</u>. 9 Vols. London: G. & W. Nicol.
     A milestone in the history of Jonsonian criticism. Introduction of "Memoirs of Ben Jonson" and critical notes are the first full scale answer to Shakespearian critics' attacks on Jonson. In his zeal to defend Jonson, Gifford may have made a stronger case than was necessary or, in fact, warranted. Jonson was neither a saint nor the father of English literature as Gifford implies. Nonetheless, Gifford's edition slightly revised in 1871 by Cunningham remained the standard edition of Jonson until Herford and Simpson (1925-52). Revised 1871.3.

2   WRANGHAM, FRANCIS. "Ben Jonson." In <u>The British Plutarch</u>. Vol. 2. London: printed for J. Mawman, et al. pp. 575-602.
     A biographical essay with brief critical remarks. Jonson's poetry is criticized for poor versification. "He is often harsh, frigid and tedious. . . ."

1818

1   ANON. Review of <u>The Works of Ben Jonson. With Notes. . .</u>, edited by William Gifford. <u>British Critic</u>, 2d ser., 10 (August):183-99.
     Objects to Gifford's exaggerated praise of Jonson and his treatment of Drummond. The reviewer concludes: "Jonson was a man of extraordinary talents and acquirements, rather than an eminent genius; a profound thinker rather than a great poet." See 1816.1.

2   ANON. "Vindication of Drummond against attack by Mr. Gifford." <u>Blackwood's Magazine</u> 2 (February):497-501.

1818

Complains that Gifford's treatment of Drummond is worse
than treatment of Jonson by earlier Shakespearian critics.

1819

1   CAMPBELL, THOMAS, ed. Specimens of the British Poets; with
    Biographical and Critical Notes. Vol. 3. London: John
    Murray, pp. 154-85.
        A selection of Jonson's poetry preceded by a brief crit-
    ical statement and an account of the poet's life. Accepts
    Gifford's defense of Jonson and welcomes this new assessment
    of the poet.

2   HAZLITT, WILLIAM CAREW. "On Shakespeare and Ben Jonson." In
    Lectures on the English Comic Writers. Vol. 1. Philadel-
    phia: M. Carey, pp. 32-54.
        A highly unfavorable assessment of Jonson which many
    critics have since tried to reconcile. "I do not deny his
    [Jonson's] power or merit; far from it: but it is to me
    a repulsive and unamiable kind. He was a great man in
    himself, but one cannot readily sympathize with him." Re-
    printed in 1903.6.

*3 SANFORD, EZEKIEL. "The Life of Ben Jonson." In The Works of
    British Poets. Vol. 3. Philadelphia: Mitchell, Ames, &
    White, pp. 217-73.
        Cited in Tannenbaum 1938.13.

4   S., B. E. "Dialogue Between Ben Jonson and Drummond of Haw-
    thornden." Blackwood's Magazine 4 (February):558-60.
        An imaginary dialogue between Jonson and Drummond.

1820

1   ANON. "The Works of Ben Jonson; Folio, 1616." Retrospective
    Review 1, pt. 2:181-200.
        We are admonished to read Jonson for his moral values.

1821

1   FARMER, RICHARD. An Essay on the Learning of Shakespeare.
    London: printed for T. and R. Rodd.
        Reprint of 1767.1.

1822

1 AIKIN, LUCY. <u>Memoirs of the Court of King James I</u>. Vol. 1.
     London: Longman, Hurst et al., pp. 151-57.
       A biographical sketch of Jonson largely derived from
     Gifford's "Memoir."

1823

1 B., J. C. Untitled. <u>Gentlemen's Magazine</u> 134 (September):227-
     28.
       Describes the opening of Jonson's grave when another
     body was buried next to him.

1824

1 GRANGER, JAMES, ed. <u>A Biographical History of England</u>. 5th
     ed. Vol. 2. London: William Baynes, pp. 124-25.
       Jonson is "frequently deficient in the harmony, and
     sometimes even in the measure, of his verses." (Earlier
     editions not seen.)

2 PROCTER, B. W. [Barry Cornwall]. <u>Effigies of Poeticae, Or,
     Portraits of the British Poets</u>. Vol. 1. London: James
     Carpenter, pp. 27-29.
       General praise for Jonson. "Jonson was a man of rare
     power. His mind, indeed, was built up by study; and he
     attained his lofty eminence in the world by casting down
     his hoards of learning, and rising upon the collected
     thoughts of others."

3 WARTON, THOMAS. <u>A History of English Poetry</u>. Edited by W.
     C. Hazlitt. London: Reeves & Turner, passim.
       Jonson's poetry is discussed in reference to the pop-
     ularity of the epigram in the early seventeenth century.

1826

*1 RYAN, RICHARD. "Ben Jonson's Sacred Poetry." In <u>Poetry and
     Poets</u>. Vol. 3. London: printed for Sherwood, Gilbert,
     & Piper, pp. 63-65.
       Cited in Tannenbaum 1938.13.

2 SCOTT, Sir WALTER. <u>Provincial Antiquities</u>. Vol. 2. London:
     John & Arthur Arch, pp. 132-38.
       Defends Drummond against Gifford's attack. Drummond was

1826

younger than Jonson and admired him greatly. It should be
no surprise that he tended to notice small disappointments
he found in Jonson's character. To suggest that Drummond
is guilty of base treachery is totally unjustified by the
facts of the situation.

1833

1 ANON. "Ben Jonson." In The Gallery of Portraitists: with
   Memoirs. Vol. 3. London: C. Knight, pp. 155-64.
      Essay recounts Jonson's life and very briefly describes
   his various publications. Author is as uncritical of Jonson as he is of others he has included in his gallery.

2 SHIRLEY, JAMES. "Prologue at the Black-Fryers." In The Dram-
   atic Works and Poems of James Shirley. Vol. 5. Edited by
   William Gifford and Alexander Dye. Vol. 5, The Sisters.
   London: John Murray, pp. 356-57.
      Reprint of 1652.1.

1834

1 SCOTT, Sir WALTER. The Life of John Dryden in Miscellaneous
   Prose Works. Vol. 1. Edinburgh: Robert Cadell, p. 227.
      Although Scott admires Jonson he does object to several
   aspects of his writing. "Many authors of that age are
   indecent, but Jonson is filthy and gross in his pleasantry,
   and indulges himself in using the language of scavengers
   and night-men." Reprinted in 1963.19.

1835

*1 COLERIDGE, SAMUEL TAYLOR. Specimens of Table Talk of the
   late Samuel Taylor Coleridge. Edited by H[enry]
   N[elson] C[oleridge]. London: John Murray.
      Source: Reprint in 1884.2.

2 GORTON, JOHN. "Jonson (Benjamin)." In A General Biographical
   Dictionary. Vol. 3. London: Whittaker, pp. 207-9.
      A biography dealing mostly in curiosities on "one of
   our most celebrated English poets."

1836

1 CATTERMOLE, R., ed. Sacred Poetry of the 17th Century. Vol.
   2. London: John Hatchard & Son, pp. 79-87.

Brief critical notes before five of Jonson's religious lyrics.

2   COLERIDGE, SAMUEL TAYLOR. "Lecture VII. Ben Jonson, Beaumont and Fletcher and Massinger." In <u>The Literary Remains of Samuel Taylor Coleridge</u>. Vol. 1. Edited by Henry Nelson Coleridge. London: William Pickering, pp. 97-113.
      Finds much to praise in Jonson. "Ben Jonson exhibits a sterling English diction, and he has with great skill contrived varieties of construction; but his style is rarely sweet or harmonious, in consequence of his labor at point and strength being so evident. In all his works in verse or prose, there is an extraordinary opulence of thought; but it is the produce of amassing power in the author, and not of a growth from within." Reprinted in 1967.5.

3   _____. "Notes on Ben Jonson." In <u>The Literary Remains of Samuel Taylor Coleridge</u>. Vol. 2. Edited by Henry Nelson Coleridge. London: William Pickering, pp. 268-88.
      Jonson appeals to Coleridge's love of classical literature. "The more I study his writings, the more I admire them; and the more my study of him resembles that of an ancient classic, in the minutiae of his rhythm, meter, choice of words, forms of connection, and so forth, the more numerous have the points of my admiration become." Reprinted in 1967.5.

<u>1837</u>

1   ANON. "Ben Jonson." <u>New Monthly Magazine</u> 51 (September):39-43.
      A biographical essay dealing largely with Jonson's excessive drinking. Author cites Herrick's poetry and two letters by Howell and argues that they had been overlooked by two previous biographers.

2   BUSBY, STANHOPE. <u>Lectures on English Poetry</u>. London: Whittaker, p. 42.
      Jonson's poems "are distinguished by an occasional tenderness and voluptuous dignity, a facility or rhyme, a manliness of thought, and a turn of mind running into epigram."

3   COLLIER, J. PAYNE. <u>A Catalogue, Bibliographical and Critical, of Early English Literature; Forming a Portion of the Library at Bridgewater House</u>. London: Thomas Rodd, passim.

1837

        Items by and about Jonson are listed and described.

*4   DUNHAM, SAMUEL ASTLEY. "Ben Jonson." In <u>Lives of the most</u>
      <u>Eminent Literary and Scientific Men of Great Britain and</u>
      <u>Ireland</u>. London: Longman, Reese, Ome et al., pp. 131-204.
      Cited in Tannenbaum, 1938.13.

1838

1   ANON. "The New Edition of Ben Jonson." <u>Spectator</u> 11 (8 Decem-
      ber):1163-64.
          Review of <u>The Works of Ben Jonson</u>, edited by B. W. Proc-
      ter. Although the reviewer regards Jonson's poems as "some-
      what constrained and pedantic in style," he finds the prose
      is far more interesting. "The <u>Sylva</u> has not the method of
      Bacon's <u>Essays</u>; but it has all their pith and depth, with
      more variety, and some instructive criticism." See 1838.3.

2   MALDEN, HENRY. "Ben Jonson." In <u>Distinguished Men of Modern</u>
      <u>Times</u>. Vol. 2. London: Charles Knight, pp. 53-65.
          Essay on life and works; touches upon the major literary
      events of Jonson's career.

3   PROCTER, B. W. [Barry Cornwall], ed. <u>The Works of Ben Jonson</u>.
      London: Edward Moxon, 819 pp.
          The introductory "Memoir" is a tribute to Jonson's life
      and works. Defends Jonson against the detractors who see
      Jonson as a plagiarizing bully. "As a censor of morals,
      as a corrector of the vices and follies of his age, he
      [Jonson] deserves especial remark."

1839

1   ANON. "New Edition of Ben Jonson." <u>Blackwoods Magazine</u> 45
      (February):114-19.
          A stinging review of <u>The Works of Ben Jonson</u>. "Ben
      Jonson by Barry Cornwall! This is really too much. The
      most masculine of intellects edited by the most effeminate
      --one of the greatest of England's poets patronized by one
      of her smallest poetasters." See 1838.3.

2   ANON. "The Works of Ben Jonson, Folio 1616." <u>Museum of For-</u>
      <u>eign Literature</u>, 9 (November):317-24.
          Review of <u>The Works of Ben Jonson</u>. . . . Even though
      Gifford's is a handsome edition, Jonson has still not
      found the reading public he deserves. See 1816.1.

1842

3   NEELE, H. <u>Lectures on English Poetry</u>. 3d ed. London: J.
      Thomas, passim.
            Points out that although Jonson is best known for his
      comedy, he is also the master of lyric purity. (Earlier
      edition not seen.)

*4   THOMAS, W. J., ed. "An Anecdote about Shakespeare and Ben
      Jonson." In <u>Anecdotes and Traditions. . . .</u> London: pp.
      2-3, 29-30.
            Cited in Tannenbaum, 1938.13.

                        1840

1   CUNNINGHAM, G. G., ed. "Ben Jonson." In <u>Lives of Eminent and</u>
      <u>Illustrious Englishmen</u>. Vol. 3. Glasgow: A Fullerton
      & Co., pp. 251-57.
            A biographical sketch. Jonson is considered a "profound
      scholar with a vigorous mind."

                        1841

1   ANON. "Beaumont and Fletcher, and Their Contemporaries."
      <u>Edinburgh Review</u> 73 (April):209-41.
            The quality of Jonson's poetry has not been fully
      appreciated. "His poetic sense pervades all that he
      wrote."

2   COLLIER, J. PAYNE. <u>Memoirs of Edward Alleyn . . . including</u>
      <u>Some New Particulars respecting . . . Ben Jonson</u>. Lon-
      don: New Shakespeare Society, pp. vi, 220.
            Documents biographical information on Jonson.

                        1842

1   ANON. Untitled. In <u>Extracts from the Accounts of the Revels</u>
      <u>at Court</u>. Edited by Peter Cunningham. London: Shake-
      speare Society, p. xlix.
            First published copy of 1634.2.

2   D'ISRAELI, ISAAC. "The 'Humors' of Ben Jonson." In <u>Amenities</u>
      <u>of Literature</u>. Vol. 2. Paris: Baudry's European <u>Library</u>,
      pp. 180-85.
            A defense of Jonson and the subject matter he treats.
      "Our poet professed to instruct as much as to delight;
      and it was in the severity of thought and the austerity of
      his genius that his nobler conceptions arose."

1842

3   LAING, DANIEL. Preface to <u>Notes of Ben Jonson's Conversations</u>
    <u>with William Drummond</u>. London: Shakespeare Society, pp.
    v-xxiv.
        Includes a discussion of the relationship between Jon-
    son and Drummond and a history of the publication of the
    <u>Conversations</u>. Laing believes Jonson and Drummond were
    much better friends than had been assumed earlier.

1843

1   SMYTH, GEORGE LEWIS. "Ben Jonson." In <u>Biographical Illustra-</u>
    <u>tions of Westminster Abbey</u>. London: Whittaker, pp. 35-38.
        A biographical sketch illustrated with excerpts of
    plays and poems with a final admonition to the reader.
    "They who judge Jonson's poetical capabilities by his plays
    only, form a very imperfect conception of his merits.
    There is in his songs and minor pieces a manly beauty,
    a vigorous imaginativeness and classical grace, which
    it would be difficult to match in the whole range of Eng-
    lish literature."

1844

1   ANON. "Ben Jonson." In <u>The Williams Monthly Miscellany</u>. Vol.
    1. North Adams, Mass.: Henry Chickering, pp. 307-10.
        General life and works essay assuring readers that Jon-
    son's "writings are in great measure free from his licen-
    tiousness."

*2 CRAIK, GEORGE LILLIE. <u>Sketches of the History of Literature</u>
    <u>. . . in Europe</u>. London: Charles Knight, pp. 202-4.
    Cited in Tannenbaum 1938.13.

1845

1   ANON. "Ben Jonson." In <u>The Cabinet Portrait Gallery of Brit-</u>
    <u>ish Worthies</u>. Vol. 5. London: C. Knight, pp. 118-28.
        A biographical summary of Jonson's life using Aubrey
    for most of the anecdotal information.

1846

1   ANON. "Ben Jonson." <u>Chamber's Edinburgh Journal</u>, 2d ser., 5,
    no. 107 (17 January):37-40.
        Reports some new biographical information about Jonson,

and in a summary statement on his work states: "His classical studies are seen in their fairest light in his
masques, and the exquisite lyrical poems scattered
throughout."

1847

1 HUNT, LEIGH. A Selection of Sketches, Essays, and Critical
   Memoirs. Vol. 2. New York: Smith, Elder, pp. 10-19.
      Is struck by the unevenness of Jonson's work. On the
   one hand Jonson writes beautiful lyrics and on the other
   he stoops to crude epigrams. "His nature included the
   contradictions of some ill-matched progenitors, and that
   while he had a grace for one parent or ancestor, he had
   a slut and fury for another." Reprinted in 1899.5.

1848

1 CAMPBELL, THOMAS. "Ben Jonson." In An Essay on English Poetry,
   with Notices of the British Poets. London: John Murray,
   pp. 198-206.
      Light biography and criticism.

2 HUNT, LEIGH. "Italian and English Pastorals." In A Jar of
   Honey from Mount Hybla. London: Smith, Elder, pp. 80-99.
      Comment on Jonson's unfinished dramatic pastoral, "the
   Sad Shepherd." Hunt believes that though Jonson was
   "burly and strong-sensation-loving . . . he could show
   a great deal of delicacy when he had a mind to it."

1849

*1 SHAW, THOMAS BUDD. Outlines of English Literature. London:
    John Murray.
       Cited in Tannenbaum, 1938.13.
       Printed in 1876.4.

1850

1 WHIPPLE, E[DWIN] P. "Old English Dramatists." In Essays and
   Reviews. Vol. 2. New York: Houghton Mifflin Co., pp.
   25-39.
      A general life and works essay but here the author de-
   fends Jonson where others have criticized him: "Jonson
   stands out from all his contemporaries, original, peculiar,

1850

leaning on none for aid, and to be tried by his own merits alone. Had his imagination been as sensitive as that of many of his contemporaries, or his self-love less, he would probably have fallen into their conscious or unconscious imitation of Shakespeare; but, as it was, he remained satisfied with himself to the last delving in his own mind."

1851

1   KNIGHT, CHARLES, ed. "Ben Jonson's London." In <u>London</u>. Vol. 1. 2d ed. London: Henry G. Bohn, pp. 365-96.
    A biography of Jonson within the context of turn-of-the century London. Poems by Jonson are cited to shed light on certain aspects of London life.

2   MILLS, ABRAHAM, ed. <u>The Literature and Literary Men of Great Britain and Ireland</u>. Vol. 1. New York: Harper & Brothers, pp. 313-38.
    A selection of poems and excerpts from plays and masques. In his headnote Mills points out the two dominant but contrasting qualities of Jonson's poetry: "One hard, rugged, gross, and sarcastic--the other, airy, fanciful, and graceful, as if its possessor had never combated with the world and its bad passions, but nursed his understanding and his fancy in poetical seclusion and contemplation."

3   MITFORD, MARY RUSSELL. "Old Authors: Ben Jonson." In <u>Recollections of A Literary Life</u>. New York: Harper & Brothers, pp. 240-46.
    Selections from Jonson's poems interspersed with complimentary remarks.

4   W., A. F. "Unpublished Verses by Ben Jonson." <u>Willis's Current Notes</u> 1 (September):68.
    Discovery of a holograph translation by Jonson of some verses beginning, "Inevitable fate to shun/Thou tak'st a world of toil. . . ."

1852

1   ANON. "Ben Jonson's Verses on the Marriage of the Earl of Somerset." <u>N&Q</u> 5 (28 February):193-94.
    Prints "To the Most Noble and above his Titles, Earl of Somerset," previously unpublished, which the author found written in a copy of <u>Works</u> 1640. The scandal surrounding the marriage that this poem celebrates probably accounts for Jonson's not having this poem published.

1853

1   AUSTIN, WILTSHIRE STANTON, AND RALPH, JOHN. "Ben Jonson." In
    Lives of the Poets-Laureate. London: R. Bentley, pp.
    49-108.
        Biographical and critical essay. The authors dispute
    Sir Walter Scott's remark that Jonson's poetry was meta-
    physical. They point out the similarities between Jonson's
    Discoveries and Bacon's Essays. Though Discoveries is
    written in a "concise and pregnant style," it does not
    contain as much "sententious wisdom" as the Essays.

2   GOUGH, HENRY. "Burial in an Erect Position." N&Q 8 (5 Nov-
    ember):455.
        When Jonson's grave was opened, he was found buried in
    an erect position.

1854

1   KNIGHT, CHARLES. "Ben Jonson's Mother," and "English Poets in
    Scotland." In Once Upon a Time. Vol. 1. 2d ed. London:
    J. Murray, pp. 154-74.
        The first chapter is a speculative biography of Jonson's
    early life. The second chapter deals largely with John
    Taylor, the Water Poet, touching on his relationships with
    Jonson.

2   RIMBAULT, EDWARD F. "Shakespeare's Rime Which He Made at the
    Mytre." N&Q 9 (13 May):440.
        Questions the attributions of a MS poem previously cred-
    ited to Shakespeare. Rimbault answers one reader who sug-
    gests Jonson as the author.

1855

1   FOSS, EDWARD. "Ben Jonson and the Lawyers." N&Q 12 (21 July):
    38.
        Suggests that Jonson's epigrams on lawyers might have
    been inspired by the hope of monetary reward.

2   MacCARTHY, D. F. "Eugene Scribe, Ben Jonson, and the Quaker."
    N&Q 11 (16 June):255.
        Why is Jonson referred to as a Quaker in Le Quaker et
    la Danseuse?

1856

1 ANON. "Ben Jonson." Bentley's Miscellany 40 (1856):157-66.
   Review of The Poetical Works of Ben Jonson, edited by Robert Bell.
      Points out the familiar aspects of Jonson's verse, but
   the author also notes, "Jonson's imagination fastens
   instinctively . . . on some mask or sign by which he designates the individual, and never lets it go, for fear of
   not meeting with any other means to express itself by."
   See 1856.3. Reprinted in 1860.1.

2 ANON. "Ben Jonson." SatR 2 (12 July):252-54.
      Review of The Poetical Works of Ben Jonson, edited by
   Robert Bell. A general evaluation of Jonson s poetry with
   an attempt to correct what the author considers misconcep-
   tions of his genius. "There are many indications that his
   genius was of the masculine and rugged type of the Elizabethan
   age; but he has too much respect for his art to throw its
   creations before the world in their unpolished roughness.
   The jewel never left his hands till its natural lustre
   was displayed in a thousand glittering facets." See
   1856.3.

3 BELL, ROBERT, ed. Introduction to The Poetical Works of Ben
   Jonson. London: John W. Parker, 288 pp.
      "The predominant merit of his poems lie in their practi-
   cal wisdom. . . . His lines are pregnant with thought ap-
   plicable to the conduct of life; and without any of the
   affectation of aphorisms, multitudes of his couplets might
   be separated from the text, and preserved apart for their
   axiomatic completeness."

4 MASSON, DAVID. Review of The Works of Ben Jonson, edited by
   William Gifford. North British Review 24, no. 48 (February):447-78.
      Complains of Gifford's polemical style in defending Jon-
   son against every critic who ever questioned Jonson's
   ability. Deals largely with Jonson's life and attempts to
   balance Gifford's defense and the attitude of Jonson's
   earlier critics. See 1816.1. Reprinted in 1856.5.

5 _____. Littell's Living Age 54 (9 August):321-38.
   Reprint of 1856.4.

6 VILLEMAIN, ABEL FRANÇOIS. "The Works of Ben Jonson." Journal
   Des Savants (May):257-75.
      Review of The Works of Ben Jonson, edited by William
   Gifford.

Discusses nineteenth-century editions of Renaissance
English dramatists. See 1816.1.

1857

1   ANON. Review of The Works of Ben Jonson, edited by William
        Gifford, and The Poetical Works of Ben Jonson, edited by
        Robert Bell. The British Quarterly Review 50 (1 April):285-320.
           A life and works essay with the emphasis on Jonson's
        life. Shows an appreciation for Jonson's poetry, and
        notes that most people are unfamiliar with it. See
        1816.1; 1856.3. Reprinted in 1857.2.

2   ANON. Littell's Living Age 55, no. 687 (July):193-212.
        Reprint of 1857.1.

3   BATHURST, C. Remarks on the Differences in Shakespeare's Ver-
        sification. London: John W. Parker, pp. 168-74.
           Jonson probably had some influence on Shakespeare's
        verse style.

4   HYDE, EDWARD, Earl of Clarendon. The Life of Edward Earl of
        Clarendon . . . Written by Himself. Vol. 1. Oxford:
        Oxford University Press, pp. 28-29.
           Reprint of 1670.1.

1858

*1   AMOS, ANDREW. Martial and the Moderns. London: Bell & Daldy,
        passim.
           Cited in Tannenbaum 1938.13.

2   ANON. "Ben Jonson." National Review 6, no. 11 (January):112-46.
           Review of The Poetical Works of Ben Jonson, edited by
        Robert Bell and The Works of Ben Jonson, edited by
        William Gifford. Because people are familiar with only
        a few beautiful lyrics of Jonson's, they are likely to think
        that more would be available in his complete works. That
        is not the case, according to the reviewer who character-
        izes Jonson's poetry as "for the most part inexpressibly
        tedious reading." See 1856.3; 1816.1. Reprinted in 1858.3;
        1858.4.

3   ANON. Eclectic Magazine 44, no. 1 (May):1-21.
        Reprint of 1858.2.

1858

4   ANON. Littell's Living Age 56, no. 718 (February):542-61.
     Reprint of 1858.2.

1859

1   ANON. "Ben Jonson in Scotland." Eclectic Magazine 47, no. 1
     (May):142.
         Reports of notes in Edinburgh's City Treasure's accounts
     of a dinner for Jonson on his visit to Scotland in 1618.

2   ANON. "Ben Jonson's Skull." Athenaeum, no. 1640 (2 April):
     455-56.
         A skull found while opening a grave next to Jonson's.

3   MEZIERES, ALFRED. "Les Contemporains Shakespeare." Le Mag-
     asin de Librairie. 2:565-608; 3:77-123; 210-42; 368-
     408; 540-60.
         A survey of Elizabethan and Jacobean literature. Jon-
     son is recognized for his contributions to drama, his
     friendship with Shakespeare, and his criticism.

1859-69

1   GRAESSE, JEAN GEORGE THEODORE. "Ben Jonson." In Tresor de
     Livres Rares et Precieux. Vol. 3. Dresde: R. Kuntze,
     pp. 476-77.
         A bibliography of editions of Ben Jonson's works to
     1650.

1860

1   ANON. "Ben Jonson: His Life and Works." Littell's Living
     Age 65, no. 828 (April):69-82.
         Reprint of 1856.1.

2   DELACOURT, RAYMOND. "Ben Jonson." N&Q 22 (22 November):367-
     68.
         Queries on certain biographical information.

1863

1   HARPER, J. A. "Ben Jonson and Mrs. Bulstrode." N&Q 28
     (22 August):150.
         Perhaps Cecily Bulstrode was the subject of Jonson's
     poem, "An epigram on the Court Pucell."

*2   TAINE, H. A.   "Ben Jonson."   In Histoire de la littérature
      anglaise. Paris: L. Hachette.

                              1864

1   ANON. "Ben Jonson," and "A Cabinet of Gems, from Ben Jonson's
      Discoveries." In The Book of Days: A Miscellany of Pop-
      ular Antiquities. Vol. 2. Edited by Robert Chambers.
      London: W. R. Chambers, pp. 181-83.
          Recounts the standard information about Jonson's life
      and laments the loss of Jonson's papers in his famous
      fire. The second article reprints selections from
      Discoveries with the remark that "very few books contain
      as much wisdom in as little space."

2   ANON. "Lyrists." Dublin University Magazine 63, no. 376
      (April):380-84.
          A comparison of Jonson, Herrick, and Carew, all of whom
      wrote at a time when poets "Looked merely for beautiful
      ideas, and let the thoughts or fancies evolve themselves
      with rhythmical naturalness."

3   FULLOM, S. W. History of William Shakespeare. London:
      Saunders, Otley, pp. 293-99.
          Short discussion of some of Jonson's criticism of
      Shakespeare.

4   KENNY, THOMAS. "Shakespeare and Ben Jonson." In The Life and
      Genius of Shakespeare. London: Longman, Green et al., pp.
      410-14.
          Although Jonson made critical statements regarding
      Shakespeare, he later took a more favorable attitude toward
      his work.

5   NEIL, SAMUEL. "Ben Jonson's Lines on Shakespeare's Portrait."
      N&Q 29 (23 April):340.
          Lines by Mulherbe on Montaigne's portrait "seem strange-
      ly like" Jonson's on Shakespeare's.

                              1865

1   AXON, WM. E. A. "Ben Jonson." N&Q 32 (2 September):195.
          Prints a previously uncollected poem of Jonson's the
      first line of which is "Temporibus lux magna fuit Juven-
      alis avitis."

                               41

1865

2   COLLIER, J. PAYNE. "Ben Jonson and Alexander Gill."
    Athenaeum, no. 1957 (29 April):587-88.
        Transcription of Alexander Gill's abusive poem to Jonson
    after the production of The Magnetic Lady. Jonson's answer
    is also printed.

3   DRACO [pseud.]. "Ben Jonson." N&Q 32 (5 August):115-16.
        Presents evidence for the standard spelling of Jonson's
    name.

4   ERIC [pseud.]. "Jonson or Johnson?" N&Q 32 (8 July):27-28.
        Argues Jonson should be spelled with an "h."

5   LOWNDES, WILLIAM THOMAS. The Bibliographer's Manual. Vol. 3.
    Bell & Dalby, pp. 1230-32.
        Lists editions of Jonson and selected items about Jonson.

6   STEPHENS, GEORGE. "Ben Jonson." N&Q 32 (11 November):403.
        Presents additional evidence for the standard spelling
    of Jonson's name.

7   WALLACE, OSWALD. "Ben Jonson and Bartholomeus Anulus." N&Q
    32 (2 September):187.
        Jonson's poem beginning, "Follow a shadow and it still
    flies you," may have been borrowed from Anulus. See
    1925.13.

                              1866

1   COLLIER, J. PAYNE. A Bibliography and Critical Account of the
    Rarest Books in the English Language. 4 Vols. New York:
    David E. Francis, Charles Scribner, passim.
        Identifies first editions of Jonson's minor poems.

2   CORNEY, BOLTON. "Ben Jonson and James Mabbe." N&Q 32
    (21 April):314-15.
        Prints a poem not previously collected "On the author,
    work and translator," in Mates Aleman's La vide y hechos
    del picars Guzman de Alfaracle translated by James Mabbe
    in 1622.

3   MACRAY, WILLIAM DUNN, ed. "Manuscripts by and Relating to
    Ben Jonson." In Index to the Catalogue of the Manuscripts
    of Elias Ashmole. Oxford: Clarendon Press, p. 89.
        An index to W. H. Black's A Descriptive, Analytical and
    Critical Catalogue of the Manuscripts Bequeathed . . .
    by Elias Ashmole, which is part 10 of Catalogi Codicum
    Manuscriptorum Bibliothecae Bodleianae pars Prima, etc.

1868

1 KNIGHT, CHARLES. <u>Studies of Shakespeare</u>. London: George
   Routledge, pp. 260-64.
       Correlation of Jonson's and Shakespeare's lives.

2 MANNINGHAM, JOHN. <u>Diary of John Manningham</u>. Edited by John
   Bruce. Westminster: J. B. Nichols, passim.
       Short notes on Jonson's poetry.

*3 WHIPPLE, EDWIN P. "Ben Jonson." In <u>The Literature of the Age</u>
   <u>of Elizabeth</u>. Boston: Fields, Osgood & Co.
       See 1891.2.

4 WOOD, ANTHONY. <u>Anthenae Oxonienses</u>. Oxford: T. Combe.
   Reprint of 1691-92.1.

1870

1 ANON. "Ben Jonson." In <u>A Historical Description of Westmin-</u>
   <u>ster Abbey</u>. London: Truscott, pp. 114-15.
       A description of Jonson's monument in Westminster Abbey.

2 ANON. "Ben Jonson's Quarrel with Shakespeare." <u>North British</u>
   <u>Review</u> 52, no. 104 (July):203-21.
       Looks for a balanced position on Jonson and Shakespeare's
   personal relationships. The author says one cannot dismiss
   evidence of a strong Jonsonian criticism as Gifford does,
   nor should we think that the two writers were at each
   other's throats as earlier critics suggested. Rather Jonson respected and admired much of Shakespeare's work, a
   fact that did not prevent him from criticizing those aspects he did not care for.

3 NICHOLSON, BRINSLEY. "Ben Jonson's Folios and the Bibliographers." <u>N&Q</u> 41 (18 June):573-75.
       A discussion of the 1616 and 1640 folios. Considers
   also the possibility of a 1641 edition which Lowndes
   mentions in his bibliography.

1871

1 C., R. "Scribimus indocti doctique epigrammata passim." In
   <u>Times' Whistle</u>. Edited by J. M. Cowper. London: N.
   Trubner & Co. for the Early English Text Society, pp. 132-
   33.
       First publication of 1615.1. Reprinted 1922.4.

1871

2 CLARKE, CHARLES COWDEN. "On the Comic Writers of England: Ben Jonson." Gentleman's Magazine 230, no. 5 (May):631-50. Argues that Jonson's lyrics are among the finest in English because he "has a higher classical tone and finish as might be expected from his learned education."

3 GIFFORD, WILLIAM, and CUNNINGHAM, FRANCIS, eds. The Works of Ben Jonson. 3 vols. London: John Camden Hotten. Cunningham's revision of Gifford was largely in the form of additional notes which are bracketed, initialed, and incorporated within Gifford's text. Revision of 1816.1. See also 1886.5.

4 NOBLE, T. C. "O Rare Ben Jonson." N&Q 43 (4 March):183-84. Speculation on the implications of a newly-discovered manuscript which relates to Jonson: "Thomas Cooke his bill 1619," a bill for Cooke's service as Jonson's messenger.

5 RUSSELL, WILLIAM CLARK, ed. "Ben Jonson." In The Book of Authors. London: Frederick Warne, pp. 44-47. Critical and biographical excerpts from such writers as Howell, Johnson, Herrick, Feltham, and David Hume.

1873

1 ANON. "Ben Jonson, 1619-1637." Pro & Con 1, no. 6 (15 May): 81-86. Biographical sketch focusing on Jonson's economic problems near the end of his life. Notes that Jonson had "an extravagant style of living," and was at least in part responsible for the poverty of his late life.

2 HARKINS, WM. "Shakespeare and Ben Jonson." Cornell Review 1 (December):141-45. A brief comparison of the two writers. Concludes: "the one produced lyrics that have never been surpassed, the other dramas which have never been approached."

3 MAIDMENT, JAMES. Introduction to Sir Thomas Overburies Vision, by Richard Niccols. [Glasgow: R. Anderson], pp. 19-26. Defends Jonson's writing of two masques and an epithalamion for the marriage of Lady Frances Howard and the Earl of Somerset, which was itself probably the greatest scandal during the reign of James I. Reprinted in 1966.11.

4 MASSON, DAVID. Life of John Milton. London: Macmillan & Co., passim.

Includes a short life of Jonson with emphasis on his personal literary dictatorship. Masson points out that Milton's early poetry showed some of Jonson's influence. Reprinted in 1946.9.

5   . "Literary London: . . . Ben Jonson's Journey to Scotland," In Drummond of Hawthornden. London: Macmillan & Co., pp. 74-114.
Describes Jonson's visit with Drummond, his <u>Conversations</u>, and reprints letters between Jonson and Drummond. Reprinted in 1969.15.

<u>1874</u>

1   ANON. Wits Recreation in Musarum Deliciae. Vol. 2. Edited by E. Dubois. London: John Camden Hotten, pp. 11, 95, 99, 124, 276, 277, 425-28.
Dubois's edition first appeared in 1817. Reprint of 1640.1 and 1663.1.

2   BROWNE, C. ELLIOT. "Ben Jonson, Junior." <u>N&Q</u> 50 (12 September):208.
Briefly discusses a book of poems printed in 1672 supposedly by Ben Jonson junior.

3   GLAPTHORNE, HENRY. "White-Hall. A Poem. Written 1642." In <u>The Plays and Poems of Henry Glapthorne</u>. Vol. 2. London: John Pearson.
Reprint of 1643.1.

4   IRELAND, WILLIAM-HENRY. "Ben Jonson." In <u>The Confessions of W. H. Ireland</u>. New York: James W. Bouton.
Reprint of 1806.1.

5   KINGSLEY, HENRY. "Ben Jonson." <u>Temple Bar</u> 42 (August):35-50.
Considers Jonson "a second-rate comic writer and a third class tragic writer," but "one of the most exquisite poets who ever wrote in our or any other language. To read his poetry is like walking in an English meadow in May time." Reprinted in 1876.3.

6   MINTON, WILLIAM. "Ben Jonson." In <u>Characteristics of English Poets</u>. Edinburgh: William Blackwood, pp. 440-50.
A life and works essay in which the author takes a different attitude toward Jonson's classical learning than one normally sees. "Jonson's domineering scholarship must not be taken for more than it was worth: it was a large and gratifying possession in itself, but he would probably have written better plays and more poetry without it."

7   SMITH, GEORGE BARNETT. "Drummond of Hawthornden." <u>New Quarterly Magazine</u>, 2 (April to July):620-39.

1874

As part of a general survey of Drummond's life and works, Jonson's association with him is described.

1875

1 ANON. "Ben Jonson." The Spectator 48 (9 October):1265-66.
Review of The Works of Ben Jonson, edited by William Gifford and Francis Cunningham. Though Jonson did not excel as a dramatist, his poetry should be taken more seriously. "Many of Jonson's minor poems are full of lyric grace and spirit and claim a need of admiration as great as that which is paid to any compositions of their class." See 1871.3.

2 FRIESEN, H. FREIH, v. "Ben Jonson. Eine Studie." Shakespeare Jahrbuch 10 (1875):127-49.
Acknowledges Jonson as a court poet capable of writing beautiful lyrics.

3 GANTILLON, P. J. F. "Rare Ben Jonson Caught Tripping." N&Q 52 (30 October):346.
Jonson made a literary historical error in Discoveries.

4 SYMONDS, JOHN ADDINGTON. Review of The Works of Ben Jonson, edited by William Gifford and Francis Cunningham. Academy & Literature 8 (2 October):352-53.
Judges that Cunningham's additions to Gifford are of very little if any use. See 1871.3.

*5 WARD, A. W. "Ben Jonson." In A History of English Dramatic Literature. Vol. 2. London: Macmillan & Co.
See 1899.9.

1876

1 HAZLITT, WILLIAM CAREW. "Ben Jonson." In Collection and Notes. London: Reeves & Turner, p. 240.
A short bibliography of works by or about Jonson.

2 HOOPER, RICHARD. "Jonson on Shakespeare." N&Q 54 (14 October):303.
Notes that a Mr. Richard Williams uses two lines from Jonson's poem on Shakespeare for a dedication in 1632 to E. Benlowes.

3 KINGSLEY, HENRY. "The Master of the Mermaid." In Fireside Studies. Vol. 1. London: Chatto & Windus, pp. 264-322.
Reprint of 1874.5.

4   SHAW, THOMAS BUDD. <u>Outlines of English Literature</u>. New York:
     Sheldon.
        Despite a certain number of undesirable characteristics,
     Jonson was "a great and good man; grateful, generous, valiant,
     free spoken, with something of the old Roman spirit in him,
     a mighty artist, and a man of a gigantic and cultivated
     genius. . . ." Reprint of 1849.1.

1877

1   INGLEBY, C. M. <u>Shakespeare: The Man and the Book</u>, Part 1.
     London: Trubner, pp. 93-97.
        Suggests that Shakespeare designated Jonson as his
     literary executor.

2   JABEZ [pseud]. "He was not of an age, but for all time."
     <u>N&Q</u> 56 (1 September):163.
        Complains that Jonson's line has been changed for the
     official seal of the National Shakespeare Committee and
     suggests that the meaning is significantly altered.

1878

1   DANIEL, GEORGE. <u>The Poems of George Daniel, Esq</u>. Vol. 1.
     Edited by A. B. Grosart. Boston, Lincolnshire: printed
     by Robert Roberts, pp. 63-66.
        Reprint of 1646.1.

2   DAVIES, JOHN of Hereford. "To my learnedly witty friend, Mr.
     Benjamin Jonson." In <u>The Complete Works of John Davies of
     Hereford</u>. Vol. 2 Edited by A. B. Grosart. Edinburgh:
     Edinburgh University Press, sec. n, p. 4.
        Reprint of 1617.2.

1879

1   ANON. "Chester's <u>Love's Martyr</u>." SatR 47 (18 January):90-92.
        Near the end of Chester's <u>Love's Martyr</u> are included
     some poems by Jonson which this writer characterizes as of
     "manly style, but with a little more of his pedantry than
     we admire nowadays."

2   DESHLER, CHARLES D. <u>Afternoons with the Poets</u>. New York:
     Harper Brothers, passim.
        Strong criticism of Jonson's poetry, particularly the
     epigrams which the author sees as half epigrams and half

1879

    sonnets. "If there are any sonnets in our language, by poets of repute, which are more devoid of merit than all of his save two, I have not been able to find them."

3 FANE, MILDMAY, Earl of Westmoreland. "In obitum Ben Johns. Poetae eximii." In Occasional Issues of Unique and Very Rare Books. Edited by A. B. Grosart. Vol. 10. [Blackburn: C. E. Sims], p. 169.
    Reprint of 1648.1.

4 INGLEBY, C. M., ed. Shakespeare's Centurie of Prayse. 2d ed. Revised by Lucy Toulmin Smith. London: Trubner, passim.
    Jonson's poetry on Shakespeare is cited.

5 MORELEY, HENRY, and TYLER, MOSES COIT. "Ben Jonson." In A Manual of English Literature. New York: Sheldon, pp. 285-94.
    A high-school survey of English literature with a standard life and works essay on Jonson.

6 NICHOLSON, B. "The Whipper's Penance." Athenaeum, no. 2716 (15 November):631-32.
    Jonson is identified as one of the individuals cited in The Whipping of the Satire, 1601.

7 TEGG, WILLIAM. Shakespeare and His Contemporaries. London, William Tegg & Co., pp. 88-90.
    Brief biographical and critical notes. Much of Jonson's poetry "is below mediocrity, but there are a few pieces which are polished into perfect gems."

1880

1 Butler, Noble. "Ben Jonson or Shakespeare." In Butler's Miscellanies. Louisville: John P. Morton & Co., pp. 157-66.
    Jonson's "To the memory of my beloved, the author, Mr. William Shakespeare" is all the evidence necessary to prove that Shakespeare did write the plays attributed to him.

2 WARD, A. W. "Ben Jonson." In The English Poets. Vol. 2. Edited by Thomas Humphrey Ward. New York: Macmillan, pp. 1-7.
    A critical introduction that points to the diversity of style in Jonson's poetry, his influence on other writers, and his lack of a readership at the present time. Reprinted in 1971.22.

1881

1   DOWDEN, EDWARD, ed. "Ben Jonson on Shakespeare's Sonnets."
    In The Sonnets of William Shakespeare. London: C. K.
    Paul, p. 45.
        Calls attention to Jonson's critical remarks on sonnets.

2   HERMANN, ERNST. "Der Beginn d. Kampfes Zwischen Ben Jonson
    and Shakespeare." In Weitere Quellenmassige Beitrage Zu
    Shakespeare's Literar. Kampfen. Vol. 1. Erlangen: A.
    Diechert, pp. 203-73.
        Jonson and Shakespeare's professional and personal re-
    lationships were not consistent. Hermann charts the pat-
    tern of their friendship arguing that the two men were
    never enemies but did disagree at times.

3   INGLEBY, C. M. "The Tongue of Shakespeare." In Occasional
    Papers on Shakespeare. London: Trubner, pp. 27-28.
        Discussion of Jonson's lyric, "Drink to me only."

4   RICHARDSON, ABBY SAGE. Familiar Talks on English Literature.
    Chicago: A. C. McClung, pp. 153-58.
        Believes that Jonson is overrated as a poet and hints
    that he maintains a kind of intimidating power over read-
    ers yet today. "I do not underrate rare old Ben when I
    say that he owes as much to his power as to his ability as
    a poet."

5   ROBINSON, C. J. "Ben Jonson's Copy of Priscian." Academy
    19 (19 February):138.
        Identifies a copy of Priscian as having been Jonson's.

1882

1   ANON. "English Poets and Oxford Critics." Quarterly Review
    153, no. 306 (April):431-63.
        Review of Ben Jonson or Shakespeare, by Noble Butler.
    On Jonson the reviewer states, "Had he never written a
    play, he would, by his songs, epigrams, epitaphs, and
    epistles, have secured for himself a poet's fame. See
    1880.1.

2   ANON. "Our Great-Great-Grandmother's Grammar." All the Year
    Round 49 (10 June):397-402.
        Gives Jonson credit for laying the groundwork for stan-
    dardized English grammar, and for basing it soundly in clas-
    sical Latin and Greek.

1882

3 BUCKLAND, ANNA. The Story of English Literature. London:
   Cassell, Petter, Galpin, pp. 171-73.
       Brief remarks on life and works concluding with a state-
   ment on Jonson's critical mind. "In all his work Ben Jonson strove with manliness and courage to lead men to live
   more serious aims, and to give the earnestness and labor
   bestowed on surface trifles to deeper things. He endeav-
   oured constantly to make them more true to an independent
   standard of perfection, and to free them from the slavish
   subjection to the custom and fashion of the hour."

4 GUEST, EDWIN. A History of English Rhythms. Edited by Walter
   W. Skeat. London: George Bell, passim.
       Focuses on a major reason for the study of Jonson: his
   contribution to English prosody. Takes up Jonson's use
   of the caesura comparing him to later writers who began
   to regularize cadences in odes and songs.

5 HALLIWELL-PHILLIPPS, J. O. Outlines of the Life of Shakespeare.
   2d ed. London: Longman's, Green & Co. pp. 106-107.
       Recounts the story of Shakespeare giving Jonson his op-
   portunity to enter the theater.

6 HOLMES, NATHANIEL. The Authorship of Shakespeare. 4th ed.
   Boston: Houghton Mifflin, pp. 165-72.
       Suggests that Bacon may have written Jonson's poem on
   Shakespeare.

7 INGLEBY, C. M. "Jonson's Censure on Shakespeare." N&Q 65
   (25 March):224.
       Jonson's famous remark on Shakespeare, "His wit was in
   his own power, would that the rule of it had been so too,"
   does not mean that someone else was writing Shakespeare's
   plays. Rather Jonson recognized that Shakespeare's wit
   was so powerful that he did not always rule it as he
   should.

8 MORGAN, APPLETON. Some Shakespearean Commentators. Cincinnati:
   Robert Clarke, p. 19.
       The fact that in Discoveries Jonson praises most highly
   Francis Bacon and does not even mention Shakespeare provides some evidence that his extended praise in his "Ode
   on Shakespeare" is actually intended for Francis Bacon.

*9 SWINBURNE, ALGERNON CHARLES. "Ben Jonson," and "The Tribe of
   Benjamin." In "Sonnets on English Dramatic Poets." In
   Tristram of Lyonesse and Other Poems. London: Chatto &
   Windus.
       See 1925.31.

1883

1   NICOLL, HENRY JAMES. <u>Landmarks of English Literature</u>. New
York: D. Appleton, passim.
Not impressed by his plays, the author finds Jonson's
songs his finest pieces.

2   PHIPSON, EMMA. <u>The Animal Lore of Shakespeare's Time</u>. London:
Kegan Paul, Trench & Co., passim.
Allusions to Jonson's use of birds, reptiles, fish, in-
sects, etc. in his poetry and prose.

3   TAINE, H. A. "Ben Jonson." In <u>The History of English Litera-
ture</u>. Vol. 2. Translated by H. Van Laun. Philadelphia:
Gebbie Publishing Co., pp. 1-49.
?   True poetry ceased to be written in England after about
1640. Jonson was one of the last and best of those poets
who really appreciated life and could write about it. Translation of 1863.2. Reprinted in 1965.16.

4   WELSH, ALFRED H. "Jonson." In <u>Development of English Literature and Language</u>. Vol. 1. 3d ed. Chicago: S. C. Griggs
& Co., pp. 444-56.
Analyzes Jonson's style. "In prose, terse, sharp, swift,
biting. In versification, peculiarly smooth and flowing;
for this literary leviathan, it strangely appears, has eminently the merits of elegance and grace."

1884

1   BEVERIDGE, A. M. "'Ed' for '-able' in Ben Jonson." <u>Shake-
speareana</u> 1 (August):254-57.
The archaic use of the passive participle as an adjec-
tive in Jonson and Shakespeare.

2   COLERIDGE, SAMUEL TAYLOR. <u>Specimens of the Table Talk of the
Late Samuel Taylor Coleridge</u>. In <u>The Complete Works of
Samuel Taylor Coleridge</u>. Vol. 6. Edited by W. G. T.
Shedd. New York: Harper & Brothers, pp. 287,426.
Coleridge admired Jonson. In brief remarks he notes,
"In Jonson you have an intense and burning art." Reprint
of 1835.1.

3   CROFTS, ELLEN. "Ben Jonson." In <u>Chapters in the History of
English Literature</u>. London: Rivingtons, pp. 232-57.
Criticizes Jonson's dependence on the classical tradition
which caused him to become more a teacher than a poet and
allowed his egotistic personality to dominate his work.

4   FLEAY, F. G. "Annals of Ben Jonson's career." <u>Shakespeareana</u>
1 (June):208-15.

1884

An extensive list of dates and events in Jonson's life
to correct mistakes in Gifford and Cunningham. See 1871.3.

5 HOFFMAN, FREDERICK A. "The Early Elizabethan Dramatic Poets."
In Poetry: Its Origin, Nature and History. London: Thur-
gate & Sons, pp. 133-38.
Impressed by Jonson's breadth of knowledge. Senses that
his poetry is strained, missing the fluency of one who writes
with more freedom.

6 HOSKYNS-ABRAHALL, J. "Ben Jonson's Song 'To Celia.'" Academy
26 (13 December):395.
Response to 1884.9. Cites passages in Jonson's poem
parallel with those in Philostratus' Epistles.

7 LEE, S[IDNEY] L. "The Epitaph on the Countess of Pembroke."
Academy 25 (5 January):12.
Explains why a portion of this poem was canceled from
Jonson's Works.

8 PAYNE, J. F. "Ben Jonson's 'To Celia.'" Academy 26 (1 Nov-
ember):291.
First of a series of notes on the source of "To Celia."
Cites lines from a letter by Angelo Poliziano as a source.
See 1884.6, 9, 12, 13.

9 SYMONDS, JOHN ADDINGTON. "Ben Jonson's 'To Celia.'" Academy
26 (6 December):377-78.
Response to 1884.8. Gives a step by step comparison of
Philostratus to Jonson's quatrains.

10 THURGOOD, ROBERT M. "Parallel Passages." N&Q 70 (8 November):
365-66.
Points out similarities between "Song to Celia" and the
Greek love letters of Philostratus.

11 VATKE, T. "Ben Jonson in seinen Anfängen." Archiv 71 (1884):
241-62.
A survey of Jonson's life along with a discussion of his
works.

12 WHARTON, HENRY T. "Ben Jonson's 'To Celia.'" Academy 26
(8 November):306.
Response to 1884.8. Suggests Philostratus as Jonson's
source.

13 WILLIAMS, J. "Ben Jonson's 'To Celia.'" Academy 26 (15 November):325.
Response to 1884.12. Agathias' Epigram v. 261, Meleager's

1886

Epigrams v. 136 and 171, and Leontius' Epigram v. 265 are
cited as more likely sources for Jonson's "To Celia" than
Philostratus.

1885

1   GREENE, G. A. "Two Queries." Academy 27 (21 March):207.
       In Jonson's "Ode on Shakespeare" the allusion, "him of
    Cordova," is a reference to Seneca.

2   HAYNES, HENRY W. "Ben Jonson and Philostratus." Nation 40
    (15 January):53-54.
       The source of Jonson's "To Celia" is Philostratus.

3   L., H. "Two Queries." Academy 27 (14 March):188
    A question answered in 1885.1.

1886

1   BEECHING, H. C. "'English Worthies': Ben Jonson." Academy
    30 (16 October):251.
       Review of Dramatic Works and Lyrics of Ben Jonson, by
    John Addington Symonds. Symonds gives a more informative
    account of Jonson's life and writings than formerly offered.
    See 1886.9.

2   FURNIVALL, FREDK. J. Some 300 Fresh Allusions to Shakespeare
    from 1594-1694. London: N. Trubner, passim.
       Jonson's allusions to Shakespeare are listed.

3   GROSS, EDMUND. Raleigh. England's Worthies. London: Long-
    mans, Green & Co., pp. 175-76.
       Jonson's Epigram XXIV, "The mind of the Frontispiece to
    a book," is printed opposite the frontispiece to Raleigh's
    History of the World. Gosse believes that the poem was
    actually written by Raleigh and transcribed by Jonson when
    he was helping prepare the History for the press. Herford
    and Simpson ascribe the poem to Jonson.

4   HALLAM, HENRY. Introduction to the Literature of Europe. 4
    vols. New York: A. C. Armstrong & Son, passim.
       Values Jonson's poetry above his drama since in his
    verse he better demonstrated his intellectual excellencies
    of "wit, observation, judgment, memory, and learning."

5   INGLEBY, C. M. "An Omitted Reference in Gifford's Jonson."
    N&Q 73 (23 January):77-78.
       Note for revisions of 1871.3.

1886

6 MACRAY, W[ILLIAM] D[UNN], ed. "The Pilgrimage to Parnassus"
   with "The Return to Parnassus." Oxford: Clarendon Press,
   passim.
       Except for the second part of "The Return to Parnassus,"
   these late sixteenth and early seventeenth century plays
   existed only in manuscript until Macray edited them. Jonson's assessment of Marston as an embarassing imitator is
   mentioned. Jonson's satire on fops, fools, and courtiers
   is also cited. Reprinted in 1949.6.

7 MORLEY, HENRY, ed. Introduction to Plays and Poems of Ben
   Jonson. 2d ed. London: George Routledge & Son, pp. 5-8.
       Brief discussion of Jonson's life and works emphasizing
   his learning and scholarship which permeates his work.

8 SANBORN, KATE. Vanity and Insanity of Genius. New York:
   George J. Combes, pp. 50-51.
       Sanborn gives "vain, irascible, and jealous" Ben Jon-
   son only two pages to support her thesis: "Vanity seems
   to be at once the source of the greatest weakeness and of
   the greatest achievements."

9 SYMONDS, JOHN ADDINGTON, ed. Introduction to Dramatic Works
   and Lyrics of Ben Jonson. London: Walter Scott, pp.
   vii-xxxv.
       Emphasizes Jonson's didacticism and his ideal of the
   poet's purpose. "The independence which marked his personal character and his theory of poetry, expressed itself
   at times in arrogance and satire; but the poems addressed
   to individuals, who might have been accounted rivals, ex-
   onerate him from the charge of envy and malignity."

10 WALFORD, E. "Ben Jonson, Rosslyn, and Hawthornden." Gentle-
    man's Magazine 261 (December):604-9.
        A description of Rosslyn Castle and the nearby country.
    estate of Hawthornden which Jonson visited in 1618.

11 [WILDE, OSCAR.] "Ben Jonson." Pall Mall Gazette 44 (20 Sep-
    tember):6.
        Review of Dramatic Works and Lyrics of Ben Jonson, edit-
    ed by John Addington Symonds. Admires Jonson's intense
    commitment to literature but is reserved and cautious in
    his remarks on Symonds' edition. See 1886.9.

1887

1 ANON. "Ben Jonson." Queries Magazine 3 (October):663-66.

Reprints a series of famous critical remarks on Jonson's
nondramatic works by Herrick, Drummond, Howell, Aubrey,
Fuller, Langbaine, Taine, Dryden, Johnson, Churchill, Dis-
raeli, Henry Hallam, Thomas Shaw, and Mary Russel Mitford,
all of which are cited in the Reference Guide.

2   ANON.   Review of <u>Dramatic Works and Lyrics of Ben Jonson</u>,
      edited by John Addington Symonds.   <u>Spectator</u> 60 (4 June):
      769-70.
         Discusses Jonson's lack of popularity and takes issue
      with some of Symonds' selections. Argues that Symonds'
      enthusiasm for Jonson may have resulted in some unworthy
      praise. See 1886.9.

3   MACKAY, CHARLES.   <u>A Glossary of Obscure Words and Phrases</u>.
      London: Sampson Low, Marston, Searle, & Rivington,
      passim.
         In his discussion of obscure words and phrases in
      Shakespeare, the author occasionally cites Jonson's use
      of the same word or phrase. For instance, oil of talc I.
      ii, "An Epigram. To the Small Poxe," from <u>Under-wood</u> is
      discussed at some length.

4   SAINTSBURY, GEORGE.   <u>A History of Elizabethan Literature</u>.
      London: Macmillan, pp. 174-84.
         Biography with comments on poems and plays and a consid-
      eration of Jonson's influence on English literature. Al-
      though Saintsbury laments Jonson's want of passion, he
      nevertheless concludes that "He could be vigorous, he
      could be dignified, he could be broadly humorous, and, as
      has been said, he could combine with these the apparently
      incompatible, or, at least, not closely connected faculty
      of grace." Reprinted in 1970.35.

5   WHEATLEY, HENRY B.   "Ben Jonson's Dedications." In <u>The Ded-
      ication of Books to Patron and Friend</u>. London: Eliot
      Stock, pp. 67-70, 77.
         Lists some of Jonson's dedications to patrons at the
      opening of his books. Comparatively speaking, Jonson
      was more noble and honorable in his dedications than were
      other writers of the time. "Jonson never disgraces him-
      self by abject flattery. He never forgets what is due
      to himself while praising his patrons."

6   WOTTON, MABLE E., ed.   "Ben Jonson." In <u>Word Portraits of Fam-
      ous Writers</u>. London: Richard Bentley, pp. 152-55.
         Excerpts from early biographies.

1888

1 DONNELLY, IGNATIUS. "Ben Jonson's Testimony." In The Great
   Cryptogram. Chicago: R. S. Peale & Co., pp. 96-99.
       Compares lines in Discoveries to lines in Jonson's "Ode
   to Shakespeare" to help prove that Bacon wrote Shakespeare's
   plays and that Jonson knew it.

2 GARNETT, J. M. "Notes on Elizabethan Prose." PMLA 4, no. 1
   (January):41-61.
       Jonson is a very significant figure in the history of
   Renaissance prose. He makes a "distinct advance upon
   Bacon" because of the modernness of his style which is
   straightforward and vigorous.

3 SWINBURNE, ALGERNON CHARLES. "Ben Jonson." Nineteenth Century 23 (April):603-16; (May):693-715.
       Stresses Jonson's moral commitment and sense of con-
   science. He directed his considerable powers, his "self-
   devotion," "self-exaction," and "self-discipline" to this
   single-minded goal in life: to perfect the lofty ideal of
   the poet. "Reversing the famous axiom of Goldsmith's pro-
   fessional art-critic, we may say of Jonson's work in
   almost every instance that the picture would have been better if the artist had taken less pains."

4 SYMONDS, JOHN ADDINGTON. Ben Jonson. English Worthies. London: Longmans, Green & Co., 202 pp.
       Looks at the poetry and prose primarily to see what they
   may tell of Jonson's masterpieces, the plays. The poetry
   is interesting only because it was written by a great playwright. Calls the reader's attention only to Jonson's most
   famous pieces. Reprinted 1970.39.

5 WATERS, ROBERT. "Ben Jonson, Bacon, and Shakespeare." In
   William Shakespeare Portrayed by Himself. New York:
   Worthington & Co., pp. 316-24.
       Jonson's mutual friendship with both Shakespeare and
   Bacon is used to defend Shakespeare's authorship of his
   plays.

1889

1 DAVIDSON, JOHN. Review of A Study of Ben Jonson, by Algernon
   Charles Swinburne. Academy 36 (23 November):331-32.
       Swinburne provides a highly readable and an excellent
   critical study of Jonson. See 1889.7.

1888

2   DAVIES, LOUISA MARY. "Meetings of Societies." <u>Academy</u> 35
    (29 June):452-53.
         Summary of a paper on Jonson and Drummond presented at
    a meeting of the Clifton Shakespeare Society.

3   GRIFFITHS, L. M. <u>Evenings with Shakespeare</u>. Bristol: J. W.
    Arrowsmith, pp. 206-11.
         A brief but comprehensive and documented life of Jonson
    with a selected bibliography.

4   MARTIN, THEODORE. "Ben Jonson's Scurrilous Sonnet on Shake-
    speare." In <u>Essays on the Drama</u>. Second Series. London:
    printed for private circulation, pp. 348-49.
         Believes that "On the Poet Ape" is addressed to Shake-
    speare.

5   MITCHELL, DONALD G. "Ben Jonson." In <u>English Lands, Letters,
    and Kings</u>. Vol. 1. New York: Scribner's & Sons, pp.
    295-303.
         Praises Jonson's lyric poetry and characterizes his
    <u>English Grammar</u> "as good as almost any man could invent
    now."

6   MORLEY, HENRY, ed. Introduction to <u>Discoveries by Ben Jonson</u>.
    London: Cassell & Co., pp. 5-9.
         An elementary introduction to a school text. Praises
    Jonson for his strong and vigorous mind.

7   SWINBURNE, ALGERNON CHARLES. <u>A Study of Ben Jonson</u>. London:
    Chatto & Windus, 213 pp.
         Swinburne is critical of Jonson's poetry and argues that
    it has been overrated. He is particularly critical of
    the scatological verse. His very best poetry approaches
    greatness but never quite achieves it. On the other hand,
    <u>Discoveries</u> cannot be praised too highly. "We find our-
    selves in so high and so pure an atmosphere of feeling and
    of thought that we cannot but recognize and rejoice in the
    presence and the influence of one of the noblest, manliest,
    finest, and most helpful natures that ever dignified and
    glorified a powerful intelligence and an admirable genius."
    Reprinted in 1969.23.

8   WAITES, A. "Did Ben Jonson Write Francis Bacon's Works?"
    <u>Shakespeareana</u> 6 (April):145-57; (June):241-59; (July):
    298-313.
         Argues that Jonson, forever in Bacon's debt for a pardon
    after killing the actor, Gabriel Spencer, wrote Bacon's
    works. Bacon could not have written what has been attributed
    to him because he was too busy with courtly duties;
    moreover, he was known to be of frail health.

1890

1   ANON. "A. C. Swinburne's Study of Ben Jonson." Athenaeum,
     no. 3255 (8 March):315-18; no. 3256 (22 March):379-81.
         Review of A Study of Ben Jonson, by Algernon Charles
     Swinburne. Argues that there was one short period in Jon-
     son's life when his imagination was free. Jonson's career
     is a "rare instance of acquired methods conquering native
     impulse--one of the most marvellous instances in all lit-
     erature of the way in which the wings of genius may be
     clipped by the shears of doctrine and clogged by cob-
     webs of conventional prescription."

2   ANON. "Swinburne's 'Ben Jonson.'" Critic 16 (1 March):101-2.
         Review of A Study of Ben Jonson, by Algernon Charles Swin-
     burne. A scathing review attacking Swinburne's judgment
     and style. The book is "Mississippi-like in the vehemence
     and fertility of its panegyric," which becomes "a discus-
     sion without method, without fruit, without conclusion."
     See 1889.7.

3   ANON. "Swinburne on Ben Jonson." Literary World 21 (15 March):
     88-89.
         Review of A Study of Ben Jonson, by Algernon Charles
     Swinburne. Though Swinburne shows good judgment and edu-
     cated taste, his own style of criticism is "extravagant
     and intense." See 1889.7.

4   ANON. Review of A Study of Ben Jonson, by Algernon Charles
     Swinburne. Nation 50 (6 March):208-9.
         Swinburne has wisely helped deflate the status of Jon-
     son's lyric poetry which had grown during the nineteenth
     century. See 1889.7.

5   BROOKS, SARAH WARNER. "Ben Jonson." In English Poetry and
     Poets. Boston: Estes & Lauriat, pp. 111-32.
         Points out the two sides of Jonson's nature: "one hard,
     rugged, gross, and sarcastic, and the other airy, fanciful,
     and graceful." In his lyrics Jonson turns to the finer
     side of his nature. Reprinted in 1972.3.

6   DAVIDSON, JOHN. "Rare Ben." Bookmart 7 (March):443-46.
         Review of A Study of Ben Jonson, by Algernon Charles
     Swinburne. A thorough evaluation of Swinburne's book.
     Praises the style as a significant factor in bringing Jon-
     son alive for the reader. See 1889.7.

7   MITCHELL, DONALD G.   "Ben Jonson Again." In <u>English Lands,</u>
    <u>Letters, and Kings</u>.   Vol. 2.   New York: Scribner's & Sons,
    pp. 26-29.
        Looks at Jonson as a major influence on English liter-
    ature. His imposing personality and his overpowering crit-
    ical views are felt through three hundred years of English
    literature. See also 1889.5.

8   RUTHERFORD, MILDRED L.   "Ben Jonson." In <u>English Authors</u>.
    Atlanta: Constitution Book & Job Print, pp. 93-97.
        As a critic Jonson's reputation was second to none.
    Reprinted in 1906.10.

9   SCHELLING, FELIX E.   "A. C. Swinburne's Study of Ben Jonson."
    <u>MLN</u> 5 (June):183-85.
        Review of <u>A Study of Ben Jonson</u>, by Algernon Charles
    Swinburne. Jonson deserves more of the kind of attention
    given to him in Swinburne's study. He has long suffered
    from too narrow a readership. See 1889.7.

1891

1   SCHELLING, FELIX E.   <u>Poetic and Verse Criticism of the Reign</u>
    <u>of Elizabeth</u>. Vol. 1. University of Pennsylvania Series
    in Philology, Literature, and Archaeology, no. 1.   Phil-
    adelphia: University of Pennsylvania Press, 97 pp.
        References to Jonson's views of major and minor Eliza-
    bethan critics.

2   WHIPPLE, EDWIN P.   "Ben Jonson." In <u>The Literature of the Age</u>
    <u>of Elizabeth</u>. Boston: Houghton Mifflin, pp. 85-118.
        Sees Jonson as an Elizabethan symbol of masculinity.
    The antithesis of the sensitive poet, he was a "man of
    muscle and brawn . . . ever ready, in all places and at all
    times, to assert the manhood of Ben by tongue and pen and
    sword." (First published 1869) Reprinted in 1972.41.

1892

1   ABBEY, C. J.   <u>Religious Thought in Old English Verse</u>.   London:
    Sampson, Low, Marston, & Co., pp. 206-8.
        Strong acclaim for Jonson's religious poetry. There is
    more vigor and impetuosity in this verse brought on by the
    fervor of religious feeling.

2   HERFORD, C. H.   "Ben Jonson." In <u>Dictionary of National Biog-</u>
    <u>raphy</u>. Vol. 30. Edited by George B. Smith. London: Smith,
    Elder. & Co., pp. 181-91.

1892

A substantial and accurate biography of Jonson which
touches briefly on the value of his work and his influence
on other writers. Herford also discusses the major con-
troversies which have surrounded Jonson, such as the extent
of his criticism of Shakespéare. Finally there is a list
of Jonson's individual works divided by genre and listed
chronologically.

3 HOWELL, JAMES. Epistolae Ho-Elianae. Vol. 2. Edited by J.
    Jacobs. London: David Nutt.
        Reprint of 1645.1 and 1647.3.

4 HUTTON, LAURENCE. "Ben Jonson." In Literary Landmarks of Lon-
    don. 3d ed. New York: Harpers, pp. 171-77.
        Descriptions of Jonson's old haunts in London. (Earlier
    editions not seen.)

5 LJUNGGREN, CARL AUGUST. The Poetical Gender of the Substan-
    tives in The Works of Ben Jonson. Lund: Collin & Zicker-
    man, 62 pp.
        Categorization of the gender of nouns in Jonson's work
    insofar as gender can be determined. Concludes that the per-
    sonification of substantives depends on the individual poet
    and does not conform to any generally accepted practice
    or usage of the time.

6 SCHELLING, FELIX E., ed. Introduction to Timber or Discover-
    ies Made upon Men and Matter by Ben Jonson. Boston: Ginn
    & Co., pp. xxi-xxii.
        Jonson's prose style is characterized by eloquence and
    classic dignity. "Jonson's condensity and directness are
    pervading, and achieved largely by a prevailing shortness
    and crispness in the construction of sentence, and an
    omission of qualifiers and connectives whenever the sense
    permits."

7 WHITE, THOMAS W. "Ben Jonson's Testimony." In Our English
    Homer. London: Sampson, Low, Marston & Co., pp. 152-64.
        Discounts Jonson's poems on Shakespeare in building
    an anti-Stratfordian case.

1893

1 ANON. A Catalogue of Original and Early Editions of . . .
    Works of English Writers from Langland to Wither. New
    York: Grolier Club, pp. 130-32.
        Bibliographic descriptions of Q Horatius Flaccus: His
    Art of Poetry and Ben Jonson's Execration against Vulcan.

1894

2   GREEN, JOHN RICHARD. A Short History of the English People.
     New York: Harpers, pp. 879-80.
        Ranks Jonson as one of the finest English lyric poets.

3   MASSON, DAVID. "Ben Jonson in Edinburgh." Blackwood's Mag-
     azine 154 (December):790-804.
        A biographical article describing Jonson's trip to Scot-
     land in 1619.

4   MORLEY, HENRY. English Writers. Vol. 10. London: Cassell
     & Co., pp. 387-94.
        A biography of Jonson with critical remarks. Emphasis
     on satire and high moral view of the poet's role blemished
     only by "an over-readiness for self assertion."

1894

1   BEERS, HENRY A. From Chaucer to Shakespeare. New York:
     Flood & Vincent, pp. 88-91.
        Jonson's drama is of interest only to the scholar will-
     ing to wade through endless footnotes, but his poetry is
     for everyone. "Jonson had a light enough touch in lyric
     poetry. His songs have not the careless sweetness of
     Shakespeare's, but they have a grace of their own."

2   C[OUCH], A. T. Q. "Ben Jonson and Drummond." Speaker 10
     (10 November):517-18.
        A comparison of the two poets along with a comment on
     their literary reputations.

3   GOSSE, EDMUND. "Ben Jonson-Chapman." In The Jacobean Poets.
     London: John Murray, pp. 23-29.
        Criticism of the epigrams which were not only bad in
     themselves, but led other poets into this "baleful depart-
     ment of seventeenth century literature." The Forest is
     written at a much higher level, though even here Jonson
     does not achieve what we might hope for him. Under-wood
     also unfortunately falls short. Though some are "elegant
     and pleasing," the vast majority are not.

*4 JUSSERAND, J. J. Histoire Littéraire du peuple anglais.
     Paris: Firmin-Didot.
        See 1909.3.

5   ROBERTSON, JANIS LOGIE. A History of English Literature.
     New York: Harpers, pp. 117-22.
        Life and works essay with a brief commentary on poetry.

1894

6   WYLIE, LAURA JOHNSON. <u>Studies in the Evolution of English</u>
        <u>Criticism</u>. New Haven: Yale University Press, pp. 13-15.
        Emphasizes Jonson's stiffness and decorum in critical
        standards. Reprinted in 1903.17.

1895

1   HOLTHAUSEN, F. Review of <u>The Poetical Gender of the Substan-</u>
        <u>tives in The Works of Ben Jonson</u>, by Carl August Ljunggren.
        <u>LGRP</u> 17 (January):13-15.
        Suggests some implications of the philologic study of
        Jonson's work. See 1892.5.

2   SCHIPPER, JAKOB. <u>Grundriss der Englischen Metrik</u>. Wien: W.
        Braumüller, passim.
        References to Jonson's poetry placing him in the neo-
        classical tradition of developing poetic style.

3   SIMPSON, P. "Field and Ben Jonson." <u>N&Q</u> 92 (19 October):301.
        New evidence of Jonson's friendship with Nathaniel Field,
        whom Jonson told Drummond "was his scholler, and he had
        read to him the Satyres of Horace, and some Epigrames of
        Martiall."

1896

1   ANON. "Ben Jonson." <u>Academy</u> 50 (14 November):390.
        Brief account of Jonson's "rollicking" life.

2   ANON. "Ben Jonson's Lyrics." Academy 50 (14 November):391;
        (21 November):432.
        Points out the enduring quality of Jonson's poetry but
        complains of the neglect which Jonson's verse is currently
        being given.

3   BROWN, T. E. "Ben Jonson." <u>New Review</u> 14 (May):514-23.
        A biographical essay venerating Jonson as an early lit-
        erary dictator.

4   GALLIENNE, RICHARD L. <u>Retrospective Reviews</u>. Vol. 1. Lon-
        don: John Lane, pp. 271-75.
        A brief discussion of Jonson's influence on Herrick and
        Milton with casual commentary on Gifford's edition of Jon-
        son.

5   STANLEY, ARTHUR PENRHYM. <u>Historical Memorials of Westminister</u>
        <u>Abbey</u>. 8th ed. London: John Murray, pp. 254-56.

1897

Biographical sketch with a description of Jonson's grave.
(Earlier editions not seen).

6 THOMSON, JAMES. "Ben Jonson." In <u>Biographical and Critical</u>
   <u>Studies</u>. London: Reeves, Turner, & B. Dobell, pp. 80-
   239.
   A long essay describing Jonson's life and works and re-
   lying heavily on excerpts of criticism to connect the narrative. Reprinted in 1972.40.

<u>1897</u>

1 CASTLE, EDWARD JAMES. <u>Shakespeare, Bacon, Jonson, and Greene</u>.
   London: Sampson, Low, Marston, & Co., pp. 171-93.
   Jonson's remarks on Shakespeare are read as evidence
   that Shakespeare did in fact write the plays attributed
   to him.

2 DOBSON, AUSTIN, and GRIFFIN, W. HALL. <u>Handbook of English</u>
   <u>Literature</u>. London: Crosby Lockwood & Son, pp. 66-67.
   Jonson's lyric poetry is of a far higher order than his
   highly topical and eminently forgettable drama.

3 GOSSE, EDMUND. "Robert Herrick." In <u>Seventeenth Century</u>
   <u>Studies</u>. 3d ed. New York: Dodd, Mead & Co., pp. 125-56.
   Description of Jonson's friendship with Herrick and his
   influence on Herrick's poetry.

4 MADDEN, D. H. "Ben Jonson and the Shakespeare Folio." In
   <u>The Diary of Mr. William Silence</u>. London: Longmans,
   Green & Co., pp. 326-28.
   Discusses Jonson's poem on Shakespeare as well as other
   critical remarks made by Jonson regarding Shakespeare. Believes that there is no question that the two men were
   friends and that Jonson had genuine respect for Shakespeare.

5 MEYNELL, ALICE. "Ben Jonson as a Lyricist." <u>Pall Mall Gazette</u>
   (4 August).
   Jonson's lyric poetry proves him "a kind of wanton
   mathematician of the fancy." Reprinted in 1965.12.

6 MITCHELL, DONALD G. "Ben Jonson." In <u>English Lands, Letters,</u>
   <u>and Kings</u>. New York: Scribner's, 1:295-303; 2:26-29.
   Survey of Jonson's work; comparison of Spenser's and Jonson's epithalamia, discussion of Shakespeare's and Jonson's
   syntax.

1897

7   ROSSI, L., and CORBOULD, E. M. Side-Lights on Shakespeare.
    London: Swan Sonnenschien. & Co., pp. 15-16, 159-60.
        Jonson and Shakespeare's friendship and their mutual
    respect for each other.

8   RUSHTON, WILLIAM LOWES. Shakespeare an Archer. Liverpool:
    Lee & Nightingale, passim.
        The meaning of words connected with archery in Jonson's
    plays and poems. Reprinted in 1973.33.

9   TENNYSON, HALLAM Lord. Alfred Lord Tennyson: A Memoir. Vol.
    2. London: Macmillan & Co., p. 73.
        In recalling the elder Tennyson's opinions of a number
    of writers, has the following to say about Jonson. "Ten-
    nyson liked Jonson's 'It is not growing like a tree,' and
    Marvell's 'To a Prude,' but he added, 'I can't read Ben
    Jonson, especially his comedies. To me he appears to move
    in a wide sea of glue.'"

10 WURZBACH, WOLFGANG Von. "John Marston." Shakespeare Jahrbuch
    33:85-94.
        Examination of the relationship between Jonson and Mars-
    ton particularly during the poets' war.

                            1898

1   CARLYLE, THOMAS. Historical Sketches of Notable Persons and
    Events in the Reigns of James I and Charles I. Edited
    by Alexander Carlyle. London: Chapman & Hall, pp. 74-76.
        Speaks of the incongruity in Jonson's poetry and his
    personal nature. "Rarer union of rough clumsy strength
    with touches of an Ariel beauty I have not met with. A
    sterling man, a true Singer-heart,--born of my native
    Valley too: to whom and to which be all honour!"

2   D-L., E. J. "A Correction." Baconiana 6 (July):53-54.
        Reference to Jonson's lines "to shake a lance,/As
    brandish't at the eyes of Ignorance" which support the
    argument that Bacon adopted the pseudonym, Shakes-peare,
    because he wanted to shake a spear at human ignorance.
    However, Shakespeare's name is not hyphenated in all quartos
    and folios as an earlier contributor, Mr. J. E. Roe, stated.

3   FOARD, JAMES T. "Some Caprices of Criticism." Papers of the
    Manchester Literary Club 24 (1898):321-49.
        Jonson has suffered at the hands of Dryden, Sir Walter
    Scott and others who pretend to be impartial and objective
    but who actually are "arrogant, arbitrary and envious."

4   FOX, ARTHUR W. "With Ben Jonson at Hawthornden." <u>Manchester</u>
      <u>Quarterly</u> 18, no. 1:61-84.
        A speculative description of Jonson and Drummond's meet-
      ing complete with imaginary dialogue. Reprinted in 1936.14.

5   GOSSE, EDMUND. <u>A Short History of Modern English Literature</u>.
      Short Histories of the Literatures of the World. London:
      William Heinemann, pp. 111-14.
        Distinguishes Jonson from his contemporaries by pointing
      to their romanticism and his classicism. Notes the over-
      powering influence of Jonson's character. "With such a
      brain and such a will as his he could not but succeed. If
      he had stuck to bricklaying, he must have rivaled Inigo
      Jones. But the most skillful and head strong master-build-
      er cannot quite become an architect of genius."

6   LEE, SIDNEY [L.]. <u>A Life of William Shakespeare</u>. New York:
      Macmillan Co., pp. 342-52.
        Numerous references to Jonson and his relationships with
      Shakespeare, the most important of which is a long commen-
      tary on the poets' war. Revised 1916.6.

7   LEVI, ANGELO RAFFAELLO. "Ben Jonson." In <u>Storia della Liter-</u>
      <u>atura Inglese</u>. Palermo: A. Reber, pp. 149-75.
        Discussion of Jonson's life and a bibliography of his
      works.

8   SCHELLING, FELIX E. "Ben Jonson and the Classical School."
      <u>PMLA</u> 13, no. 2:221-49.
        Comparison of Jonson's lyric poetry to that of Donne,
      Spenser, and other contemporaries. Jonson is not superficial
      in his imitation of classical writers, but rather he builds on
      the influence of the ancients. He characterizes Jonson's
      verse as finished rather than elaborate, reserved but nev-
      ertheless retaining a degree of spontaneity. Reprinted in
      1927.10 and 1961.15.

9   STATHAM, HENRY HEATHCOTE. <u>Architecture Among the Poets</u>.
      London: B. T. Batsford, pp. 26-29.
        The influence of building practices on "To Penshurst,"
      and Thomas Carew's "To his friend G. N., from Wrest."

10 WOODBRIDGE, ELIZABETH. <u>Studies in Jonson's Comedy</u>. Yale
      Studies in English, V. Boston: Lamson, Wolffe & Co., 102
      pp.
        Chapter 1, "Jonson's Theory of Literary Art," is a
      thorough discussion of Jonson's views outlined in <u>Discover-</u>
      <u>ies</u> and practiced in his writing. "His perception that

1898

truth is higher than authority, that laws are generaliza-
tions not causes, his suggestion of the historic method in
dealing with antiquity, prove him a philosophic and vital
thinker."

1899

1   ALDEN, RAYMOND MacDONALD. "Ben Jonson." In The Rise of Formal
    Satire in England. Philadelphia: University of Pennsylvan-
    ia Press, pp. 192-98.
       Discussion of the style and subject matter of Jonson's
    satire. Notes that Jonson is thoroughly English in his
    sincerity, occasional optimism, and the ethical quality
    of his work. Reprinted in 1961.1.

2   BAYNE, THOMAS. "Ben Jonson's Works." N&Q 99 (5 August):
    p. 113.
       Jonson used woodsy titles, Timber, Forrest, and Under-
    wood, following the ancients and meaning "works of diverse
    nature and matter congested."

3   BOWDEN, H. S. The Religion of Shakespeare. London: Bums
    & Oates, pp. 103-5.
       The significance of Jonson's conversion to Catholicism
    in the early seventeenth century. Reprinted in 1974.8.

4   CARRY, JOHN T. "An Unclaimed Poem by Ben Jonson." N&Q 100
    (16 December):491-92.
       Prints a poem on Prince Henry beginning, "Reader, wonder
    think it none," which Carry believes should be attributed
    to Jonson. He also believes that Jonson wrote some of the
    finest elegies in the language.

5   HUNT, LEIGH. "Suckling and Ben Jonson." In The World of Books.
    New York: Truslove, pp. 47-63.
       Reprint of 1847.1.

6   REINSCH, HUGO. Ben Jonson Poetik und Beziehung Zu Horaz.
    Erlangen: A. Deichert'sche verlagsbuch. nachf. G.
    Böhm, 130 pp.
       Horace's critical views and their influence on Jonson's
    poetry and Jonson's own criticism. Jonson assimilated
    Horace in a more creatively positive manner than any other
    writer of the Renaissance. Reprinted in 1918.6.

7   SPINGARN, J. E. A History of Literary Criticism in the Ren-
    aissance. New York: Macmillan Co., passim.
       Jonson's impact on criticism in drama and poetry is men-

tioned throughout. His view of the ideal poet is summar-
ized: "Mere excellence in style or versification does not
make a poet, but rather the exact knowledge of vices and
virtues, with ability to make the latter loved and the
former hated; and this is so far true, that to be a good
poet it is necessary, first of all to be a really great man."
Reprinted in 1963.20.

8   STEBBING, WILLIAM. <u>Sir Walter Raleigh</u>. Oxford: Clarendon
     Press, pp. 274-76.
          Believes that the assistance which Jonson gave Raleigh
     in preparing <u>The History of the World</u> for publication has
     been exaggerated by Jonson and later critics. Reprinted
     1972.38.

9   WARD, A. W. "Ben Jonson." In <u>A History of English Dramatic
     Literature</u>. Vol. 2. Rev. ed. London: Macmillan & Co.,
     pp. 296-407.
          A short survey with critical comments on the nondramatic
     works. Notes Jonson's ability to work with different
     poetic styles attributing this to his freedom of spirit.
     Revision of 1875.5.

1900

1   GLOEDE, O. Review of <u>Ben Jonson Poetik und Beziehung Zu Horaz</u>,
     by Hugo Reinsch. LGRP 21 (January):12-14.
          Reinsch's work will aid our understanding of seventeenth-
     century English poetry. See 1899.6.

2   HALLECK, RUEBEN POST. "Ben Jonson." In <u>History of English
     Literature</u>. New York: American Book Co., pp. 166-73.
          A school text taking up Jonson's life and works. Jon-
     son's poems are "exquisite as well for their delicacy of
     expression as for the character of the thought." As for
     the prose, "we meet with thought as vigorous and as tersely
     expressed as we find in the conversations of Dr. Jonson."

3   KELLNER, L. <u>Shakespeare</u>. Leipzig: Verlag vo E. A. Seemann
     und der Gesellschaft fur graph, passim.
          References to Jonson's friendship with Shakespeare and
     his criticism of his plays.

4   MABIE, HAMILTON WRIGHT. William Shakespeare: Poet, Dramatist,
     and Man. New York: Macmillan Co., pp. 280-84.
          Though Jonson may well have been envious of Shakespeare's
     success, he was too intelligent and had too much integrity
     to descend into petty jealousy.

1900

5   PARROTT, KATHERINE. "Ben Jonson." Radcliffe Magazine 2
    (June):115-28.
        Considers the major issues in Jonsonian criticism in
    this life and works essay. Parrott believes that Jonson's
    lyric poetry was more suited to the era of Dryden and Pope
    than Spenser and Shakespeare and that its dominant theme is
    its most enduring virtue. "The greatest thing still re-
    mains; the quality in him which stamped all his thought,
    which lifted him above his age, above the lyric artificial-
    ity that succeeded him--his moral championing of the true
    and strong in life."

6   SANDERS, H. M. "The Poems of Ben Jonson." Temple Bar 121
    (October):213-29.
        A survey of occasional poetry touching on the variety
    of a subject matter which Jonson approached. Saunders be-
    lieves that Jonson succeeded best as a satirist and that
    in his poetry his satire reaches its highest level.

7   SIDNEY, PHILIP, ed. Introduction to The Conversations of Ben
    Jonson with William Drummond. London: Gay & Bird, pp.
    1-12.
        Describes the importance of the conversations and brief-
    ly notes the historical situation under which they were
    recorded. Sidney points out that information regarding
    Jonson's love affairs has been omitted.

1901

1   DOBELL, BERTRAM. "Newly Discovered Documents of the Eliza-
    bethan and Jacobean Periods." Athenaeum, no. 3830 (23
    March):369-70; no. 3831 (30 March):403-4; no. 3832 (6
    April):433-34; no. 3833 (April 13):pp. 465-67.
        A four-part article describing a manuscript book (now
    Folger MS v.a. 321) which the author believes to have been
    by George Chapman. In the book are copies of letters be-
    tween Chapman and Jonson.

2   MENDENHALL, T. C. "A Mechnical Solution for a Literary Prob-
    lem." Popular Science Monthly 60 (December):97-105.
        A comparison of word frequency in Bacon's and Shake-
    speare's works to see if the same person wrote both, with
    a comparative discussion of word frequency in Jonson.
    There is a significant difference between the types of words
    used by Bacon and Shakespeare which cannot be totally at-
    tributed to the two different genres the authors used.

1902

3   MOULTON, CHARLES WELLS. "Ben Jonson." In The Library of Lit-
       erary Criticism. Buffalo: Moulton Publishing, pp. 745-67.
           Excerpts from critical essays on Jonson from the seven-
       teenth to the twentieth centuries. Revised in 1966.18.

4   THORNDIKE, ASHLEY H. The Influence of Beaumont and Fletcher
       on Shakespeare. Worcester, Mass.: Press of O. B. Wood,
       passim.
           Remarks on the relationship between Beaumont and Fletch-
       er and Jonson. Reprinted in 1965.18.

                              1902

1   ANON. "Ben Jonson's Prose." Academy 62 (1 February):119-21.
           A review of the current state of scholarship on Timber
       or Discoveries.

2   CRAWFORD, C. "Ben Jonson's Method of Composing Verse."
       N&Q 106 (18 October):301.
           A comparison of Jonson's prose passages with his verse
       to illustrate that he did as he told Drummond, write all
       of his poetry in prose first.

3   EICHHOFF, THEODOR. "Shakespeare und Ben Jonson." In Der Weg
       Zu Shakespeare. Halle: S. M. Niemeyer, pp. 135-38.
           Refers to Jonson's tributes to Shakespeare.

4   HERPICH, CHARLES A. "Shakespeare and Ben Jonson: Did They
       Quarrel?" N&Q 105 (12 April):282-84.
           Believes that Jonson was not above ridiculing Shake-
       speare.

5   MOODY, WILLIAM VAUGHN, and LOVETT, ROBERT MORSE. "Ben Jonson."
       In A First View of English Literature. New York: Scrib-
       ner's, pp. 119-21.
           Jonson's lyrics were outstanding even in an era of ex-
       ceptional lyric poetry. Reprinted in 1964.16.

6   PAGE, JOHN T. "Ben Jonson Imitated." N&Q 106 (11 October):
       283.
           Jonson's epitaph on Elizabeth L. H. is imitated on a
       gravestone in Stepney Churchyard.

7   SAINTSBURY, GEORGE. "Ben Jonson: his equipment." In A His-
       tory of Criticism and Literary Taste. Vol. 2. New York:
       Dodd, Mead, pp. 197-209.
           Emphasizes the importance of Timber or Discoveries and
       compares it to Bacon's Essays. Saintsbury comments on the

1902

way in which Jonson discovered his <u>Discoveries</u> and concludes
that he was in no way deceitful in his borrowings. Reprinted
in 1949.8.

1903

1   BAYNE, THOMAS. "Ben Jonson and Tennyson." <u>N&Q</u> 108 (5 Sep-
    tember):186.
        The stanzaic form of Elegy xxxix of <u>Under-wood</u> is sim-
    ilar to that which Tennyson used in <u>In Memoriam</u>.

2   BEGLEY, WALTER E. <u>Is It Shakespeare?</u> London: John Murray,
    pp. 81-106.
        Finds evidence in the poets' war to support his argu-
    ment that Bacon was the author of Shakespeare's plays.

3   ERSKINE, JOHN. <u>The Elizabethan Lyric</u>. New York: Macmillan
    Co., passim.
        Does not consider Jonson a major lyric poet or even an
    important lyricist. "The lyric emotion in Jonson never
    burns very bright; he is an intellectual artist rather
    than a singer." Reprinted in 1967.8.

4   GARNETT, RICHARD, and GOSSE, EDMUND. "Ben Jonson." In <u>English
    Literature: An Illustrated Record</u>. Vol. 2. New York:
    Macmillan, pp. 310-21.
        Jonson can be best understood as a leader in the reaction
    against pure imagination near the beginning of the seven-
    teenth century. He worked for realism and plainness in
    his writing. Reprinted 1935.8.

5   HARRISON, JOHN SMITH. <u>Platonism in English Poetry of the Six-
    teenth and Seventeenth Centuries</u>. New York: Columbia
    University Press, passim.
        Jonson sees love as an essence. Love in the present is
    only passion. Reprinted in 1965.7.

6   HART, H. C. "G. Harvey, J. Marston and Ben Jonson." <u>N&Q</u> 107
    (14 March):201-3.
        Reconstruction of the major events in the poets' war.

7   HAZLITT, WILLIAM CAREW. "On Shakespeare and Ben Jonson." In
    <u>Lectures on the English Comic Writers</u>. London: G. Bell.
        Reprint of 1819.2.

8   HEMS, HARRY. "Ben Jonson's Burial." <u>N&Q</u> 107 (13 June):465.
        Information on Jonson's burial and tomb.

1903

9   OMOND, T. S. <u>English Metrists</u>. Oxford: Clarendon Press,
    passim.
        Jonson's critical remarks on versification are noted in
    this history of the development of English versification.

10 PEET, WILLIAM H. "'Honest' Epitaphs," <u>N&Q</u> 108 (31 October):
    356.
        Anecdote of Jonson extemporizing an epitaph on a lawyer.

11 ROBERTSON, J[AMES] M. "Elizabethan Lyrics." In <u>Criticisms</u>.
    Vol. 2. London: A & B. H. Bonner, pp. 83-90.
        Comment on A. H. Bullen's assessment of Jonson. Rob-
    ertson believes that Bullen has not given proper attention
    to Jonson's best lyrics.

12 SAINTSBURY, GEORGE. "Ben Jonson." In <u>Loci Critici</u>. Boston:
    Ginn & Co., pp. 107-35.
        A short headnote with selections from <u>Discoveries.</u>

13 SECCOMB, T., and ALLEN, J. W. <u>The Age of Shakespeare</u>. Vol.
    1. London: George Bell, pp. 107-12.
        Describes Jonson's critical theories and the signifi-
    cance of <u>Discoveries</u>.

14 SYMMES, HAROLD S. "Ben Jonson et sa theorie de la critique
    positive, 1598-1616." In <u>Les Debuts de la Critique dram-
    atique</u>. Paris: Ernest Leroux, pp. 158-204.
        A discussion of Jonson's underlying critical theories.
    Makes special note of the moral and ethical content of
    Jonson's works.

15 VAN DAM, B. A. P., and STOFFEL, CORNELIS. "The Authority of
    the Ben Jonson Folio of 1616." <u>Anglia</u> 26 (1903):377-92.
        Jonson's editors have always assumed that Jonson sup-
    ervised the printing of his 1616 folio with meticulous
    care; however, that may not be the case. A careful anal-
    ysis of the quarto and folio editions of <u>Every Man out of
    His Humour</u> raises serious questions on Jonson's editorial
    care.

16 WAINWRIGHT, JOHN B. "Ben Jonson and Tennyson." <u>N&Q</u> 108 (3
    October):277-78.
        Cites a number of possible sources, including Jonson,
    for the <u>In Memoriam</u> stanza form.

17 WYLIE, LAURA JOHNSON. <u>Studies in the Evolution of English
    Criticism</u>. Boston: Ginn & Co., pp. 13-15.
        Reprint of 1894.6.

1904

1   COLLINS, JOHN CHURTON. Studies in Shakespeare. Westminster:
     Archibald Constable & Co., passim.
         Jonson's remarks on Shakespeare are used to help refute
     the charge that Bacon wrote Shakespeare's plays.

2   DOBELL, BERTRAM. "An Unknown Poem of Ben Jonson's." Athenaeum,
     no. 4014 (1 October):447; no. 4016 (15 October):517.
         In the first article the author argues that a poem he
     recently discovered, "The Goodwife's Ale," is by Ben Jon-
     son. In the second article the author acknowledges a num-
     ber of letters he received that point out that the poem
     had been published before. Herford and Simpson do not
     attribute this poem to Jonson.

*3   FLETCHER, P. "English Blank Verse." Colorado College Studies:
     Language Studies 2 (1904):41-65.
         Cited in Tannenbaum, 1947.10.

4   GWYNN, STEPHEN LUCIUS. "Ben Jonson and Herrick." In The Mas-
     ters of English Literature. London: Macmillan & Co., pp.
     68-82.
         Compares Jonson and Shakespeare and calls attention to
     Jonson's influence on Herrick, "the most representative
     poet of the Caroline age." Reprinted in 1972.14.

5   HESSEN, ROBERT. Leben Shakespeare's. Berlin: Derlag von
     W. Spemann, pp. 151-56.
         Biographical sketch of Jonson showing his relationship
     with Shakespeare.

6   LEE, SIDNEY [L.]. "Ben Jonson on the Sonnet." Athenaeum, no.
     4002 (9 July):49.
         Suggests that Stefano Guazzo's seventh dialogue in Dialoghi
     Piaceuoli is the source of Jonson's criticism of the son-
     net form which Drummond recorded in his Conversations.

7   ROLFE, WILLIAM J. A Life of William Shakespeare. Boston:
     Dana Estes, passim.
         Biographical and critical references to Jonson. Re-
     printed in 1973.31.

8   RUEHL, ERNEST. "Ben Jonson." In Grobianus in England. Ber-
     lin: n.p., p. xxv.
         The influence and importance of the epigram on the de-
     velopment of Jonson's dramatic characters.

9   SANDERS, H. M. "Drummond of Hawthornden." Gentleman's Mag-
       azine 297 (October):360-75.
         Biographical essay which discusses Drummond's meeting
    with Jonson in 1618.

10 SCHELLING, FELIX E. The Queen's Progress. Boston: Houghton
       Mifflin Co., pp. 223-52 and passim.
         A book of sketches which seek to convey the flavor of
    Elizabethan and Jacobean life. Jonsonian anecdotes add
    salt to the sumptuous delights Schelling serves his read-
    ers.

11 WENDELL, BARRETT. The Temper of the Seventeenth Century.
       New York: Scribners, passim.
         Jonson's life, poetry, drama, and prose are touched upon
    throughout. Wendell believes that Jonson's combination
    of the classical with the vernacular leads to nearly
    perfect poetry.

                        1904-1906

1   ANON. "Ben Jonson and Bacon." N&Q 110 (10 December 1904):469;
       111 (14 January 1905):35; 111 (4 February 1905):94; 113
       (13 January 1906):31.
         A brief query: Did Jonson work for Bacon between 1620-
    23? Three responses, none of which turn up any sound ev-
    idence that Jonson did work for Bacon.

                          1905

1   COLLINS, JOHN CHURTON. Studies in Poetry and Criticism. Lon-
       don: George Bell & Sons, pp. 275-78.
         Jonson's concept of the role of the poet is discussed in
    relation to other poets' and critics' theories.

2   HERPICH, CHARLES A. "Shakespeare, Ben Jonson, Pliny, and the
       First Folio." Nation 81 (13 July):33.
         The Heminge and Condell authorship of the dedication of
    Shakespeare's first folio is questioned. Jonson may have
    written the dedication.

3   SPINGARN, J. E. "The Sources of Discoveries." MP 2, no. 4
       (April):451-60.
         Parallel texts of passages of Discoveries with their
    sources from Heinsius, Pontanus, and Buchler.

1906

1 ANON. Review of Underwoods. Athenaeum (17 March):324-25.
Review of a fine-printing limited edition of Under-wood
(Underwoods) [Cambridge: University Press, 1905], 165 pp.
Points out that this is an unusual case of Jonson being
given some of the respect he so richly deserves.

2 ARONSTEIN, ph. Ben Jonson. Literarhistorische Forschungen, no.
34. Berlin: Verlag von Emil Felber, 378 pp.
Contains chapters on both prose and poetry. Discusses
the sources of Jonson's poetry as well as the circumstances
surrounding the occasional verse. Admires Jonson's contribution to late Renaissance criticism.

3 BANG, W. "Memorandums of the Immortal Ben." MLR 1, no. 2
(January):111-15.
Reprints Jonson's famous "Memorandums" and defends their
authenticity. For further information on the "Memorandums"
see 1717.1; 1925.15; and 1936.12.

4 BAYNE, THOMAS. "Ben Jonson's Under-wood xli." N&Q 113 (3
January):25.
Questions a word dropped in "Ode. To Himself."

5 BENSLY, EDWARD. "Under-wood xli." N&Q 113 (28 April):337.
Continues the discussion of the dropped word.

6 CURRY, JOHN T. "Et Tu Brute." N&Q 113 (17 February):125.
This phrase appears to have been used first by Jonson in
Every Man Out Of His Humour. Jonson may have been piqued
with Shakespeare for the apparent poaching as he criticized Julius Caesar on two separate occasions.

7 EVANS, H. A. "Ben Jonson's Works, 1616." N&Q 113 (6 January):7.
The 1616 folio does not contain a portrait of the poet
by Vaughan.

8 GOSSE, EDMUND. "Ben Jonson." In Chambers Cyclopedia of English Literature. Vol. 1. London: W. & R. Chambers, pp.
401-13.
A detailed biography with prefatory comments on Jonson's
writings.

9 GRIERSON, HERBERT J. C. The First Half of the Seventeenth
Century. Periods of European Literature. London: William
Blackwood & Sons, pp. 160-65.

A sensitive discussion of the similarities and differences between Donne and Jonson. Grierson finds value in
nearly all of Jonson's poetry. For instance, of his eulo-
gistic verse Grierson says: "Jonson's most characteristic
and classical eulogies are relevant and appropriate ap-
preciations, compliments a man might be proud to receive,
because they tell something about him to posterity, couched
in a style and verse often obscure and harsh, but often
vigorous and felicitous."

10 RUTHERFORD, MILDRED [L.]. "Ben Jonson." In English Authors.
     Atlanta: Franklin Printing Co.
     Reprint of 1890.8.

11 TUPPER, FREDRICK. "Legacies of Lucian." MLN 21, no. 3
     (March):76-78.
     Discusses Jonson's indebtedness to Lucian in drama and
     poetry.

<u>1907</u>

1   ANON. "A French Critic on Ben Jonson." Living Age 254, no.
     3293 (17 August):444-47.
     Review of Ben Jonson: L'Homme et l'Oeuvre (1572-1637),
     by Maurice Castelain.
     See 1907.5. Reprint of 1907.3.

2   ANON. Early English Printed Books in the University Library
     of Cambridge 1457-1640. Vol. 4. Cambridge: University
     Press, p. 205.
     A list of books by Jonson or which have Jonson's works
     in them printed before 1641 in the Cambridge University
     Library.

3   ANON. "Musing without Method--A French Critic on Ben Jon-
     son." Blackwood's Magazine 181 (June):839-43.
     Review of Ben Jonson: L'Homme et l'Oeuvre (1572-1637),
     by Maurice Castelain. Castelain, in part because of his
     knowledge of Latin literature, has prepared an excellent
     edition of Discoveries. "Whatever Ben Jonson discusses,
     be it morals or letters, he speaks with the voice of
     authority and tradition; and his Discoveries cannot but
     magnify our respect for the wisdom of the ancients."
     See 1907.5. Reprinted 1907.1.

4   BEGLEY, WALTER E. "Ovid's Elgies: Translated by C. M."
     Baconiana (January):24-28.

1907

> Jonson may have translated two of the Ovidean elegies
> normally attributed to Marlowe.

5   CASTELAIN, MAURICE. Ben Jonson: L'Homme et l'Oeuvre (1572-
>   1637). Paris: Librairie Hachette, 980 pp.
>   A major study of Jonson's life and works. Castelain
>   discusses the different types of poetry Jonson writes and
>   how he adopts specific techniques to his occasional poetry.
>   He defends the epigrams that other late nineteenth-century
>   scholars and critics condemned. He discusses at length
>   many of Jonson's epistles and elegies.

6   _____, ed. Introduction to Discoveries: A Critical Edition.
>   Paris: Librairie Hachette, pp. vii-xxv.
>   Carefully traces the sources of Jonson's short essays
>   to such classical writers as Euripides, Paterculus, Gellius,
>   Quintiaian, Seneca, Vives, and others. So numerous and so
>   complete are these borrowings that the editor maintains
>   "the book is not his; or, at least, that the merit and
>   interest of it are for the most part attributable to other
>   men."

7   _____. "Shakespeare et Ben Jonson." Revue Germanique 3
>   (January):21-65; (March):133-80.
>   Reviews Jonson's criticism of Shakespeare and seeks a
>   balanced assessment of Jonson's true critical sense of
>   Shakespeare.

8   DAVIES, RANDALL. "'Our Fellow Shakespeare' Interpreted."
>   Academy 73 (30 November):191.
>   Assessment of Jonson and Shakespeare's relationship,
>   based on the famous passage from Discoveries.

9   EDMUNDS, E. W. "Ben Jonson." In Story of English Literature.
>   Vol. 1. London: John Murray, pp. 318-29.
>   "Though poetry is by no means absent, Jonson's nature
>   was essentially not poetic but intellectual. . . . He
>   is clever, often very witty, always clear, and generally
>   obtains the effect he desires, but that effect is not
>   poetical, nor does it yield us natural pearls of phrase,
>   so much as a very glittering but artificial diamond."

10 JUSSERAND, J. J. "Ben Jonson's Views on Shakespeare's Art."
>   In The Works of William Shakespeare. Vol. 10. Stratford:
>   Shakespeare Head Press, pp. 297-319.
>   A thorough discussion of Jonson's criticism of Shake-
>   speare including definitions of the general critical views
>   both men held. Despite their differences Shakespeare and
>   Jonson never had a lasting quarrel because both were aware

of each other's genius and both appreciated each other's geniality.

11   SHELLEY, HENRY C. Inns and Taverns of Old London. Boston: L. C. Page & Co., passim.
      Descriptions of Jonson's old haunts with some anecdotal information on Jonson.

12   SIDNEY, PHILIP. "The Subject of All Verse": Being An Inquiry into the Authorship of a Famous Epitaph. London: Oxford University Press, 40 pp.
      Authorship of the epitaph "On the Countesse Dowage of Pembroke" is discussed in this book. Both Whalley and Gifford attributed the epitaph to Jonson though it did not appear in Jonson's Works (1640). Sidney is the first to present a documented case for William Browne's authorship. This view is also supported by Herford and Simpson. See 1947.5.

13   SIMPSON, PERCY. "Tanguam explorator: Ben Jonson's Method in the Discoveries." MLR 2, no. 3 (April:201-10.
      Probably nothing in Discoveries is Jonson's original thought. Though Jonson borrowed much from the ancients, Simpson also makes a case for borrowings from the Renaissance humanists.

14   WOODHOUSELEE, ALEXANDER FRASER TYTLER, Lord. Essay on the Principles of Translation. Everyman Library. London: J. M. Dent & Co., pp. 36-38.
      Reprint of 1797.1.

1908

1   ARONSTEIN, Ph. Review of Ben Jonson: L'Homme et l'Oeuvre (1572-1637), by Maurice Castelain. Shakespeare Jahrbuch 44 (1908):371-74.
      A review of Jonsonian scholarship, points out the need for this new and useful assessment of Jonson's work. See 1907.5.

2   BANG, W. Review of Discoveries: A Critical Edition, edited by Maurice Castelain. Shakespeare Jahrbuch 44 (1908), 368-71.
      Discusses the format of Discoveries and speculates on Jonson's intention for the book. See 1907.6.

3   BRIGGS, WILLIAM DINSMORE. "Sources of Jonson's Discoveries." MLN 23, no. 2 (February):43-46.

1908

Additional information on Jonson's sources for <u>Discover-ies</u>.

4 BRYAN, J. INGRAM. "Shakespeare, Jonson, and Donne." In <u>The Feeling for Nature in English Pastoral Poetry</u>. Tokyo: Kyo-Bun-Kwan, pp.64-73.

Jonson was too intellectual and conservative, too philo-sophical and reflective "to sympathize very deeply with the less subjective content of pastoral poetry; but on its in-tellectual side it represented an attitude to nature that would have made the pastoral more sane and human if less rustic."

5 FURNIVALL, F[REDK.]. J. and MURO, JOHN. <u>Shakespeare: Life and Work</u>. London: Cassell & Co., passim.

References to Jonson's friendship and criticism of Shake-speare.

6 GREENWOOD, G[EORGE] G. <u>The Shakespeare Problem Restated</u>. New York: John Land, passim.

Jonson's inconsistent critical remarks on Shakespeare can be easily explained. When Jonson praises Shakespeare he is really praising the great playwright who wrote under the pseudonym of Shakespeare. When he criticized Shake-speare he had in mind the actor who occasionally wrote plays of no distinction. Reprinted in 1970.20.

7 PARSONS, EDWARD S. "Ben Jonson and John Milton." <u>Nation</u> 87 (12 November):459-60.

Comparison of poems by Jonson and Milton on Shakespeare suggests that Milton derived his lines from Jonson's.

8 PLATT, I. H. "On Ben Jonson's Lines on the Shakespeare Por-trait." <u>Baconiana</u> (October):267-68.

Questions the meaning of "hid" in Jonson's lines on Shakespeare's portrait.

9 POSCHER, ROBERT. <u>Andrew Marvell's Poetische Werk</u>. Wien: Wil-helm Braumuller, pp. 116-17.

Brief discussion of Jonson's contribution to pre-Restor-ation satire.

10 SAINTSBURY, GEORGE. <u>A History of English Prosody</u>. 3 vols. London: Macmillan & Co., passim.

The most significant comment on Jonson's poetry is found in Vol. 2, pp. 153-58. Here Saintsbury notes, "some of the daintiest and most delightful of English lyrics stand to his [Jonson's] credit, and that in lyric he hardly ever gives us anything harsh or crude." Reprinted in 1961.14.

1909

11 SPINGARN, J. E., ed. "The Jacobean Outlook: Bacon and Ben
    Jonson." In Critical Essays of the Seventeenth Century.
    Vol. 1. Oxford: Clarendon Press, pp. ix-xxi.
        Describes Jonson's understanding of Sidney's criticism
    and the way in which he altered it for his own purposes.
    The differences between Sidney and Jonson tell us a good
    deal about what was happening in Renaissance criticism.
    Reprinted in 1968.16.

12 UPHAM, ALFRED HORATIO. The French Influence in English Lit-
    erature. New York: Columbia University Press, passim.
        The influence of Du Bartas, Rabelais, Montaigne, and
    other French writers on Jonson. Reprinted in 1965.19.

13 WESTCOTT, A. E. "Traces of Classical Style in Poetry of the
    Early Seventeenth Century." SR 16, no. 3 (July):257-76.
        Argues that Schelling (1898.9) is misleading in sev-
    eral respects and attempts to clarify the significance of
    classical scholarship on Jonson and his followers.

14 WOLFF, MAX J. Shakespeare der Dichter und Seine Werk. Mun-
    chen: n.p., passim.
        The relationship between Jonson and Shakespeare is fully
    outlined and documented. Jonson's criticism of Shake-
    speare is discussed.

1909

1 BOOTH, WILLIAM STONE. Some Acrostic Signatures of Francis
   Bacon. Boston: Houghton Mifflin Co., pp. 290-301,
   322-25, 569-71.
       Tries to prove that Bacon's name is spelled numerous
   times in Shakespeare's works, and that Jonson participated
   in these acrostic exercises also.

2 CRAWFORD, C. "England's Parnassus, 1600." N&Q 119 (5 June):
   443-45.
       There are fourteen quotations from Jonson in England's
   Parnassus.

3 JUSSERAND, J. J. A Literary History of the English People.
   Vol. 3. New York: G. P. Putnam, pp. 369-409.
       A detailed account of Jonson's life and a discussion of
   his aesthetics. Translation of 1894.4.

4 KOTTAS, KARL. T. Randolph, sein Leben und seine Werke. Wein:
   W. Braumüller, passim.
       Randolph imitated Jonson's poetry.

1909

5 THORN-DRURY, G. "Ben Jonson and Suckling." N&Q 120 (30
   October):345.
        In Suckling's play, The Sad One, a character, Signior
   Multercarni, is supposed to represent Ben Jonson.

6 WAITE, ALICE VINTON. "Ben Jonson's Grammar." MLN 24, no. 5
   (May):137-40.
        Establishes the importance of Jonson's Grammar, incom-
   plete as it is, in the developing systemization of the English language.

7 _____, ed. Introduction to Ben Jonson: The English Grammar.
   New York: Sturgis & Walton, pp. v-xii.
        Restates, often verbatum, information given in 1909.6.

1910

1 B., G. F. R. "Goulands in Ben Jonson." N&Q 122 (31 December):
   532-33.
        Gowland is the name given to a number of different yel-
   low or golden flowers. Response to 1910.10 and 1911.5.

2 COLLINS, JOHN CHURTON. Greek Influence on English Poetry.
   London: Sir Isaac Pitman & Sons, pp. 89-90.
        Jonson was the most considerable critic of the Eliza-
   bethan Age. He derived three important principles from
   classical criticism: "the definition and true scope of
   poetry, the essential connexion aesthetics and ethics, and
   the nature of the relation between poetry and painting."

3 COURTHOPE, W. J. A History of English Poetry. Vols. 3 & 4.
   London: Macmillan & Co., 3:178-87; 4:267-303.
        Discussion of the quality of Jonson's poetry and the
   influence of classicism along with biography and commentary
   on drama. Reprinted in 1962.6.

4 GRIFFINHOOFE, C. G. Celebrated Cambridge Men. Cambridge: A.
   P. Dixon, n. p.
        Biographical sketch noting Jonson's short stay at Cam-
   bridge.

5 KLEIN, DAVID. "Ben Jonson." In Literary Criticism from the
   Elizabethan Dramatists: Repertory and Synthesis. New
   York: Sturgis & Walton, pp. 81-152.
        Points to fundamental differences in seventeenth-cen-
   tury dramatic criticism. "Shakespeare was creative, Jonson assimilative. . . . Shakespeare was romantic, Jonson
   was classic." But he finally concludes that Jonson's
   influence on criticism has been overestimated.

1910

6   LEE, SIDNEY [L.]. The French Renaissance in England. Oxford:
    Clarendon Press, passim.
        Frequent references to Jonson throughout with a special
    note on his views on poetry as revealed in Discoveries.
    Also, Jonson recognized Montaigne's influence on English
    writers as seen in passages from Volpone and Discoveries.
    Drummond reports in Conversations that Jonson criticized
    DuBartas. Reprinted 1968.7.

7   MOORMAN, F. W. Robert Herrick: A Biographical and Critical
    Study. London: T. Nelson, passim.
        Herrick was a devoted disciple of Jonson, who was "his
    father as head of the tribe of which he had been sealed
    a member, but he was also his poetic father to whom he
    looked for guidance in the composition of his verses."
    Reprinted in 1962.13.

8   SCHELLING, FELIX E. English Literature during the Lifetime
    of Shakespeare. New York: Henry Holt & Co., pp. 245-48.
        Jonson had a well developed sense of poetic form which
    involved "brevity and condensity of expression, a feeling
    on the part of the poet that the effect may be spoiled
    by a word too much, a feeling notably in contrast with the
    diffuseness, the continuousness and want of concentration
    characteristic of the Spenserian mode of the day."

9   SCHIPPER, JAKOB. A History of English Versification. Oxford:
    Clarendon Press, passim.
        Jonson's poetry is referred to in various chapters which
    take up various metrical and verse techniques.

10 T., W. "Goulands in Ben Jonson." N&Q 122 (26 November):429.
        Query on the meaning of goulands. See 1910.1 and
    1911.5.

11 THOMPSON, FRANCIS. "The Prose of Poets: 3. Ben Jonson." In
    A Renegade Poet and Other Essays. Boston: Ball, pp. 253-
    65.
        Recognition of Discoveries and general appreciation of
    the prose style. Reprint in 1965.17.

12 THORNDIKE, ASHLEY H. "Ben Jonson." In The Cambridge History
    of English Literature. Edited by A. W. Ward and A. R.
    Waller. Vol. 6, part 2. New York: G. P. Putnam, pp.
    1-30.
        A succinct and informative essay which takes up the ma-
    jor critical issues surrounding Jonson's works. Notes
    again, for instance, that nearly all of Discoveries is

1910

translated material. On Jonson's poetry: "Few of the odes,
epistles, and epigrams show aught but careful writing, but
there are also few that can be praised unreservedly or
read with delight. The Epigrams (1616) are characteristic-
ally coarse. . . . The great majority of his poems are
lacking in melodoy, charm, or distinction. They are the
work of a forerunner of classicism, of one who departs from
Spenser, and looks forward to Dryden."

1911

1 BUTLER, H. B.: FLETCHER, C. R. L.: and WALKER, EMERY.
   "Benjamin Jonson." In Historical Poetraits 1600-1700.
   Oxford: Clarendon Press, pp. 62-64.
      Illustrated biography with critical assessment. "Indeed,
   it is to his genius as a satirist and a critic, rather than
   as a playwright, that Jonson owes his final position in
   literary history."

2 DAVIDSON, THOMAS. "Ben Jonson's Testimony as to William
   Shakespeare: What He Really Said." New Shakespeareana 10,
   no. 2 (July):41-48.
      A systematic discussion of Jonson's comments on Shake-
   speare. Davidson concludes that Jonson "knew Shakespeare
   personally and thought he had more virtues than vices."

3 HUNT, MARY LELAND. "The Quarrel with Jonson; the Close of the
   Henslowe Period, 1601-1602." In Thomas Decker. Columbia
   University Studies in English. New York: Columbia
   University Press, pp. 64-85.
      Describes the quarrel between Jonson, Decker, and Mars-
   ton, commonly known as the poets' war. Jonson's play
   Poetaster is perhaps the most interesting work to come out
   of the quarrel. Reprinted in 1964.10.

4 KENDALL, F. A. William Shakespeare and His Three Friends, Ben,
   Anthonie, and Francis. Boston: W. A. Butterfield, passim.
      Conjecture of Jonson's social and literary relationships
   with Shakespeare.

5 SKEAT, WALTER W.; HILL, N. W. and RATCLIFFE, THOMAS. "Gar-
   lands in Ben Jonson." N&Q 123 (18 February):136.
      Further, and evidently final thoughts on the meaning of
   goulands. See 1910.1. and 1910.10.

6 SUDDARD, [S. J.] MARY. "Ben Jonson and Shakespeare." Contemporary Review 99 (March):316-28.

Emphasizes the balance and evenness of Jonson's thought. "In this sense, balance means constant equilibrium between the moral and the intellectual qualitites, an equilibrium whose very constancy suppresses the disturbing element of emotion."

7   THOMAS, EDWARD. Feminine Influence on the Poets. New York: John Lance & Co., pp. 340-42.
    Jonson's connections with Lady Venetia Digby.

8   WESTCOTT, A. E., ed. Introduction to New Poems by James I of England. New York: Columbia University Press, pp. lxxix-lxxxii.
    Cites Jonson's remarks to James I on poetry.

1912

1   ADAMS, JOSEPH QUINCY, Jr. "Notes on Ben Jonson, From a Seventeenth Century Common-Place Book." MLR 7, no. 3 (July): 296-99.
    A reprint and comment on Alexander Gill's scurrilous attack on Jonson (see 1633.1). Adams claims to have found a better original copy of the poem than Gifford used in his edition of Jonson.

2   BEAUMONT, FRANCIS. "Mr. Francis Beaumont's Letter to Ben Jonson, . . ." In The Works of Francis Beaumont and John Fletcher. Vol. 10. Edited by A. R. Waller. Cambridge: University Press, pp. 199-201.
    Reprint of 1647.1.

3   BRIGGS, WILLIAM DINSMORE. "Studies in Ben Jonson. I." Anglia 36:463-93.
    A description and examination of Harl. MS 4955, referred to by Gifford as "the Newcastle MS." Many of Jonson's poems and masques are found in the MS and Briggs collates them with Gifford's edition. Briggs reproduces three poems to Jonson not found elsewhere before. Publication of 1629.2.

4   CARY, LUCIUS Viscount FALKLAND. "An Epistle to his Noble Father, Mr. Jonson," and "An Anniversary Epistle on Sir Henry Morison, with an Apostrophe to My Father. Jonson." "Studies in Ben Jonson. I." Anglia 36 (1912):474-78.
    Published 1632.1.

5   CRUICKSHANK, A. H. Ben Jonson: A Paper Read Before the Durham Branch of the English Association, May 9, 1912. Durham: Durham County Advertiser Office, 20 pp.

1912

A general survey of Jonson's life and works concluding
with a final judgment that Jonson is among the thirty
finest writers in the English language.

6 DIXON, W. MACNEILE. English Epic and Heroic Poetry. London:
J. M. Dent, passim.
Alludes to Jonson's criticism of other poets particular-
ly Shakespeare and Spenser.

7 LANG, ANDREW. "Ben Jonson." In Shakespeare, Bacon and the
Great Unknown. London: Longmanns, Green & Co., pp. 247-
54.
Reads Jonson's "Ode on Shakespeare" as further evidence
that Shakespeare did exist and write the plays attributed
to him.

8 REED, EDWARD BLISS. English Lyrical Poetry. New Haven: Yale
University Press, pp. 223-33.
Discusses Jonson's theory of poetry in light of his
criticism, poems, and conversations with Drummond.

9 SAINTSBURY, GEORGE. A History of English Prose Rhythm. London: Macmillan & Co., pp. 204-8.
Jonson was not a plagiarist in Discoveries, "for what
ever be the origin of their thought, the vehicle of their
expression is pure English, and English of a type remarkable
in itself, to a great extent novel and extremely germinal."

10 SUDDARD, S. J. MARY. "A Parallel Between Ben Jonson and
Shakespeare." In Studies and Essays in English Literature.
Cambridge: University Press, pp. 182-204.
Contrasts the two theories of dramatic criticism. "Jon-
son asks himself how the drama is to be built up; Shake-
speare asks himself what its purpose is."

1913

1 BRIGGS, WILLIAM DINSMORE. "Ben Jonson: Notes on Underwoods
xxx and on the New Inn." MP 10, no. 4 (April):573-85.
At least a third of Jonson's epistle to Sackvile, Earl
of Dorset is taken from Seneca's De beneficiis.

2 _____. "Ben Jonson's Epigram on Sir Horace Vere." Athenaeum
(7 June):623.
Notes the discovery of an holograph of Jonson's Epigram
XCI "To Sir Horace Vere."

3 _____. "Certain Incidents in Ben Jonson's Life." MP 11, no.
    2 (October):279-88.
        Jonson's participation in a theological dispute may in-
    directly supply some possible reasons for the 1616 folio
    not appearing in 1612 when it was originally licensed.

4 HALLECK, RUEBEN POST. "Ben Jonson." In Halleck's New English
    Literature. New York: American Book Co., pp. 199-205.
        A schoolbook including an account of Jonson's life and
    works.

5 MILLER, GEORGE MOREY. The Historical Point of View in English
    Literary Criticism. Heidelberg: Carl Winter, pp. 72-74.
        Describes Jonson's modest role in English criticism. He
    "was the founder in England of a reasonable, mild, but def-
    inite neoclassic system of conscious art, and therefore
    little was to be expected of him in the matter of genetic
    criticism."

6 RHYS, ERNEST. Lyric Poetry. London: J. M. Dent, pp. 180-81.
        Summarizes the paradox of Jonson's personality which
    made him not necessarily a great writer but an interesting
    individual. "Jonson's personality was huge and irrepres-
    sible; yet he was one of the most subservient and imitative
    of writers. He loved books too well, and men, so far as
    they did not help him to extend his own estate, too little."

7 ROBERTSON, J[AMES] M. The Baconian Heresy. London: Herbert
    Jenkins, passim.
        Reviews Jonson and Shakespeare's relationship in refuting
    the theory that Bacon wrote Shakespeare's plays.

8 SCHELLING, FELIX E. The English Lyric. Boston: Houghton
    Mifflin Co., pp. 77-80, 82-86, 94-96.
        Jonson's metrics and versification are "finished and
    informed with a sense of design; the idea is often both
    happy and novel, and carried out with artistic logic and
    insistent completeness."

9 SMEDLEY, WILLIAM T. "An Astronomical Similitude." Baconiana
    10 (July):160-63.
        In Jonson's tribute to Shakespeare are the following
    lines:

        "But stay! I see in the Hemisphere
        Advanc'd, and made a constellation.
        Shine forth, thou Starre of Poets."

    Smedley argues that the "constellation" is Francis Bacon.

1913

10 SMITHSON, E. W. "Ben Jonson's Pious Fraud." <u>Nineteenth Century</u> 74, no. 441 (November):965-72.
    Jonson's poem on Shakespeare is really ironic. Jonson knew who Shakespeare really was, an illiterate actor, and the poem is nothing more than a contemptuous sneer. See 1913.11.

11 SULLIVAN, E. "A Libel on Ben Jonson." <u>Nineteenth Century</u> 74, no. 442 (December):1294-1310.
    A systematic and detailed response to 1913.10.

12 STEBBING, W[ILLIAM]. "Ben Jonson." In <u>Five Centuries of English Verse</u>. Vol. 1. London: Oxford University Press, pp. 52-60.
    A general affirmation of the value of Jonson's poetry. Special appreciation for the beauty and simplicity of his verse.

13 THOMPSON, FRANCIS. "Ben Jonson's Prose." In <u>The Works of Francis Thompson</u>. Vol. 3. London: Burns & Oates, pp. 159-63.
    Jonson is a prose writer of strength and character. His prose "has not the sweetness and light of modern culture; it is ursine: but it sticks in the memory."

14 ZEITLIN, JACOB, ed. <u>Hazlitt on English Literature</u>. New York: Oxford University Press, pp. 423-24.
    Short biographical sketch of Jonson under the section "Notes."

1914

1 BRIGGS, WILLIAM DINSMORE. "Ben Jonson and the First Shakespeare Folio." <u>TLS</u>, 12 November, p. 502.
    Discusses Jonson's remarks on Shakespeare's method of composing and writing. Attributes the "Address" at the beginning of the first folio to Jonson. See 1914.11; 1915.3 and 6.

2 _____. "Did Ben Jonson Write a Third Ode to Himself?" <u>Athenaeum</u> (13 June):828.
    Argues that a newly discovered manuscript poem is by Jonson on a theme similar to that of "Ode to Myself."

3 _____. "Recovered Lines of Ben Jonson." <u>MLN</u> 29, no. 5 (May): 156-57.
    Reports the discovery of the concluding lines to no. xii of <u>The Forrest</u> in Harleian MS 4064, f. 243.

4   _____ . "Studies in Ben Jonson. II." Anglia 38:101-20.
          Collation of Jonson's 1640 quarto and twelve miscellan-
     eous poems printed by John Benson with Gifford's edition
     of the same poems.

5   CURRY, JOHN T. "The 'Monstrous' Possessive in Ben Jonson."
          N&Q 130 (12 September):204-5.
          In his English Grammar Jonson provides an early and ac-
     curate explanation for the use of the apostrophe in form-
     ing the possessive case.

6   GRAY, WILLIAM FORBES. The Poets Laureate of England. London:
          Sir Isaac Pitman & Sons, pp. 20-32.
          Describes the relationships between James I, Charles I,
     and Jonson. Details are given of Jonson's pay and the
     duties required of him.

7   KEENE, H. G. "English Classics." East & West 13, no. 158
          (December):1130-41.
          "It is in his lighter poetry that Jonson lives and that
     the reputation he enjoyed in his own day finds its com-
     plete justification."

8   MACKENZIE, A. S. "Ben Jonson." In History of English Liter-
          ature. New York: Macmillan Co., pp. 170-75.
          Biographical sketch with positive remarks on Jonson's
     literary contribution.

9   MASSON, DAVID. "Ben Jonson." In Shakespeare Personally. Ed-
          ited and arranged by Rosaline Masson. London: Smith, El-
          der, & Co., passim.
          Points out that Jonson wrote a great deal of occaisional
     poetry whereas Shakespeare wrote none at all.

10   SAINTSBURY, GEORGE. Historical Manual of English Prosody.
          London: Macmillan & Co., passim.
          General remarks on Jonson's role in the development of
     prosody.

11   SIMPSON, PERCY. "Ben Jonson and The First Shakespeare Folio."
          TLS, 19 November, p. 518.
          Response to 1914.1. Simpson does not think Jonson wrote
     "Address." See 1915.3 and 6.

12   TATLOCK, JOHN S. P. "Origin of the Closed Couplet." Nation
          98 (9 April):390.
          Though Jonson was the father of English classicism in
     general, Thomas Heywood was the first English author to
     use closed couplets.

1915

1   BENSLY, EDWARD. "Ben Jonson: Pindar." N&Q 132 (3 July):17.
    A Pindaric echo is to be found in The Forrest x,
    "Praeludium." Response to 1915.2.

2   BOURGEOIS, BON A. F. "Ben Jonson: Pindar." N&Q 132 (3 April):267.
    A query on Jonson and Pindar. See 1915.1 for response.

3   BRIGGS, WILLIAM D[INSMORE]. "Ben Jonson and The First Shake-
    speare Folio." TLS, 23 April, pp. 135-36.
    Response to 1914.11. Defends position that Jonson did
    write the "Address" because of "striking parallels" between
    the "Address" and Discoveries which are similar to paral-
    lels between other works Jonson is known to have written.
    See 1914.1 and 11; 1915.6.

4   CHURCH, A. H. "Ben Jonson: Another Epitaph." Athenaeum
    (20 March):272.
    Prints Thomas Willford's "An Epitaph upon the most
    learned Comedian and Modern Poet, Benjamin Jonson."

5   KRAPP, GEORGE PHILLIP. The Rise of English Literary Prose.
    New York: Oxford University Press, pp. 465-68.
    Jonson followed Bacon in his prose styling. He regarded
    prose as so important that he wrote all of his poems first
    in prose and, of course, much of his drama is prose.

6   SIMPSON, PERCY. "Ben Jonson and The First Shakespeare Folio."
    TLS, 20 May, p. 170.
    Response to 1915.3. Argues again that Heminge and Con-
    dell who signed the "Address" must still be considered
    its authors since no compelling or irrefutable evidence to
    the contrary has been advanced. See 1914.1 and 11; 1915.3.

7   VIZETELLY, ERNEST ALFRED. "Some English Poets of Tudor and
    Stuart Days." In Loves of the Poets. London: Holden &
    Hardingham, pp. 71-72.
    Jonson had no great love in his life, possibly because
    he was so egocentric, perhaps because he simply liked the
    company of men more.

1916

1   BRIGGS, WILLIAM DINSMORE. "Source Material for Jonson's Ep-
    igrams and Forrest." Classical Philology 11, no. 2
    (April):169-90.

1916

A list of selected borrowing from such Latin poets as Martial, Seneca, Lucian, Horace, Ovid, Sallust, and others.

2 _____. "Studies in Ben Jonson. III & IV." Anglia 39 (1916): 16-44, 209-52.
Part III takes up various bibliographical and textual questions associated with Jonson as well as an examination of the unpublished epigrams of Henry Tubbe to determine Jonson's influence on him. Part IV is a listing of poems ascribed to Jonson by Gifford which Briggs believes are doubtful, and a list of poems not previously ascribed to Jonson which he believes should be given serious consideration for the Jonson canon.

3 CARGILL, ALEXANDER. "Shakespeare, Ben Jonson, and Scotland." In Shakespeare the Player. London: Constable & Co., pp. 97-108.
A comparison of Shakespeare's possible journey to Scotland and Jonson's actual journey there.

4 CLARK, J. S., and ODELL, J. P. "Ben Jonson." In A Study of English and American Writers. Chicato: Row, Peterson & Co., pp. 40-53.
Discusses Jonson's personal characteristics as revealed in his writing under such topics as: arrogance, classicism and coldness, insolent satire, and sweetness of lyric. Reprinted in 1974.12.

5 GREENWOOD, G[EORGE] G. "The Jonsonian Utterances and the Shakespeare Folio of 1623." In Is There a Shakespeare Problem? London: John Lane, pp. 371-432.
A lengthy explanation of why Jonson's remarks on Shakespeare do not alter the case against Shakespeare writing his own plays.

6 LEE, SIDNEY [L.]. A Life of William Shakespeare. New York: Macmillan Co.
Revision of 1898.6.

7 LUCE, MORTON. "Ben Jonson on Shakespeare." Spectator 116 (1 April):438.
Comment on a phrase from Jonson's "Ode on Shakespeare."

8 Madden, D. H. "Ben Jonson." In Shakespeare and His Fellows. New York: D. H. Madden, pp. 114-36.
Concludes that Shakespeare and Jonson were not friends during Shakespeare's lifetime. It was only after Shakespeare died that Jonson mellowed and revealed the kind side of his nature.

1916

9   SCOTT, MARY AUGUSTA. <u>Elizabethan Translations from the Ital-</u>
    <u>ian</u>. Vassar Semi-Centennial Series. Boston: Houghton
    Mifflin, passim.
        References to Jonson's involvement with Italian trans-
    lations. Reprinted 1969.21.

1917

1   BRIGGS, WILLIAM D[INSMORE]. "Source-Material for Jonson's
    <u>Under-wood</u> and Miscellaneous Poems." <u>MP</u> 15, no. 6 (Sep-
    tember):277-312.
        Identifies more of Jonson's poetic sources.

2   HOOPER, EDITH S. "The Text of Ben Jonson." <u>MLR</u> 12, no. 3
    (July):350-52.
        Questions the accuracy of Jonson's 1616 folio.

3   PAUL, FRANCIS. "Two Elizabethans." <u>American Catholic Quar-</u>
    <u>terly Review</u> 42 (January):149-64.
        Biographical comparison of Jonson and Lodge. "Jonson
    knew the Elizabethan age as only that man knows who has
    tried its adventures and undergone its hardships." Admir-
    ation for Jonson's strength and his will to struggle up-
    ward from his humble origins.

1918

1   BRIGGS, WILLIAM DINSMORE. "The Birth-Date of Ben Jonson
    <u>MLN</u> 33, no. 3 (March):137-45.
        Argues that June 11, 1572 or 1573 was Jonson's birthday.

2   CLARK, DONALD LEMEN. "The Requirements of a Poet: A Note on
    the Sources of Ben Jonson's <u>Timber</u>, Paragraph 130." <u>MP</u>
    16, no. 8 (December):413-29.
        Considers question, which is most important in the com-
    position of poetry: inspiration or rhetoric? Jonson ac-
    knowledged the significance of both.

3   COLBY, ELDRIDGE. "Ben Jonson and the Colby Family." <u>N&Q</u> 136
    (April):103.
        Who is the Colby whom Jonson addresses in "An Epistle
    to a Friend, to a Friend, to Persuade him to the Warres"?

4   GUINEY, L[OUISE] I[MOGENT]. "Henslowe and Ben Jonson." <u>N&Q</u>
    136 (October):271.
        Was Henslowe's letter to Alleyn, 26 September 1598, a
    forgery? In it Henslowe refers to Jonson's slaying of Gab-

riel Spencer and his subsequent incarceration and conver-
sion to Catholicism.

5   MAGNUS, LAURIE. A General Sketch of European Literature. Lon-
     don: Kegan Paul, Trench, Trubner & Co., pp. 366-68.
        Considers Jonson's lyric poetry of greater interest and
     of more enduring quality than his plays.

6   REINSCH, HUGO. Jonsons Poetik und seine Beziehungen zu Horaz.
     Naumberg: n.p.
        Reprint of 1899.6.

7   SHAFER, ROBERT. "Ben Jonson and His Followers," In The Eng-
     lish Ode to 1660: An Essay in Literary History. Princeton:
     Princeton University Press, pp. 109-19.
        Jonson was heavily influenced by both Horace and Pindar.
     Though he wrote only a few odes they are among his best
     poems and among the best odes in English literature. Re-
     printed in 1966.16.

8   WRIGHT, H. "Jonson on Elizabethan Translation of Homer and
     Virgil." MLR 13, no. 3 (July):322-23.
        Explanation of a remark on translation which Jonson
     made to Drummond.

1919

1   ADAMS, JOSEPH QUINCY, Jr. "The Bones of Ben Jonson." SP 16,
     no. 4 (July):289-302.
        Summarizes the history of Jonson's grave.

2   ANON. "Ben Jonson." TLS, 13 November, pp. 637-38.
        Review of Virgil and the English Poets, by E. Nitchie.
     Laments the fact that although Jonson has a fine literary
     reputation, he is largely ignored by the reading public.
     Author believes he deserves better. See 1919.8.

3   BENSLY, EDWARD. "Samuel Jonson and Ben Jonson." N&Q 137
     (April):103.
        A note on Carlyle's reference to Ben Jonson.

4   BUTLER, GEOFFREY. "Autographs of Ben Jonson." TLS, 3 July,
     p. 364.
        Notes the discovery of Jonson's autograph in a book
     Hadrianai Amerotic Compendium Graec: Gramm, etc.

5   ELIOT, T. S. "Ben Jonson." TLS, 13 November, pp. 637-38.
        Primarily on Jonson's drama, but makes general observa-

tions on Jonson's style and his themes. Suggests that Jonson writes "poetry of the surface," which "cannot be understood without study." "The immediate appeal of Jonson is to the mind; his emotional tone is not in the single verse, but in the design of the whole. But not many people are capable of discovering for themselves the beauty which is only found after labor; and Jonson's industrious readers have been those whose interest was historical and curious, and those who have thought that in discovering the historical and curious interest they have discovered the artistic value as well." Jonson requires a total immersion, and "intelligent saturation in his work as a whole; we mean that in order to enjoy him we must get to the center of his work and his temperament. . . ." Reprinted in 1920.2 and 1963.9.

6   HILL, N. W. "Henslowe and Ben Jonson." N&Q 137 (March):81-82.
     Response to 1918.4. Presents evidence that the letter in question is authentic.

7   HUXLEY, ALDOUS. "Ben Jonson." London Mercury 1 (December): 184-91.
     Review of Ben Jonson, by Gregory G. Smith. "One cannot honestly call him [Jonson] a good poet or a supreme dramatist. And yet, unsympathetic as he is, uninteresting as he often can be we still go on respecting and admiring him, because, in spite of everything, we are conscious, obscurely but certainly, that he was a great man." See 1919.9.

8   NITCHIE, E. Virgil and the English Poets. New York: Columbia University Press, pp. 98-99, 122-23.
     Jonson was strongly influenced by the classics in general and more so by Virgil in particular than most critics have recognized.

9   SAINTSBURY, GEORGE. Review of Ben Jonson by Gregory G. Smith. Bookman 57 (December):105-7.
     Describes the difficulties in writing about Ben Jonson because of the complexity of his personality and his work. Reprinted in 1947.13. See 1919.10.

10   SMITH, G. GREGORY. Ben Jonson. English Men of Letters. London: Macmillan & Co., 310 pp.
     Includes a thorough discussion of Jonson's poetry emphasizing the classical quality of his verse. Discounts Jonson's heavy borrowing from ancient writers, but finally concludes that he will not be remembered for his poetry. "The general failure of his efforts as a poet is in part

the effect of his theoretical prejudices on verse technique.
No one dare say, with the finer passages in memory, that
Jonson had a bad ear, or was indifferent to the nicer values
in words, but few will fail to see that he worked under
difficulties of his own making, and either could not or
would not move freely."

11   WYNDHAM, GEORGE. "The Poems of Shakespeare." In Essays in
     Romantic Literature. London: Macmillan & Co., pp. 290-
     309.
        Considers the professional relationship between Jonson
     and Shakespeare and particularly their roles in the poets'
     war in the early 1600s. Reprinted in 1968.20.

1920

1   BAYFIELD, M. A. "An Examination of the 1616 Folio of Ben Jon-
    son's Works." In A Study of Shakespeare's Versification.
    Cambridge: University Press, pp. 295-313.
       Compares Jonson's and Shakespeare's versification in the
    folio editions of their work noting that Jonson probably
    corrected his own proof sheets. Reprinted 1969.1.

2   ELIOT, T. S. "Ben Jonson." In Sacred Wood. London: Methuen
    & Co., pp. 95-111.
       Reprint of 1919.5.

3   HARRIS, L. H. "Three Notes on Ben Jonson." MP 17, no. 12
    (April):679-85.
       The second note deals with the source of Epigram CXII,
    "To a weak Gamester in Poetry." Harris cites Martial's
    Epigram 12.94. Notes one and three refer to Catiline.

4   LAWRENCE, J. W. "The Casting-out of Ben Jonson." TLS,
    8 July, p. 438.
       Jonson satirizes Samuel Daniel in the character of
    Matheo or Matthew the gull in Every Man in His Humour. See
    1920.6.

5   LOONEY, J. THOMAS. Shakespeare Identified. New York: Duell,
    Sloan, & Pierce, pp. 27-30.
       The fact that Jonson is not mentioned in Shakespeare's
    will is evidence, according to the author, that Shakespeare
    was not a playwright or man of letters.

6   SIMPSON, PERCY. "The Casting-out of Ben Jonson." TLS, 15
    July, p. 456.

1920

        Response to 1920.4. Matheo or Matthew is not a carica-
ture of Daniel since in the play the character plagarizes
one of Daniel's sonnets.

*7   WHIMBLEY, C. "Ben Jonson." <u>Observer</u>, 8 February, p. 6.
       Cited in Tannenbaum, 1947.10.

8   WENDELL, BARRETT. <u>The Tradition of European Literature</u>. New
       York: Scribner's & Sons, pp. 310-11.
       Jonson's indebtedness to Martial.

1921

1   ANON. "Ben Jonson's Hack-work." <u>SatR</u> 132 (3 September):298.
       Review of <u>Ben Jonson and Shakespeare</u>, by George G. Green-
wood. Argues that Jonson's statements on Shakespeare are
not evidence that Jonson, Heminge, and Condell were con-
spirators in a plot. See 1921.6.

2   ANON. Review of <u>Ben Jonson and Shakespeare</u>, by George G. Green-
       wood. <u>TLS</u>, 4 August, p. 502.
       Lists a number of arguments to counter Greenwood's the-
sis. See 1921.6.

3   BROADUS, EDMUND KEMPER. "Ben Jonson and William Devenant."
       In <u>The Laureateship: A Study of the Office of Poet</u>
<u>Laureate in England</u>. Oxford: Clarendon Press, pp. 40-58.
       Although Jonson was not an official poet laureate, it is
clear "that the popular conception of such an office--an
officially appointed court poet who should be styled poet
laureat--began to take shape during his lifetime." Reprint in 1966.4.

4   BROWN, HORATIO F. "Ben Jonson and Robert Browning." <u>Specta-</u>
<u>tor</u> 127 (6 August):165-66.
       Lists similarities between the poetry of Browning and
Jonson. "The wood of their instruments is from the same
tree, equally seasoned, and yields a like pitch of note."

5   DUNN, S. G. "A Jonson Copyright." <u>TLS</u>, 28 July, p. 484.
       Notes some manuscript changes in the 1640 edition of
<u>Under-wood</u>.

6   GREENWOOD, GEORGE [G.]. <u>Ben Jonson and Shakespeare</u>. London:
       Cecil Palmer, 60 pp.
       After examining Jonson's comments on Shakespeare and his
contributions to Shakespeare's first folio, concludes
that Jonson was in a plot with Heminge and Condell to print

a book of plays which were not written by the man, William Shakespeare, whose name appeared on the title page.

7   _____. "Ben Jonson and Shakespeare." TLS, 11 August, p. 517.
        Response to 1921.2. Continues to assert his theory of
        conspiracy.

8   GREG, W. W. "'Berigemenes Jonsones Share.'" MLR 16, nos.
        3-4 (July-October):323.
        Takes exception to Thaler's interpretation of informa-
        tion presented in 1921.12.

9   LANG, ANDREW. "Jonson and Jonson's Prose." In History of Eng-
        lish Literature. London: Longmans, Green & Co., pp. 233-
        41.
        Discoveries filled with trite aphorisims and chronic com-
        plaining is not all that the critics of late have suggested.
        Bacon's Essays are far superior. Reprinted in 1969.12.

10   MORLEY, CHRISTOPHER DARLINGTON. "By the Fireplace." In Plum
        Pudding. Garden City, N. Y.: Doubleday, Page & Co., pp.
        206-9.
        Comments about Jonson's views of his fellow poets.

11   SIMONDS, WILLIAM EDWARD. A Student's History of English Lit-
        erature. Boston: Houghton Mifflin Co., pp. 147-50.
        Short notes on the poetry and prose.

12   THALER, ALVIN. "'Bengemenes Johnsones Share.'" MLR 16, no.
        1 (January):61-65.
        Jonson's financial dealings with Henslowe.

13   WARD, A. W. "Ben Jonson's Prose." In Collected Papers. Vol.
        3. Cambridge: Cambridge University Press, pp. 364-66.
        A brief and measured note on Discoveries. "The general
        style of these aphorisms, or notes for essays never in-
        tended to be written, is quite unforced; and we may perhaps
        have reason to be glad that they were not over-elab-
        orated for publication.

1922

1   ACHESON, ARTHUR. Shakespeare's Sonnet Story 1592-1598. Lon-
        don: Bernard Quaritch, passim.
        A number of remarks about Shakespeare's and Jonson's
        relationship including the belief that Jonson's epigram
        "The Poet-Ape" is directed against Shakespeare.

1922

2   ALDEN, RAYMOND MacDONALD. Shakespeare. New York: Duffield
    & Co., pp. 86-90.
        Comparison of the two playwrights. Comment on Jonson's
    critical remarks on Shakespeare.

3   BARTLETT, HENRIETTA COLLINS. "Bibliographical Data Regarding
    Ben Jonson." In Mr. William Shakespeare. New Haven: Yale
    University Press, pp. 154-57.
        Bibliographic descriptions of some of Jonson's early
    works including Works 1616 and 1640.

4   BRADLEY, JESSE FRANKLIN, and ADAMS, JOSEPH QUINCY, [Jr.],
    The Jonson Allusion-Book: A Collection of Allusions to
    Ben Jonson from 1579 to 1700. Cornell Studies in English,
    no. 6. New Haven: Yale University Press, 472 pp.
        A listing of allusions to Jonson and to his dramatic,
    poetic and prose works. Parodies, complementary poems,
    epitaphs, etc., are often printed in full. Provides a
    wide view of seventeenth-century opinion on Jonson. Re-
    printed in 1971.2.

5   CLARK, D. H. Rhetoric and Poetry in the Renaissance. New
    York: Columbia University Press, pp. 93-95, 156-59.
        As a critic Jonson insisted on the didactic element of
    poetry maintained through the fiction of the genre.

6   MATHEW, FRANK. "Ben Jonson's Opinion." In An Image of Shake-
    speare. London: Butler & Tanner, pp. 317-51.
        Summarizes the poetic and prose commentary on Shake-
    speare by Jonson. Contemporary opinions on the relation-
    ships between the two writers are also noted.

7   SMITHSON, E. W. "Ben Jonson and Shakespeare," In Baconian
    Essays. London: Cecil Palmer, pp. 97-119.
        Discusses Jonson's "Ode on Shakespeare," and the crit-
    icism found in Discoveries.

                              1923

1   ADAMS, JOSEPH QUINCY, Jr. A Life of William Shakespeare.
    Boston: Houghton Mifflin Co., passim.
        An account of the professional and personal relation-
    ships of Shakespeare and Jonson.

2   ANON. "Jonson and Drummond." TLS, 9 August, p. 529.
        Review of Ben Jonson's Conversations . . . , edited
    by Richard F. Patterson. "An alluring and baffling
    book." Lists a number of misprints or misleading statements.

3   ANON. "Literary Conversations." SatR 136 (7 July):18-19.
Review of Ben Jonson's Conversations . . . , edited by
Richard F. Patterson. Description of Conversations. Judges
that this is the best edition yet published of "one of the
most important literary documents of Elizabethan times."
See 1923.9.

4   BAKER, ERNEST. Review of Ben Jonson's Conversations . . . ,
edited by Richard F. Patterson. New Statesman 21 (28
July):473.
Welcomes a new and accurate edition of Conversations.
See 1923.9.

5   DRINKWATER, JOHN. "S. Godolphin and Ben Jonson." TLS, 25
October, p. 708.
Identifies the author of an anonymous tribute to Ben
Jonson as Sidney Godolphin based upon the discovery of a
manuscript book in William Godolphin's hand.

6   GRAVES, THORNTON S. "Jonson in the Jest Books." In The Manly
Anniversary Studies in Language and Literature. Chicago:
University of Chicago Press, pp. 127-39.
Discusses jests by and about Jonson. Points out that
the compilers of seventeenth- and eighteenth-century jest
books often falsely attributed jests to famous figures.

7   HERBERT, EDWARD, Lord Herbert of Cherbury. "To his Friend
Ben Jonson, of his Horace made English." In The Poems English and Latin of Edward, Lord Herbert of Cherbury. Edited by G. C. Moore Smith. Oxford: Clarendon Press, pp.
19-20.
Reprint of 1640.6.

8   HUXLEY, ALDOUS. "Ben Jonson." In On The Margin: Notes and
Essays. London: Chatto & Windus, pp. 184-202.
Sees Jonson as a realistic and moralistic writer, though
he may not be a good poet. "Unsympathetic as he is, un-
interesting as he often can be, we still go on respecting
and admiring him, because, in spite of everything, we are
conscious, obscurely but certainly, that he was a great
man."

9   PATTERSON, R[ICHARD] F., ed. Introduction to Ben Jonson's
Conversations with William Drummond of Hawthornden. Lon-
don: Blackie, pp. iii-xv.
Discusses the background to Conversations by amplifying
some of Drummond's cryptic comments. Takes up in detail
Jonson's remarks on Donne.

1923

10   RHODES, R. COMPTON. <u>Shakespeare's First Folio</u>. Oxford:
     Basil Blackwell, pp. 9-13, 52-54.
          Discusses Jonson's "Ode to Shakespeare," as well as his
     criticism of Shakespeare in <u>Discoveries</u>.

11   SAINTSBURY, GEORGE. "Drummond and Ben Jonson." <u>Bookman</u> 66
     (August):279.
          Review of Ben Jonson's <u>Conversations . . .</u> , edited by
     Richard F. Patterson. Questions the validity though not
     the authenticity of <u>Conversations</u>. How are we ever to
     know how true or misconceived Drummond's record is? See
     1923.9.

12   SQUIRE, J. C. "Ben Jonson's Conversations with Drummond."
     <u>Observer</u> (21 October), p. 4.
          Review of <u>Ben Jonson's Conversations . . .</u> , edited by
     Richard F. Patterson. Summarizes the contents of <u>Conver-
     sations</u> and notes the importance of the work. See 1923.9.

13   WOOLF, LEONARD. "Ben Jonson." <u>Nation and The Athenaeum</u>, 33
     (23 June):396.
          Review of <u>Ben Jonson's Conversations . . .</u> , edited by
     Richard F. Patterson. The <u>Conversations</u> give the reader a
     very personal look at Jonson in a way we cannot view most
     other early English writers. Jonson is "the first English
     critic, a first rate prose writer, an original thinker,
     and a great character. He could afford to do without
     genius." See 1923.9.

14   "Rare Ben Jonson." <u>Liguistica Antrerpiensia</u> 318
     (11 August):281-82.
          Review of <u>Ben Jonson's Conversations . . .</u> , edited by
     Richard F. Patterson. Reprint of 1923.13. See 1923.9.

                              <u>1924</u>

1   ANON. Forward to <u>The Songs and Poems of Ben Jonson</u>. London:
     Philip Allan, pp. iii-vii.
          Brief biographical sketch with general remarks on the
     lyrical quality of Jonson's songs.

2   HEBEL, J. WILLIAM. "Drayton's Sierena." <u>PMLA</u> 39, no. 4
     (December):814-36, particularly pp. 830-36.
          Argues that there was some animosity between Drayton
     and Jonson.

3   JUSSERAND, J. J. "Ben Jonson's Views on Shakespeare's Art."
     In <u>The School for Ambassadors and Other Essays</u>. London:
     Fisher Unwin, pp. 275-330.
          Reprint of 1907.9.

4   K., J. "The 'but' of Ben Jonson." N&Q 147 (19 July):45.
    Syntactical confusion in "Drink to me only."

5   KELLER, WOLFGANG. "Shakespeare, Ben Jonson, und die Folio von
    1623." Shakespeare Jahrbuch 59 (1924):123-29.
    Discusses the influence Jonson might have exerted on the
    printing of Shakespeare's first folio.

6   LEGOUIS, EMILE HYACINTHE. Histoire de la litterature anglaise.
    Paris: Hachette, 1312 pp.
    Translated 1926.7, which see for abstract.

7   SMITH, G. C. MOORE. Review of The Jonson Allusion-Book . . . ,
    by Jesse Franklin Bradley and Joseph Quincy Adams. MLR
    19, no. 1 (January):111-13.
    Although very useful in gaining some sense of seventeenth-
    century opinion of Jonson, contains a number of errors. A
    long but only partial list is provided. See 1922.4.

*8 ZWAGER, N. H. M. "Ben Jonson's Religion." Tydschr van Rall
    and Lettergen. 12:182-91.
    Cited in Tannenbaum 1938.13.

                                1925

1   ALDINGTON, RICHARD. "Conversations with William Drummond of
    Hawthornden." Nation and The Athenaeum 38 (5 December):
    356.
    Review of Jonson and Drummond, their Conversations . .
    . , by C. L. Stainer (1925.30). Discusses major objec-
    tions to Stainer's hypothesis and vigorously criticizes
    his work.

2   ANON. "Are Drummond's 'Conversations' Forgeries?" Black-
    wood's Magazine 218 (December):878-81.
    Review of Jonson and Drummond, their Conversations . . . ,
    by C. L. Stainer. Believes that Satainer's argument
    is singularly unconvincing. See 1925.30.

3   ANON. "Ben Jonson." TLS, 30 July, pp. 501-2.
    Review of Ben Jonson, by C. H. Herford and Percy Simpson.
    Biography in Volume I is not only the best available but
    is a great service to Jonson and his readers. "The Ben
    Jonson that we find here is an awe inspiring person. He
    is a greater bully than the eighteenth century Jonson, with
    whom he has often been compared. . . . Yet Jonson's was
    a noble arrogance, and it helped him immensely to do his
    work in life. No less than Milton he felt himself a ded-

1925

icated man, and the work to which he was dedicated was
nothing less than educating the people of England." The
rest of the material in these two volumes is also excellent.
Herford and Simpson have brought together significant items
on Jonson heretofore either unknown or scattered. See
1925.17.

4   ANON. "In Brief Review." Bookman 57 (November):348-49.
        Short publication announcement of Ben Jonson, by C. H.
    Herford and Percy Simpson. See 1925.17.

5   ANON. Review of Ben Jonson, by C. H. Herford and Percy Simp-
    son. N&Q 149 (8 August):107-8.
        Description with some grudging praise. See 1925.17.

6   B., J. N. "The Oxford Jonson." Oxford Magazine 1 (22 Octo-
    ber):45-47.
        Review of Ben Jonson, by C. H. Herford and Percy Simpson.
    Description of the volumes calling attention to the edi-
    tor's discoveries of new information on Jonson's life.
    See 1925.17.

7   BIRRELL, FRANCIS. "Ben Jonson." The Empire Review, 42 (Oc-
    tober), 392-96.
        Review of Ben Jonson, by C. H. Herford and Percy Simp-
    son. Welcomes a long overdue new edition of Jonson. "Ben
    Jonson was above all a literary writer. He appeals to us
    by the texture of his writings, by the monstrous extravagance
    of his conceptions, not by any direct appeals to our human
    emotions." See 1925.17.

8   BRAWLEY, BENJAMIN GRIFFITH. A New Survey of English Litera-
    ture. A Textbook for Colleges. New York: F. S. Crofts,
    pp. 118-20.
        Points out that "Jonson by his fine taste and precision
    helped to mold the Cavlier lyric."

9   CHAMBERS, E. K. Review of Ben Jonson, by C. H. Herford and
    Percy Simpson. Library, 4th ser., 6, no. 2 (September):
    179-82.
        General praise for Herford and Simpson's work. Questions
    the authenticity of "Memorandums of the Immortal Ben"
    which are presented without comment. It has since been
    proven that they are not authentic. See 1925.17.

10 CHEW, SAMUEL C. Review of Ben Jonson, by C. H. Herford and
    Percy Simpson. Nation 121 (23 September):333-34.
        Discusses the scholarly problems associated with the
    work and concludes with a generous tribute for the editors'
    efforts. See 1925.17.

11   COLVIN, SIDNEY, JOHN KEATS. New York: Macmillan Co., passim.
     References to Jonson's influence on Keats' poetry.

12   DUNN, ESTHER CLOUDMAN. Ben Jonson's Art: Elizabethan Life
     and Literature as Reflected Therein. Northampton, Mass.
     Smith College, 176 pp.
        Stresses the moral purpose of Jonson's poetry but does
     not interpret it in a strictly didactic or ethical way.
     "One might say that while Jonson could only proceed by
     intellectual processes in the practice of poetry and while
     he must see for it a definite moral aim, both intellect
     and morality transcended their limits, were transmuted in
     fires of his own burning conception of the divinity of his
     art." Reprinted in 1963.8,

13   FORSYTHE, ROBERT S. "The Pursuit of Shadows." N&Q 148 (7
     March):165-66.
        Reference to 1865.7. Although Jonson probably did trans-
     late Anulus's poem in his epigram to the Countess of Pem-
     broke, the comparison of women to men's shadows was known
     in England through other sources.

14   GOLLANCZ, ISRAEL. "Ben Jonson's Ode to 'The Phoenix and the
     Turtle.'" TLS, 8 October, p. 655.
        Reports on discovering a new prelude by Jonson to "The
     Phoenix and the Turtle."

15   GREG, W. W., et al. "Benjamin Jonson." In English Literary
     Autographs. 1550-1650. London: Oxford University Press,
     n.p.
        Reproduces four Jonson holographs. Comment that Jonson
     "wrote a characteristic but not particularly tidy hand,
     rather less humanistic in style than one might have expected.
     The general impression is Italian, but it is by no
     means pure.

16   GREG, W. W. "Ben Jonson's 'Conversations.'" TLS, 27 August,
     p. 557.
        Reference to 1925.22, 23, and 27. Sums up the difference
     between Simpson and Patterson. "I have a good deal of
     sympathy with 'the ordinary reader' who desires a plain,
     readable text unencumbered with critical details. But, af-
     ter all, he has been pretty generously catered for, and to
     suppose that he can combine his easy pleasures with criti-
     cal scholarship is an idle superstition. For serious work,
     far from the pendulum having swung too much in the direc-
     tion of exact reproduction, we are merely beginning to
     appreciate the importance of rigorous methods."

1925

17   HERFORD, C. H., AND SIMPSON, PERCY, eds. <u>Ben Jonson</u>. Vols.
     1 & 2. Oxford: Clarendon Press.
        This eleven-volume edition was not completed until 1952.
     Volume 8 <u>The Poems and Prose Works</u> was published in 1947.
     Two volumes of commentary, literary record and notes com-
     pleted the project. Here publication of the dramas and
     masques is not noted.
        Volume 1 contains a life of Jonson, contemporary letters
     and records, and concludes with a list of books in his
     library. Volume 2 contains introductions to the plays,
     poems, and prose. The biography of Jonson is a descrip-
     tion of the man. "Jonson figures in our current analysis
     as the staunch asserter of classic tradition, instructed
     reason, and enlightened common sense, against the imagin-
     ative individualism of Elizabethan romancers. But the
     Jacobean world saw in this doughty champion of unpopular
     traditions the most incisive individual personality, the
     most commanding personal force which had, within its mem-
     ory, mingled in the world of letters."
        Few editors have had such a demonstrable impact upon
     their authors as Herford and Simpson had on Jonson. Aca-
     demic interest was greatly stimulated as critics became
     less concerned about when Jonson would get his just re-
     ward and more interested in the scholarly analysis of his
     individual works.

18   KENDON, FRANK. Review of <u>Ben Jonson</u>, by C. H. Herford and
     Percy Simpson. <u>London Mercury</u> 13 (December):214-15.
        Summary comment on Jonson's character. "The unqualified
     admiration that he desired he never won; in many efforts
     to prove himself superior to criticism he spattered him-
     self with the mud of controversy: he used the art he
     boasted to defend his self-esteem, and damaged it a little
     in the process." See 1925.17.

19   LUCAS, F. L. "Ben Jonson." <u>New Statesman</u> 26 (28 November):
     209-10.
        Review of <u>Ben Jonson</u>, by C. H. Herford and Percy Simp-
     son. Favorable review of Herford and Simpson but asks if
     Jonson really justifies the effort. "We would gladly give
     his faults some indulgence, if he ever showed any to others;
     we could forget them in concentrating on his works, which
     are after all our real concern, if he would but let us for-
     get his more intolerable virtues. . . Not nobility, nor com-
     passion, nor sensitiveness to beauty, are his qualities;
     but stark force and personality and intensity. What he
     meant, he meant vehemently." See 1925.17.

20 MacMECHAN, ARCHIBALD. Review of Ben Jonson, by C. H. Herford
    and Percy Simpson. Dalhouise Review 5 (October):419-20.
        Announcement and short description of the volumes with
    a brief complaint that the British do not acknowledge Am-
    erican scholars of English literature. See 1925.17.

21 MACNAGHTEN, HUGH. "Ben Jonson's Celia." National Review 84
    (January):721-24.
        Points out once again that "Drink to me only," is large-
    ly lifted from Philostratus.

22 _____. "Ben Jonson and Celia." National Review 84 (February):
    956.
        Clarifies which of Philostratus' love letters Jonson
    used.

23 PATTERSON, RICHARD F. "Ben Jonson." TLS, 6 August, 521.
        Takes issue with Herford and Simpson's criticism
    (appearing in 1925.17) of his edition of Conversations.
    In turn Patterson finds some questionable readings in
    Herford and Simpson.

24 _____. "Ben Jonson's 'Conversations.'" TLS, 3 September, p.
    569.
        Response to 1925.27. Patterson continues to defend his
    view of textual editing.

25 REA, JOHN D. "'This Figure that Thou Here Seest Put.'" MP
    22 (May):417-19.
        Possible sources Jonson may have used in writing his
    lines on Shakespeare's portrait.

26 SAINTSBURY, GEORGE. "Jonson's Discoveries." Bookman 68
    (September):279-81.
        Review of Ben Jonson, by C. H. Herford and Percy Simpson.
    In a bewildering and ingenious way Jonson uses the words
    of ancients to comment on contemporary writers. See
    1925.17.

27 SIMPSON, PERCY. "Ben Jonson." TLS, 13 August, p. 533.
        Response to 1925.23. Brief discussion of the editor's
    role and responsibility in preparing an edition of a fam-
    ous author.

28 SQUIRE, J. C. "Ben Jonson's Conversations with Drummond."
    Observer, 1 November, p. 4.
        Review of Jonson and Drummond, their Conversations . . . ,
    by C. L. Stainer. Believes that the evidence of a
    forgery is very convincing but reserves final judgment.
    See 1925.30.

1925

29 ____. "Volumes 1 and 2 of Herford and Simpson's Ben Jonson."
Observer, 19 July, p. 4.
Review of Ben Jonson, by C. H. Herford and Percy Simpson. Admires the edition much more than Jonson. See
1925.17.

30 STAINER, C. L. Jonson and Drummond, their Conversations: A
Few Remarks on an 18th Century Forgery. Oxford: B. Black-
well, 80 pp.
Argues that Sir Robert Sibbald's transcription of Conversations, which is the only extant document since Drummond's own MS was either lost or destroyed, is a forgery.
The case rests largely on speculation.

31 SWINBURNE, ALGERNON CHARLES. "Ben Jonson," and "The Tribe of
Ben." In The Complete Works of Algernon Charles Swinburne.
Vol. 5. Edited by Sir Edmund Gosse and Thomas James Wise.
London: William Heinemann, p. 173, 185.
Both sonnets are a general tribute to the lasting quality
of Jonson. In the first he is seen as something of a
timeless but fearless critic.

"Nor less, high-stationed on the grey grave heights,
High-thoughted seers with heaven's heart-kindling lights
Hold converse: and the herd meaner things
Knows or by fiery scourge or fiery shaft
When wrath on thy broad brows as risen, and laughed,
Darkening thy soul with shadow of thunderous wings."

The second sonnet lists the more prominent members of the
tribe and mentions their relationship to Jonson. Reprint
of 1882.9.

32 WHIMBLEY, CHARLES. "Ben Jonson, the Man." Blackwood's Mag-
azine, 218 (November):680-91.
Review of Ben Jonson, by C. H. Herford and Percy Simp-
son. Herford and Simpson "have given us a picture of Ben
Jonson, the man, which is neither blurred not indistinct.
Their judgment matches their erudition; and when their
work is complete we shall have such an edition of Ben
Jonson's plays and poems as will be an enduring credit to
English scholarship." See 1925.17.

33 WHIPPLE, T. K. "Ben Jonson." In Martial and the English Ep-
igram from Sir Thomas Wyatt to Ben Jonson. University of
California Publications in Modern Philology, vol. 10.
Berkeley: University of California Press, pp. 384-406.
A general survey of the epigrams with particular empha-
sis on Martial's influence on Jonson. Discusses the

1926

closeness of Jonson to Martial in their style, structure, rhetoric, subject matter, and uses of irony and satire, but concludes that Jonson's "epigrams are as thoroughly English and characteristic of himself as Martial's are Roman and typical of their author." Reprinted in 1970.45.

34 WOOLF, LEONARD. "Ben Jonson." Nation and The Athenaeum 37 (25 July):516.
Review of "Benjamin Jonson," by W. W. Greg et al. "Admirable examples of learning without pedantry." See 1925.15.

1926

1 ARONSTEIN, PH. "Herford & Simpson's Ben Jonson." Anglia Beibl, 37, no. 1 (January):10-14.
Review of Ben Jonson, by C. H. Herford and Percy Simpson. Touches upon the highlights of Jonson's life and the major items of significance concerning his writings and his reputation. See 1925.17.

2 BROOKE, TUCKER. Review of Ben Jonson, by C. H. Herford and Percy Simpson. SatR 2 (27 February):592.
Takes exception to some points in the biography but generally regards the first two volumes as "shrewd and learned." See 1925.17.

3 GREG, W. W. Review of Ben Jonson, by C. H. Herford and Percy Simpson. MLR, 21 (April), 201-10.
A highly favorable and very thorough treatment of Herford and Simpson's work. Some mistakes and problems are noted. See 1925.17.

4 _____. "Notes on Ben Jonson's Works." RES 2, no. 6 (April): 129-145.
Takes up textual questions raised in Herford and Simpson's edition.

5 _____. "The Riddle of Ben Jonson's Chronology." Library, 4th ser. 6, no. 4 (March):340-47.
"After publishing the first volume of his Works, Jonson altered his customary dating from the Calendar to the Legal use. After his death his first editor, Sir Kenelm Digby, reverted, errors and ignorance apart, to the more rational and more popular method."

6 HOUSTON, PERCY HAZEN. Main Currents of English Literature. New York: F. S. Crofts & Co., passim.

1926

"Jonson was the first of the great literary dictators,
as Dr. Samuel Johnson was the last, to make the laws of
literary taste for a large section of the reading public.
The pseudo-classical period really has its beginnings in
his severity, his pedantry, and his strong didactic bent."

7   LEGOUIS, EMILE [HYACINTHE]. A History of English Literature,
     650-1660. Translated by Helen Douglas Irvine. Vol. 1.
     London: J. M. Dent, pp. 213-15.
        The most notable feature of Jonson's poetry is its vari-
     ety of theme, subject matter, style and temper, perhaps
     because "Jonson was a glorious egoist, very strongly in-
     dividualized, with fixed ideas which he asserted arrogant-
     ly. His pride, his contempt for ignorance and hypocrisy,
     his love of frankness and loyalty, his straightness, the
     manly affection of which he was capable: all these are
     manifest in his verse." See 1924.6. Revised 1935.14. Re-
     printed 1957.5.

8   McKERROW, R. B. "Herford and Simpson's Ben Jonson." RES 2,
     no. 6 (April):227-30.
        Review of "Benjamin Jonson," by W. W. Greg et al.
     The life of Jonson is an excellent study that makes use of
     all new information on Jonson which has come out over the
     past twenty years. It suffers slightly from a comparative
     absence of documentation. See 1925.15.

9   MAGNUS, LAURIE. A Dictionary of European Literature. London:
     George Routledge, p. 263.
        Short life and works essay. Reprinted in 1970.28.

10   SIMPSON, PERCY. "The Genuineness of the Drummond 'Conversa-
     tions.'" RES 2, no. 5 (January):42-50.
        Review of the transmission of Sibbald's transcription
     with a defense of its authenticity.

11   WILDER, M. L. "Did Jonson Write 'The Expostulation' Attribu-
     ted to Donne?" MLR 21, no. 4 (October):431-35.
        On internal evidence Wilder believes that "The Expostu-
     lation" was more probably written by Jonson than Donne.
     See also 1939.12 and 1978.4.

12   ZWAGER, N. [H.M.] Glimpses of Ben Jonson's London. Amster-
     dam: Swets & Zeitlinger, 215 pp.
        Contemporary accounts of social customs and avocational
     recreations alluded to in Jonson's poetry, prose and drama.

1927

1   ARONSTEIN, PH. Review of "The Genuineness of the Drummond
    'Conversations'," by Percy Simpson. Anglia Beibl 38, no.
    7 (July):204-5.
        Description with summary of comments on Jonson's con-
    temporaries. See 1926.10.

2   BRIGGS, WILLIAM DINSMORE. Review of Ben Jonson's Art . . . ,
    by Esther Cloudman Dunn. MLN 42, no. 8 (December):543-
    45.
        Professor Dunn's book is a reasonable survey of informa-
    tion on Jonson, although she is in many cases superficial
    and in some inaccurate. See 1925.12.

3   _____. Review of Ben Jonson, by C. H. Herford and Percy Simp-
    son. MLN, 42, no. 6 (June):404-11.
        Although some of the assertions and conclusions in the
    first two volumes are questioned, argues, "These volumes
    contain much of the best writing that has ever appeared on
    the subject of Jonson's character, his artistic genius, his
    methods, and the enduring value of his work." See 1925.17.

4   BYRNE, M. St. CLARE. Review of Glimpses of Ben Jonson's Lon-
    don, by N. H. M. Zwager. RES 3, no. 12 (July):481-82.
        "The glimpses are isolated ones, and are taken, as is
    natural when Jonson is the starting point from the satiric
    angle." See 1926.12.

5   CLARK, EDWIN. Review of O Rare Ben Jonson, by Francis Steeg-
    muller. New York Times, 18 September, p. 6.
        An engaging and entertaining narrative. Scholarship
    not to be taken seriously. See 1927.12.

6   GEROULD, GORDON HALL. "Ben Jonson in His Habit." SatR, 4
    (22 October), 236.
        Review of O Rare Ben Jonson, by Francis Steegmuller.
    Apart from the type of biography this is, it is a dull
    book which never gives the reader a picture of the inner
    Jonson. "The vacuity, one fears, is merely in this little
    book, of which M. Maurois, Mr. Lytton Strachey, and Mr.
    Erskine should be set down as godparents." See 1927.12.

7   NOYES, ROBERT G. Untitled. SatR 4 (31 December):494.
        Letter quoting some lines about Jonson's statue.

*8 PRAZ, MARIO. "Ben Jonson." La Cultura 6 (15 October):543-51.
    Cited in Tannenbaum 1938.13.

1927

9 SAWYER, CHARLES J., and DARTON, F. J. HARVEY. English Books, 1475-1900. Vol. 1. Westminster: C. J. Sawyer, pp. 120-33.

A discussion of Jonsonian editions and books which Jonson owned.

10 SCHELLING, FELIX E. "Ben Jonson and the Classical School," In Shakespeare and Demi-Science. Philadelphia: Univ. of Pennsylvania Press, pp. 59-64.

Reprint of 1898.8. Also reprinted in 1961.15

11 SHADWELL, THOMAS. The Complete Works of Thomas Shadwell. Vol. 1. Edited by Montague Summers. London: Fortune Press, pp. 183-89, 254-55.

Reprint of 1671.3.

12 STEEGMULLER, FRANCIS [Byron Steel]. O Rare Ben Jonson. New York: Alfred A. Knopf, 158 pp.

A "constructed" narrative of Jonson's life. The author makes the following observation on the book: "After one has read the large mass of tradition and scholarship concerning the life and works of Ben Jonson, one emerges into the more vivifying air of independent meditation, and discovers that one has despite the set-backs of contradictions and uncertainities evolved a definite conception of the man Ben Jonson, his friends, and his surroundings. This poetically true conception I have set down on paper. The fragmentary and scattered data have been the 'bricks' and 'stones' of my construction."

13 WILSON, F. P. The Plague in Shakespeare's London. Oxford: Clarendon Press, pp. 112-13.

Anecdote recounting the death of Jonson's son in the plague of 1603.

14 WOOLF, LEONARD. "Ben Jonson." In Essays on Literature, History, and Politics. New York: Harcourt, Brace & Co., pp. 11-18.

A discussion or recreation of Jonson's character based upon Drummond's conversations, Jonson's letters, and other contemporary documents.

1928

1 ALBRECHT, WALTER. Uber das "Theatrum Poetarum" von Milton's Neffen Edward Phillips. Weimar: Druck von G. Uschmann, 114 pp.

Comparison of Phillip's life of Jonson to other seventeenth-century commentators.

1928

2   ALLEN, PERCY. <u>Shakespeare, Jonson, and Wilkins as Borrowers</u>.
    London: C. Palmer, passim.
        Jonson's remarks on borrowing and imitation are used to
    support the central thesis, that there was an almost un-
    believable amount of borrowing among Renaissance dramatists.

3   _____. "Shakespeare, Jonson and Wilkins as Borrowers." <u>SatR</u>
    (Eng) (31 March):388.
        Response to 1928.10. The parallels the author points
    out are not mere coincidences as Brown argued in his review.

4   ANON. "Horace in English." <u>TLS</u>, 22 March, p. 203.
        Review of <u>Horace on the Art of Poetry</u> . . . , edited by
    Edward Henry Blakeney. Jonson's translation of Horace is
    infamous. Swinburne said, "A worse translator than Ben
    Jonson never committed a double outrage on two languages
    at once." See 1928.8.

5   ANON. Review of <u>Shakespeare, Jonson and Wilkins as Borrowers</u>,
    by Percy Allen. <u>Nation</u> 43 (14 April):50-51.
        Questions Allen's interpretation of borrowing. See
    1928.2.

6   ANON. Review of <u>How Shakespeare "Purged" Jonson</u> . . . , by
    Arthur Gray. <u>TLS</u>, 3 May, p. 330.
        Very skeptical of Gray's argument. See 1928.13.

7   BASKERVILLE, CHARLES REED. Review of <u>Ben Jonson</u>, by C. H.
    Herford and Percy Simpson. <u>MP</u> 25, no. 3 (February):366-68.
        "A sympathetic and constructive analysis that is gener-
    ally excellent and frequently brilliant. The emphasis
    given, however, to Jonson's dominant personal traits, his
    outstanding literary qualities, and his dogmatism as critic
    causes Herford at times to obscure and even underestimate
    the range and complexity of the man and his work." See
    1925.17.

8   BLAKENEY, EDWARD HENRY, ed. <u>Horace on the Art of Poetry</u>:
    <u>Latin Text, English Prose Translation, Introduction, Notes</u>,
    <u>with Ben Jonson's English Verse Rendering</u>. London: Schol-
    artis Press, pp. 107-35.
        An edition of Jonson's translation with notes. Reprint-
    ed in 1970.7.

9   BRINKLEY, ROBERTA FLORENCE. <u>Nathan Field, The Actor-Playwright</u>.
    New Haven: Yale University Press, pp. 72-77.
        Discussion of the relationship between Jonson and one
    of his "sons."

1928

10 BROWN, IVOR. "Shakespeare, Jonson and Wilkins." SatR (Eng)
    145 (7 April):432-33.
        Response to 1928.3. Brown clarifies his position stat-
    ing that he simply cannot see the parallel nature or
    quality of the passages Allen cites as parallel. Brown
    does not see any close similarity.

11 _____. "The Theatre: Merchandise Marks." SatR (Eng) 145
    (24 March):348-49.
        Review of Shakespeare, Jonson and Wilkins as Borrowers,
    by Percy Allen. Allen's work is not only futile and ped-
    antic, it is also misleading. See 1928.2.

12 ELIOT, T. S. Dial 85 (July):65-68.
        Review of Ben Jonson, by C. H. Herford and Percy Simp-
    son. "As fine and final an edition of an Elizabethan
    dramatist as has yet been received." Of Jonson Eliot
    remarks, "We get an impression of the man essentially the
    same as that of his tradition, but merely graven deeper.
    It was through an immensely impressive personality, as
    much as by the greatness of his work, that Jonson influenc-
    ed, more than any other one man, the whole course of Eng-
    lish literature." See 1925.17.

13 GRAY, ARTHUR. How Shakespeare "Purged" Jonson: A Problem
    Solved. Cambridge: W. Heffer & Sons, 34 pp.
        Argues that Shakespeare caricatured Jonson as Jaques in
    As You Like It. Reprinted in 1973.14.

14 _____. "Shakespeare's 'Purge' of Jonson." TLS, 10 May, p. 358.
        Response to 1928.6.

15 HENLEY, PAULINE. Spenser in Ireland. Dublin: Cork Univer-
    sity Press, passim.
        Notes Jonson's remarks on Spenser.

16 LEO, BROTHER. "Ben Jonson," In English Literarure. Boston:
    Ginn & Co., pp. 181-83.
        Summarizes Jonson's major critical tenets.

17 LODGE, OLIVER F. W. "Ben Jonson, Stow, & Strummond." TLS,
    31 May, p. 412.
        A gloss on Conversations.

18 McKNIGHT, GEORGE HARLEY. Modern English in the Making. New
    York: D. Appleton-Century, passim, particularly pp. 234-
    36.
        Jonson's impact on the English Language is discussed.

19   PROESTLER, MARY. "'Caesar did Never Wrong But With Just
        Cause,'" PQ 7, no. 1 (January):91-92.
            Discussion of the famous criticism Jonson leveled against
        Shakespeare.

20   ROGERS, KENNETH. The Mermaid and Mitre Taverns in Old London.
        London: Homeland Association, passim, particularly pages
        29-34.
            Jonson's name comes up frequently as literary allusions
        to taverns in London are noted.

21   RYAN, M. J. "'Tanquam Explorator.'" TLS (19 July):536.
            Jonson took the motto from Seneca, Tanquam Explorator,
        which he inscribed on the title pages of his books.

22   SMART, JOHN S. Shakespeare: Truth and Tradition. London:
        Edward Arnold, passim.
            Explains why Jonson wrote tributes to Shakespeare while
        knowing full well that Francis Bacon wrote all the plays.

23   TURNER, CELESTE. Anthony Mundy: An Elizabethan Man of Let-
        ters. University of California Publications in English,
        vol. 2, no. 1. Berkeley: University of California Press,
        pp. 120-23.
            Mundy was a minor playwright who knew Jonson.

24   WELLS, HENRY W. "Jonson's Criticism of Shakespeare." In The
        Judgement of Literature. New York: W. W. Norton, passim.
            Jonson was "one of the first and one of the greatest
        formal critics in England." He had a much more systematic
        concept of art than Shakespeare.

                                   1929

1   ANON. "Plagiarism: Ben Jonson and L. Sterne." Blackwood's
        Magazine, 225 (March):431-34.
            Review of Shakespeare, Jonson and Wilkins as Borrowers,
        by Percy Allen. Plagiarism is not a literary crime.
        "Practiced with skill and tact, it even smacks of virtue."
        Jonson is a good example of a successful plagiarist. See
        1928.2.

2   BASKERVILLE, CHARLES REED. The Elizabethan Jig. Chicago:
        University of Chicago Press, passim.
            Discussions of Jonson's satiric songs. Reprinted in
        1965.2.

1929

3   BROWN, HUNTINGTON. "Ben Jonson and Rabelais." MLN, 44, no. 1
     (January), 6-13.
         Discusses Jonson's borrowings from Rabelais, particu-
     larly those dealing with the inspirational qualities of
     wine.

4   DRAPER, JOHN W. The Funeral Elegy and the Rise of English Rom-
     anticism. New York: New York University Press, passim.
         "The Funeral Elegy and the Cavaliers" examines the
     elegiac tradition with reference to Jonson and his follow-
     ers. Reprinted in 1967.7.

5   EVANS, WILLA McCLUNG. Ben Jonson and Elizabethan Music. Lan-
     caster, Penn.: Lancaster Press, 131 pp.
         Discusses the technical devices with which Jonson made
     his verse peculiarly suitable for singing. "Smooth-flowing
     symmetrical patterns present a striking contrast to the
     heavy, scholarly verse written for the printed page." Re-
     printed in 1965.4.

6   FRIJLINCK, W. P. Review of Ben Jonson, by C. H. Herford and
     Percy Simpson. ES 11, nos. 1-6 (June):102-7.
         A description of the volumes and a tribute to the care-
     ful scholarship that went into the work. See 1925.17.

7   G., P. B. "Ben Jonson to Drummond of Hawthornden." N&Q 157
     (28 December):457-58.
         Prints a letter supposedly from Jonson to Drummond
     alluding to a visit by Shakespeare to Edinburgh. The
     letter was reproduced in an early nineteenth-century news-
     paper clipping.

8   GAVIGAN, WALTER V. "The Modern School of Biography," Thought
     4, no. 2 (September):181-204.
         Discusses 1927.12. Although it is not a scholarly work,
     "one is forced to agree, nevertheless, that the author
     has succeeded in capturing all of the significant details
     of the famous dramatist's life and has agreeably fused
     them into an unusually interesting literary portrait."

9   PAULL, HENRY MAJOR. Literary Ethics. New York: Dutton,
     passim.
         Jonson is not one of the major literary criminals of
     England, but he is a kind of fellow traveller with the
     forgers and imposters.

10   RANDOLPH, THOMAS. The Poems of Thomas Randolph. Edited by
     G. Thorn-Drury. London: Frederick Etchells & Hugh Mac-
     donald.
         Reprint of 1638.3.

1930

11   REYNOLDS, GEORGE F. "Ben Jonson." In <u>English Literature in</u>
        <u>Fact and Story</u>. New York: Century Co., pp. 128-29.
            General remarks on prose and poetry notes that Jonson
        was the first literary dictator of England.

12   STEEGMULLER, FRANCIS [Byron Steel]. <u>L'aventureuse Existence</u>
        <u>de Ben Jonson</u>. Translated by Jeanne Odier. Paris:
        Firmin-Didot, 204 pp.
            Translation of 1927.12.

13   THORN-DRURY, G., ed. Introduction to <u>The Poems of Thomas</u>
        <u>Randolph</u>. London: Frederick Etchells & Hugh Macdonald,
        pp. vii-xxviii.
            Discussion of Jonson's influence on Randolph, and Ran-
        dolph's poetic commentary on Jonson.

<u>1930</u>

*1   BRULE, A. "Le titre des Discoveries." <u>Revue Anglo-Americ-</u>
        <u>aine</u> 7 (August):538-39.
            Cited in Tannenbaum 1938.13.

2   BUTLER, PIERCE. <u>Materials for the Life of Shakespeare</u>. Chapel
        Hill: University of North Carolina Press, pp. 16-18.
            Relates the story of Shakespeare "discovering" Jonson.

3   CONTTRELL, GEORGE W., and FAIRCHILD, HOXIE N. "Ben Jonson."
        In <u>Critical Guide . . . in World Literature</u>. New York:
        Columbia University Press, pp. 217-18.
            "The verses on Shakespeare refute the claim that Shake-
        speare was not rightly estimated in his own time."

4   HAMER, ENID. <u>The Metres of English Poetry</u>. London: Methuen
        & Co., passim.
            Mentions Jonson's contributions to English verse par-
        ticularly to the elegy and the ode.

5   HERRICK, MARVIN THEODORE. <u>Poetics of Aristotle in England</u>.
        Cornell Studies in English. New Haven: Yale University
        Press, pp. 36-43.
            Argues that Jonson was the major critic of the early
        seventeenth century. He was highly influenced by Aristotle
        and understood him better than any of his contemporaries.

6   H., H. C. "Ben Jonson and Hoskyns." <u>TLS</u>, 8 May, p. 394.
            Shows some variant readings between Jonson's <u>Discoveries</u>
        and Hoskyns' manuscript. See also 1930.10.

1930

7   H., F. "Ben Jonson to Drummond of Hawthornden." <u>N&Q</u> 158
(4 January):16.
Points out that the letter reproduced in 1929.7 has
never before been attributed to Jonson and that it is
much different in style from his others.

8   MARCHAM, FRANK. "Thomas Walkley and Ben Jonson's Works of
1640." <u>Library</u>, 4th ser. 11, no. 2 (September):225-29.
Reproduces the Chancery suit by Thomas Walkley against
John Benson and Andrew Crooke for Benson and Crooke's publication of Jonson's 1640 <u>Works</u>.

9   McCLURE, NORMAN EGBERT, ed. Introduction to <u>The Letters and</u>
<u>Epigrams of Sir John Harington</u>. Philadelphia: University
of Pennsylvania Press, pp. 3-53.
Harington's "epigrams are more thoroughly English and
less classical in tone and matter than Jonson's."

10   OSBORNE, LOUISE B[ROWN]. "Ben Jonson and Hoskyns." <u>TLS</u>,
1 May, p. 370.
Jonson borrowed three pages of <u>Discoveries</u> from a friend,
Benedict Hopkyns's "Directions for Speech and Style," MS
Harl. 4604. See 1930.6.

11   SCOTT-JAMES, R. A. "Ben Jonson." In <u>The Making of Literature</u>.
New York: Henry Holt & Co., pp. 120-28.
"In a world in which he saw chaos, Jonson endeavored,
in the light of ancient learning, to reimpose the classic
order. . . . Seeking principles of order, restraint, harmony, he takes his stand upon the precepts and the examples
of the Greeks."

12   SIMPSON, PERCY. "Ben Jonson and Cecilia Bulstrode." <u>TLS</u>,
6 March, p. 187.
Prints a letter Jonson wrote to Cecilia Bulstrode re-
tracting the slanderous statements he made about her in
"The Court Pucelle."

13   WARREN, AUSTIN. "Pope and Ben Jonson." <u>MLN</u> 45, no. 2 (February):86-88.
Reports on Alexander Pope's annotations in his 1692
folio of Jonson's <u>Works</u>. Speculates that Pope was planning
an edition of Jonson similar to his Shakespeare.

<u>1931</u>

1   ALLEN, PERCY. "Ben Jonson." In <u>The Oxford Shakespeare Case</u>
<u>Corroborated</u>. London: C. Palmer, pp. 43-164.

Discussion of the friendship between Jonson and Shakespeare.

2 ANON. Review Of <u>Ben Jonson and King James</u> . . . , by Eric
Linklater. <u>TLS</u>, 22 October, p. 816.
"Much of his book resembles what in one sort of jour-
nalism is known as a 'write up'; in which the writer's ob-
ject is to make a great display out of little matter."
See 1931.17.

3 B., I. "Too Rare Ben Jonson." <u>Week-End Review</u> 4 (17 October):
490.
Review of <u>Ben Jonson and King James</u> . . . , by Eric
Linklater. "The survey of Jacobean England is brilliant;
had the blue pencil been freely used upon the purple patch
this book would have been better than good." See 1931.17.

4 BROADUS, E[DMUND] K[EMPER]. <u>The Story of English Literature</u>.
New York: Macmillan, pp. 107-9.
Notes the care with which Jonson wrote. "This matter
of 'composition'--the careful planning of the whole poem,
the fitting together of every link, the definite coming
to a stop when the poem had said what it had to say--Jon-
son saw as vital; and beyond that he strove for sharper,
more clear images, less flow and more precision."

5 CLARK, ARTHUR MELVILLE. <u>Thomas Heywood</u>. Oxford: Basil Black-
well, passim.
Discussions of the relationships between Heywood and
Jonson as well as Heywood's criticism of Jonson.

6 CRAIG, HARDIN. <u>Shakespeare: A Historical and Critical Study</u>.
Chicago: Scott, Foresman & Co., pp. 989-93.
Short discussion of Jonson's part in Shakespeare's world.

7 DOUGLAS, MONTAGUE WILLIAM. <u>The Earl of Oxford as Shakespeare</u>.
London: C. Palmer, passim.
Argues that Jonson conspired with the Earl of Oxford
writing under Shakespeare's name. Jonson's poem, "To
the memory of . . . Mr. William Shakespeare" should be
read as ironic.

8 EDDY, WILLIAM ALFRED. "Dryden Quotes Ben Jonson." <u>MLN</u> 46,
no. 1 (January):40-41.
A line from Dryden's "A Song for St. Cecilia's Day" is
taken from Jonson's "The Musical Strife: A Pastoral Dialogue."

1931

9 GREG, W. W. "Walkley and Ben Jonson's <u>Works</u>." <u>Library</u>, 4th
   ser. 11, no. 4 (March):461-65.
      Comments on 1930.8. Gregg concludes that the so-called
   third volume of Jonson's <u>Works</u> (1640) came about as a
   result of this suit and was printed by Walkley.

10 HEIDLER, JOSEPH BUNN, and PECKHAM, HARRY HOUSTON. <u>A History
    of English Literature</u>. New York: Richard R. Smith, p. 210.
       Remarks that Jonson is the founder of seventeenth-century
    English poetry as both a critic and a poet.

11 HOWELL, A. C. "Jonson's Literary Methods." <u>SP</u> 28, no. 4
    (October):710-19.
       Surveys the scholarship on Jonson's composing and trans-
    lating processes and concludes with his own findings.

12 JOHNSON, STANLEY. "Donne's Autumnall Elegy." <u>TLS</u>, 30 April,
    p. 347.
       Points out echoes of Donne in Jonson's poetry and con-
    cludes that Jonson may indeed have tried the metaphysical
    style.

13 JOHNSTON, GEORGE BURKE. "Notes on 'Execreation Upon Vulcan,'"
    <u>MLN</u>, 46, no. 3 (March):150-53.
       In an "Excreation Upon Vulcan," probably written in
    November, 1623, Jonson mentions the loss of a play manu-
    script. Presents evidence to suggest that <u>The Staple of
    News</u> (1626) was the manuscript destroyed.

14 KITCHIN, GEORGE. <u>A Survey of Burlesque and Parody in English</u>.
    Edinburgh: Oliver & Boyd, pp. 74-75.
       Discusses "Ode to Himself" and two parodies written on
    it. Reprinted 1967.11.

15 LAVER, JAMES. "A Biography of Ben." <u>Spectator</u> 147 (24 Oc-
    tober):535-36.
       Review of <u>Ben Jonson and King James</u> . . . , by Eric
    Linklater. The biography is written in an affected style,
    but it does "provide some vivid pictures of the men who
    flourished in Elizabethan Bohemia." See 1931.17.

16 LEWIS, B. ROLAND. <u>Creative Poetry</u>. Stanford, Calif.: Stan-
    ford University Press, passim.
       Notes on Jonson's lyric poetry and criticism.

17 LINKLATER, ERIC. <u>Ben Jonson and King James: Biography and
    Portrait</u>. London: Jonathan Cape, 328 pp.
       A biography that rests heavily on background material.
    There is a strong emphasis on the flavor of Elizabethan

life, very little literary criticism. Reprinted in 1972.24.

18 _____. "Ben Jonson." TLS, 29 October, p. 842.
Response to 1931.2. Defends the use of background information rather than providing background material.
Reviewer counters that Linklater inserts false
information rather than providing background material.

19 SHIPLEY, JOSEPH T. The Quest for Literature: A Survey of
Literary Criticism and Literary Forms. New York: Richard
R. Smith, passim.
Discusses Jonson's role in the history of literary crit-
icism.

20 THEOBALD, BERTRAM GORDON. "Ben Jonson and the 1623 Folio."
In Exit Shakespeare. London: C. Palmer, pp. 70-77.
Argues that Jonson knew Bacon to have written Shakespeare's
plays, and that he indicates this fact in a cryptic way in
both the epigram on Shakespeare's picture and his dedicatory poem.

21 THOMAS, P. G. Aspects of Literary Theory and Practice, 1550-
1870. London: Heath Cranton, pp. 26-28.
"Stress must be laid upon the debt to Heinsius since
this explains the position occupied by Jonson as a forerunner of classical criticism."

1932

1 ANON. Review of Collation of the Ben Jonson Folios . . . ,
by H. L. Ford. TLS, 1 September, p. 610.
Announcement describing the book. See 1932.7.

2 BUCHAN, JOHN. A History of English Literature. New York:
Thomas Nelson & Sons, pp. 122-28.
"As a poet pure and simple Jonson had his fortunate
moments, but his verse is throughout distinguished by
strength and accuracy of form rather than by inspiration."

*3 CHAIT, R. "Satire of Ben Jonson." Master's thesis, Cornell
University.
Cited in Tannenbaum, 1938.13.

4 CHESTER, ALLAN GRIFFITH. Thomas May: Man of Letters 1595-
1650. Philadelphia: University Pennsylvania Press,
passim.
Jonson influenced the work of May, who was a member of
his tribe.

5 DRAYTON, MICHAEL. "To My Most Dearly-Loved Friend Henery
Reynolds Esquire, of Poets and Poesie." In The Works of

1932

<u>Michael Drayton</u>. Vol. 3. Edited by J. William Hebel.
Oxford: Shakespeare Head Press, p. 229.
Reprint of 1627.1.

6   DUNN, ESTHER CLOUDMAN. Review of <u>Ben Jonson and King James</u> . . . ,
by Eric Linklater. <u>SatR</u> 8 (9 April):647.
Finds a light, fast-moving though reasonably accurate
narrative of Jonson against the backdrop of his times.
Sometimes Linklater is a bit free and easy with his facts
or a little romantic with his interpretation. See 1931.17.

7   FORD, H. L. <u>Collation of the Ben Jonson Folios, 1616-13-1640</u>.
Oxford: Oxford University Press, 30 pp.
Partial listing of variants in 1616 copies of Jonson's
<u>Works</u> and in 1640 copies of <u>Works</u>. Commentary on the
history and value of the volumes. Reprinted in 1973.9.

8   FRIEDERICH, WERNER P. <u>Spiritualismus & Sensualismus in d</u>
<u>engl Barocklyrick</u>. Wien: Wilhelm Braumuller, passim.
Jonson is discussed in the context of all early seventeenth century English poetry. Though he did not have the
power or beauty of Donne or Herbert, Jonson's influence
was highly significant.

9   GILETT, E. Review of <u>Ben Jonson and King James</u> . . . , by Eric
Linklater. <u>London Mercury</u> 25 (April):600-601.
Finds that though there are some inaccuracies and in
places the book is "over written," the author accomplishes
what he set out to do: "to re-create the personality of
a remarkable man of letters who won a place for himself
among his colleagues by sheer weight of character and intellectual ability." See 1931.17.

10 HETT, FRANCIS PAGET. "Refutation of the Charge against Sir
Robert Sibbald of Forging Ben Jonson's <u>Conversations</u>."
In <u>The Memoris of Sir Robert Sibbald</u>. London: Oxford
University Press, pp. 12-43.
Argues against the view expressed in 1925.30. System-
atically sets forth reasons to indicate that there is no
substance to the charge that Sibbald's transcription of
Drummond's <u>Conversations</u> is not authentic.

11 KINGMAN, TRACY. <u>An Authenticated Contemporary Portrait of</u>
<u>Shakespeare</u>. New York: William Edwin Rudge, pp. 7-11,
21-23, 56-58.
Portrait by Karel Van Mander is said to be of Jonson
and Shakespeare playing chess.

*12 RICHARDSON, VIOLA ENLOE. "Ben Jonson's Critical Ideas."
      Master's thesis, University of Colorado.
            Cited in Tannenbaum, 1938.13.

13 ROBINSON, HERBERT SPENCER. English Shakespearean Criticism
      in the 18th Century. New York: H. W. Wilson Co., passim.
            A brief general comparison of Jonson's and Shakespeare's
      reputations in the 18th century, based upon critical re-
      marks.

14 SIMPSON, PERCY. "Ben Jonson on Chapman." TLS, 3 March, p.
      155.
            Prints Jonson's marginalia on Chapman's Homer which
      was published in 1616.

15 SMITH, JAMES HARRY, and PARKS, EDD WINFIELD, eds. "Ben Jon-
      son." In Great Critics. New York: W. W. Norton & Co., pp.
      212-21.
            Introductory comments on Jonson's criticism. "Jonson
      did not escape the classical limitation by any means, but
      he tempered that limitation with strong and fearless common
      sense."

16 TOCH, M. "Portrait of Ben Jonson and Shakespeare." New York
      Times, 2 May, p. 19.
            News story of Karel Van Mander's portrait of Jonson and
      Shakespeare.

1933

1 BAKER, H. KENDRA. "'Swan of Avon'" N&Q 164 (3 June):393-94.
            Jonson's use of this phrase, "Swan of Avon," might be
      an allusion to Orlado Furioso. Response to 1933.4. See
      1933.2.

2 _____. "'Swan of Avon'" N&Q 165 (15 July):29.
            Response to 1933.4. Wilton House is not on the Avon but
      on two tributaries leading to it. See 1933.1.

3 BROWN, HUNTINGTON. Rabelais in English Literature. Cambridge,
      Mass.: Harvard University Press, pp. 81-94.
            Jonson and Rabelais had a shared interest in scatologi-
      cal imagery. "Ben came under Rabelais's influence only
      because the two men shared important traits of mind and
      temperment. Both were intellectually as tough and inde-
      pendent as any two men who ever lived."

4 COMTE, F. C. G. "Memorabilia." N&Q (20 May):343.

1933

The Avon to which Jonson refers in "Swan of Avon" may
actually be the Avon in Wiltshire. See 1933.1 and 1933.2.

5   DAVIS, B. E. C. Edmund Spenser: A Critical Study. London:
    Cambridge University Press, passim.
        Several references to Jonson's assessment of Spenser.
    Reprinted in 1962.5.

6   ELTON, OLIVER. The English Muse. London: G. Bell & Sons,
    passim.
        Finds that though Jonson is a major figure in the his-
    tory of the drama, he does not hold a central position in
    the history of poetry. Nevertheless, "no one has a higher
    conception of his art, or can word it with more state and
    dignity."

7   HARRISON, G. B. Shakespeare at Work 1592-1603. London:
    George Routledge & Sons, passim.
        Comments on the way in which Jonson's and Shakespeare's
    careers corresponded.

8   HILBERRY, CLARENCE BEVERLY. Ben Jonson's Ethics in Relation
    to Stoic and Humanistic Ethical Thought. Chicago:
    University of Chicago Press, 31 pp.
        Jonson's Stoicism is more the product of sixteenth-cen-
    tury humanists than a strict adherence to classical Stoic
    views. Reprinted in 1969.10.

9   HOLLAND, H. H. "Jonson's Commendatory Verses in the First
    Folio." In Shakespeare, Oxford and Elizabethan Times.
    London: Morrison & Gibb, pp. 163-67.
        A close reading of Jonson's poem that provides evidence
    for the author that Shakespeare did not write most of the
    plays attributed to him and that Jonson was aware of this.

10 LATHROP, HENRY BURROWES. Translations from the Classics into
    English, From Caxton to Chapman; 1477-1620. University of
    Wisconsin Studies in Language and Literature, no. 35. Madi-
    son: University of Wisconsin Press, passim.
        The change in intellectual thought near the end of the
    reign of Elizabeth is noticed in translations as writers
    turned away from Ovid and Virgil "to the stern authors of
    the Silver age. Ben Jonson is a leader of the movement;
    and his works wide as is their range in ancient literature
    draw particularly upon Juvenal and the Senecas, Tacitus,
    and Suetonius."

11 MAYNARD, THEODORE. Preface to Poetry. New York: Century Co.,
    pp. 324-26.
        Short comment on Jonson's strict use of the Pindaric
    structure in his odes.

12   RADFORD, W. L.   "Ben Jonson and Brome Jonson." <u>N&Q</u> 164 (1
     April):228.
          Response to 1933.13.   Finds no connection between these
     individuals.

13   WARLING, ALFRED.   "Ben Jonson and Brome Jonson."   <u>N&Q</u> 164
     (18 March):187.
          Asks if the unusual name, Brome Jonson, has any connec-
     tion with Richard Brome or Ben Jonson.   See 1913.12.

14   WHITING, GEORGE W.   "The Hoe-Huntington Folio of Ben Jonson."
     <u>MLN</u> 48, no. 8 (December):537-38.
          Remarks on the collation of this 1616 Folio with others
     referred to in 1932.7.

15   WYLD, HENRY CECIL.   <u>Some Aspects of the Diction of English
     Poetry</u>.   Oxford: Basil Blackwell, pp. 17-18.
          Jonson's remarks noted from <u>Discoveries</u> on inven-
     tion, eloquence, and archaism.

1934

1   ANON.   "Ben Jonson 'Greatest of English Worthies.'"   <u>SatR</u>
     (Eng.) 157 (16 June):705.
          Review of <u>Ben Jonson</u>, by John Palmer.   The book "ad-
     mirably succeeds" in placing Jonson in the proper per-
     spective which he so richly deserves.   See 1934.16.

2   ANON.   Review of <u>Ben Jonson</u>, by John Palmer.   <u>TLS</u>, 3 May,
     p. 319.
          Palmer believes that a biographer should reveal the
     mind of this subject, and he has found Jonson more hum-
     anist and realist than a romantic.   See 1934.16.

3   BENET, WILLIAM ROSE.   "A Mighty Cliff of a Man."   <u>SatR</u>
     10 (12 May):687.
          Review of <u>Ben Jonson</u>, by John Palmer.   Palmer's book
     is thorough and readable.   It is "scholarly yet never
     pedantic, thoroughly and precisely documented yet never
     dry. . . ."   See 1934.16.

4   BROADUS, EDMUND KEMPER.   <u>The Story of English Literature</u>.
     New York: Macmillan, pp. 175-78.
          Jonson's down-to-earth, common-sense attitude toward
     poetry is contrasted.with Spenser's dreamy, smooth-
     flowing style.

1934

5   EASTON, EMILY. <u>Youth Immortal: A Life of Robert Herrick</u>.
    Boston: Houghton Mifflin Co., pp. 44-46, 77-83.
        A general discussion of Herrick's adoration of Jonson
    as reflected in Herrick's poems.

6   ERVINE, St. JOHN. "O Rare Ben Jonson." <u>Observer</u>, 27 May,
    p. 15.
        Review of <u>Ben Jonson</u>, by John Palmer (1934.16). Al-
    though a "sober analysist" nevertheless, Palmer too often
    wants to provide an apology for Jonson rather than simply
    admire that which is admirable and leave the rest alone.

7   GEBHARDT, ERMA R. "Jonson's Appreciation of Chaucer as
    Evidenced in <u>The English Grammar</u>." MLN 49, no. 7 (Novem-
    ber):452-54.
        In the second part of <u>The English Grammar</u> Jonson uses
    twenty-five illustrations from Chaucer in his remarks on
    syntax; however, there are numerous errors in Jonson's
    quotations.

8   GILBERT, A[LLAN] H. "Volume on Ben Jonson." <u>SAQ</u> 33, no. 4
    (October):430-32.
        Review of <u>Ben Jonson</u>, by John Palmer. An interesting,
    enthusiastic but nonscholarly work. "So far as any con-
    tact of art with life, or of fulfillment of the function
    of art, whatever it may be is concerned, he is better off
    who spends an hour reading the poorest and least intelligi-
    ble of Jonson's plays than is he who peruses all of Mr.
    Palmer's pleasant pages." See 1934.16.

9   GILDER, ROSAMOND. "Palmer's 'Ben Jonson.'" <u>Theatre Arts
    Monthly</u> 18, no. 10 (October):801-2.
        Review of <u>Ben Jonson</u>, by John Palmer. Praise for Palm-
    er's recreation of Ben Jonson and the exciting times in
    which he lived.

10 GOLDEN, MARCUS SELDEN. <u>Sir Philip Sidney and The Arcadia</u>.
    Illinois Study in Language and Literature, 17, nos. 1 & 2.
    Urbana: University of Illinois.
        Briefly discusses Jonson's comments and speculations on
    <u>The Arcadia</u>.

11 GRIERSON, H[ERBERT[J. C., and BULLOUGH, GEOFFREY. Preface
    to <u>The Oxford Book of Seventeenth Century Verse</u>. Oxford:
    Clarendon Press, pp. v-xv.
        Little is said about Jonson; few pages are given to his
    poetry.

12 HUGHEY, RUTH. "Forgotten Verses by Ben Jonson, George Wither

and Others to Alice Sutcliffe." RES 10, no. 38 (April):
156-64.
    Reports on the finding of a book of poetry: Meditations
of Man's Mortality (1634) by Alice Sutcliffe. There appears to be a dedicatory poem by Jonson which Hughey says
is an addition to his Celia poems.

13   KRUTCH, JOSEPH WOOD. "Shakespeare's Rival." Nation 138 (30
       May):623.
    Review of Ben Jonson, by John Palmer. "Mr. Palmer is
an excellent guide, with scholarship enough to furnish
the clew to what a modern could not devine for himself and
with an admirable gift which enables him to make his auth-
or mean something to us." See 1934.16.

14   LUCAS, E. V. "Benjamins." In A Saunterer's Rewards. Phil-
       adelphia: J. B. Lippincott, pp. 153-58.
    While listening to the solemn strokes of Big Ben, the
author ruminates on the Benjamins of British history. Jonson is most remembered for his epitaph.

15   NETHERCOT, ARTHUR H. "Milton, Jonson and the Young Cowley."
       MLN 49, no. 3 (March):158-62.
    Presents evidence showing a close association in the
1630s between Abraham Cowley, about thirteen years old at
the time, and Ben Jonson.

16   PALMER, JOHN. Ben Jonson. London: George Routledge, 330 pp.
    A study of the literary achievement of Jonson through
both his works and his personality. Recreates the figure
instead of providing a critical guide to the works. Chapter on Jonson's poetry is entitled "Anthology," and mainly
reproduces stanzas making brief appreciative comments on
them. Reprinted in 1967.15.

17   PARROTT, THOMAS MARC. William Shakespeare: A Handbook.
       New York: Scribners, pp. 214-15.
    Takes up Jonson's criticism of Shakespeare.

18   SPARROW, JOHN. "Jonson Warm and Large." Spectator 62 (8
       June):895.
    Review of Ben Jonson, by John Palmer. Points out a num-
of factual errors in the book and complains that this type
of popular history is misleading. "If this is history
'writ warm and large' there are some who will prefer it
cooler and a little smaller--as small, for instance, as
life." See 1934.16.

1934

19 TAYLOR, WALT. "Arabic words in Ben Jonson." <u>Leeds Studies
    in English and Kindred Languages</u>, no. 3:44-50.
        Lists words of Arabic derivation in Jonson's works.

20 THORNTON, JAMES, ed. "Ben Jonson." In <u>Table-Talk</u>. Everyman's
    Library. New York: E. P. Dutton, pp. 1-17.
        Prints part of Drummond's <u>Conversations</u> and notes that
    this is a major source of information on Jonson's life and
    character.

21 WALKER, RALPH S. "Ben Jonson's Lyric Poetry." <u>Criterion</u> 3,
    no. 52 (April):430-48.
        Argues that Jonson is an experimental poet in the sense
    "he had something new to express, an ideal of beauty never
    before expressed in English poetry. . . . There is not
    the normal opposition between art and inspiration--for art
    is its inspiration. And it is because this truth has
    never been duly recognized, that Ben Jonson's poetry has
    been so long a stumbling block for criticism--its success
    the cause of insincere applause, its influence a mystery."
    Revised in 1953.14.

22 WECTER, DIXON. "Two Great Chams." <u>VQR</u> 10, no. 2 (July):471-
    75.
        Review of <u>Ben Jonson</u>, by John Palmer. Judges the work
    an interesting though perhaps simplified biography that
    unfortunately does not make use of the best and most re-
    cent American scholarship.

23 YATES, FRANCIS A. <u>John Florio</u>. Cambridge: University Press,
    pp. 277-83.
        Florio was a good friend of Jonson's and probably had
    considerable influence on him.

24 YOUNG, STARK. "Passionately Kind and Angry." <u>New Republic</u>
    79 (6 June):103.
        Review of <u>Ben Jonson</u>, by John Palmer. Calls the work
    a good compromise between scholarship and Steegmuller.

1935

1 BENSLY, EDWARD. "Ben Jonson Queries." <u>N&Q</u> 169 (26 October):
   229.
        Response to 1935.19. Explains that "Socket" in "An
   Epistle to Arthur Squib" probably means a taper or candle.
   The "ring" and the "Lance" in "Ode . . . in celebration
   of her Majesties Birthday" refers to a practice of tilters.

2 _____. "Ben Jonson Query." N&Q 169 (9 November):335.
Response to 1935.22. Jonson's translation of rhombus
and scarus from Horace are the same as those given in
Bishop Thomas Cooper's Thesaurus Linguae Romanae et Brit-
annicae (1573). Both words refer to types of fish.

3 _____. "'Civill Soldierie,' 1625." N&Q 169 (7 December):409.
Response to 1935.27. Identifies a number of proper
names in Jonson's "A speech according to Horace."

4 _____. "Jonson's answer to Alexander Gill, and Two Taverns."
N&Q 169 (3 August):86.
Response to 1935.25. Suggests "Denis" in "Jonson's answer to Alexander Gill" might be a reference to Dionysius.
Notes that there is still a "Half Moon Passage" on the
west side of Aldersgate Street which is apparently cited
in Jests or the Wits Pocket Companion. See 1935.16.

5 BRULE, A. "Sur Ben Jonson." Revue Anglo American 13 (October):1-17.
Biographical summary of Jonson as a man of the people:
forceful, honest, steeped in the classics.

6 CHESTER, ALLAN GRIFFITH. "Thomas Walkley and the 1640 Works
of Ben Jonson." TLS, 14 March, p. 160.
Describes two pieces of information picked up among
manuscripts of the House of Lords that support the theory
that Thomas Walkley was involved in a law suit over the
publication of Jonson's 1640 Works.

7 DODDS, M. H. "Ben Jonson Queries." N&Q 169 (31 August):157.
Response to part three of 1935.18. Phillip Grey, son
of Edward Grey of Horwick, died in 1615/16 and may have
been the subject of Jonson's poem.

8 GARNETT, RICHARD, and GOSSE, EDMUND. English Literature: An
Illustrated Record. Vol. 2. New York: Macmillan.
Reprint of 1903.4.

9 HARBAGE, ALFRED. Sir William Davenant: Poet Venturer 1606-
1668. Philadelphia: University of Pennsylvania Press,
pp. 60-66.
References to literary and personal relationship between
Davenant and Jonson.

10 HUDSON, HOYT H[OPEWELL], ed. Introduction to Directions for
Style and Speech, by John Hoskins. Princeton Studies in
English, no. 12. Princeton: Princeton University Press,
pp. ix-xl.

1935

Jonson's personal and intellectual relationship with
Hoskins is discussed in the introduction to a modern edition of this seventeenth-century work on rhetoric.

11   JOHNSTON, GEORGE BURKE. "Notes on Ben Jonson." TLS, 14 February, p. 92.
Describes two poems found by the author on the fly leaf
of volume 1 of his 1640 Folio of Jonson's Works: "An extem-
pore Epilogue spoken by Ben. Johnson. . . ." and "Ben
Johnson's Epitaph made by Fletcher for him. . . ."

12   LAWRENCE, W. J. Those Nut-Cracking Elizabethans. London:
Argonaut Press, pp. 141-47.
Discusses the union of song, poetry, and theater. Re-
printed in 1969.13.

13   LEAVIS, F. R. "English Poetry of the Seventeenth Century."
Scrutiny 4, no. 3 (December):236-56.
Review of The Oxford Book of Seventeenth Century Verse,
by H. J. C. Grierson and Geoffrey Bullough. Attempts to
establish Jonson's position in the tradition of seventeenth-
century poetry and points to his influence on later writers.
Tries to define Jonson's classicism and discriminates it
from other kinds of classicism in late Renaissance, Restoration, and eighteenth-century poetry.

14   LEGOUIS, EMILE [HYACINTHE]. A History of English Literature.
New York: Macmillan.
Revision of 1926.7.

15   M., T. O. "Ben Jonson Queries." N&Q 1969 (17 August):123.
Response to 1935.25. Denis in "Jonson's answer to
Alexander Gill" may refer to a headless saint.

16   _____. "Ben Jonson Queries." N&Q 169 (7 September):177.
Further discussion of 1935.4 and 1935.25. Additional
support for the headless saint being Jonson's source for
Denis in "Jonson's answer to Alexander Gill."

17   NEWDIGATE, BERNARD H. "Ben Jonson Queries." N&Q 169 (6 July):
10.
Queries on "Inviting a friend to Supper," and "On The
Famous Voyage."

18   _____. "Ben Jonson Queries." N&Q 169 (August):119.
Queries on Jonson's "An Epistle to a Friend to Persuade
him to the Warres," and "An Epitaph on Master Philip Gray."
See 1935.7.

19 _____. "Ben Jonson Queries." N&Q 169 (12 October):262.
    Queries on "An Epistle to Arthur Squib" and "Ode by all
    the Muses in celebration of her Majesties Birthday." See
    1935.1.

20 _____. "Ben Jonson Queries." N&Q 169 (2 November):313-14.
    Queries on two poems: an anagram on Thomas Coryat
    printed in his Crudities and "On the Kings Birthday."

21 _____. "Ben Jonson Queries." N&Q 169 (9 November):332.
    Queries on "Execration upon Vulcan" and "The Painter
    to the poet."

22 _____. "Ben Jonson Query." N&Q 169 (26 October):296.
    Query on Jonson's translation of Horace. See 1935.2.

23 _____. "Ben Jonson Query: Uvedale: Cary." N&Q 169 (7 Dec-
    ember):406.
    Who was Sir William Uvedale's wife, Epigram 125.

24 _____. "Ben Jonson Sources Wanted." N&Q 169 (26 October):298.
    Asks for suggestions of sources for two poems. Jonson's
    lines on Thomas Palmer and "An Epigram on the Princes Birth,"
    1630.

25 _____. "Ben Jonson's Answer to Alexander Gill, and Two Tav-
    erns." N&Q 169 (20 July):47.
    Queries on Jonson's poem answering Gill, and the Angel
    Tavern at Basinstoke and the Half-Moon in Aldersgate both
    of which Jonson was supposed to have frequented. See 1935.4,
    15, 31, 32, and 35.

26 _____. "Ben Jonson's 'Under-wood.'" TLS, 7 February, p. 76.
    Argues that "Under-Woods" is a misprint for "Under-Wood."

27 _____. "Civill Soldierie." N&Q 169 (23 November):368.
    Queries on "A speech according to Horace." See 1935.3.

28 _____. Untitled. N&Q 169 (7 December):409.
    Announces the receipt of the Journals of the H A C
    (Honorable Artillery Company) from a correspondent, which
    contains a fully annotated copy of "A speech according to
    Horace." See 1935.27.

29 OSGOOD, CHARLES GROSVENOR. The Voice of England: A History
    of English Literature. New York: Harper Brothers, pp.
    197-202.
    A general survey of life and works.

1935

30 PERRY, H. T. E. "Palmer's Ben Jonson." YR 24, no. 3 (March):
    641-43.
        Review of Ben Jonson, by John Palmer. Palmer, a good
    critic, takes a simplistic approach to his subject. Jon-
    son was not the last great humanist courageoulsy holding
    out against the vulgar puritan masses. He does come at
    the conclusion of a tradition, and we see in his works,
    particularly the later ones, the collapse of that trad-
    ition. It is because Jonson did not change and grow
    with the times that he "died a disappointed and neglected
    old man." See 1934.16.

31 ROGERS, K[ENNETH]. "Two Taverns." N&Q 169 (3 August):86-88.
        Response to 1935.25. Cites early records and books on
    taverns to shed more light on the Sun and Half-Moon tav-
    erns.

32 _____. Untitled N&Q 169 (17 August):123-24.
        Response to 1935.25. Extracts taken from the church
    warden's accounts of St. Botolph's Aldersgate which refer
    to the Sun and Half-Moon taverns.

33 THOMPSON, EDWARD JOHN. Sir Walter Raleigh. London: Mac-
    millan & Co., passim.
        Discussion of Jonson's assistance on The History of the
    World.

34 WALLERSTEIN, RUTH C. "The Development of the Rhetoric and
    Metre of the Heroic Couplet, Especially in 1625-1645."
    PMLA 50, no. 1 (March):166-209.
        Discusses Jonson's place in the development of the heroic
    couplet and draws heavily upon Felix E. Schelling's essay,
    1898.7. Reprinted in 1961.16.

35 WHITE, E. A. "Two Taverns." N&Q 169 (3 August):86.
        Response to 1935.25. Speculates on the location of the
    Half-Moon Tavern on Aldersgate Street.

36 WHITE, HAROLD OGDEN. Plagiarism and Imitation during the
    English Renaissance: A Study of Critical Distinctions.
    Cambridge, Mass.: Harvard University Press, pp. 128-45.
        A full discussion of Jonson's views on imitation in
    drama, poetry, and prose. In many of his plays, a number
    of his poems, and in Conversations, Jonson attacks the
    practice of plagiarizing which was fairly common during
    the time. He is particularly critical of the poet who
    translates another's work and calls it his own. Reprint
    of 1965.20.

37 WILLIAMSON, GEORGE. "The Rhetorical Pattern of Neo-Clas-
        sical Wit." <u>MP</u> 33, no. 1 (August):55-81.
        Jonson was a major figure in establishing the heroic
    couplet in English poetry. "To look for the remarks of
    Jonson which bear upon the heroic couplet is to find the
    most significant statements he ever made about metrics."
    Reprinted in 1961.17.

<u>1936</u>

1 ALLEN, DON CAMERON. "A Jonson Allusion." <u>TLS</u>, 18 April, p.
        336.
            Mentions an allusion to Jonson in the "de Providentia
    Dei" by the puritan zealot Richard Crakanthorp.

2 ANON. Review of <u>The Poems of Ben Jonson</u>, edited by Bernard
        H. Newdigate. <u>N&Q</u> 171 (18 July):53.
            "This is a noble edition, worthy of the Shakespeare
    Head Press and edited with ample care and skill." See
    1936.23.

3 BAKER, ERNEST. "Drink to me only." <u>Spectator</u> 157 (10 Novem-
        ber):890-91.
            Jonson's poem was taken from one of Philostratus's let-
    ters.

4 BENSLY, EDWARD. "Ben Jonson Query." <u>N&Q</u> 170 (8 February):103.
            Response to 1936.20. Believes the Virgin is the goddess
    Astraea, the patroness of justice.

5 _____. "Banks, A Ben Jonson Victim." <u>N&Q</u> 171 (28 November):
        395.
            Response to 1936.15. "Chuff" may not be a personal
    name but rather "a term of reproach for a miserly or avari-
    cious person."

6 BOWERS, FREDSON T. "Dekker and Ben Jonson." <u>TLS</u>, 12 Septem-
        ber, p. 729.
            Comment on the quarrel between Jonson and Dekker.

7 [CHILD, HAROLD.] "The Triumph of Ben Jonson: Tests of poetic
        Magic." <u>TLS</u>, 4 July, pp. 549-50.
            Review of <u>The Poems of Ben Jonson</u>, edited by Bernard H.
    Newdigate. Takes as point of departure A. E. Housman's
    test for what he would consider "pure poetry." Admits
    that Jonson's poetry is unlikely to make one "go goosey"
    and in fact it surely was not Jonson's intention that this

1936

should happen. Nevertheless, Jonson is not a lesser poet.
"He accomplished poetry as well as influenced it." See
1936.23. Reprinted in 1948.4.

8 COLBY, ELBRIDGE. "Ben Jonson." In English Catholic Poets.
   Milwaukee: Bruce Pub. Co., pp. 84-96.
   "Like the great Samuel Jonson of a century and a half
   later, he himself is more interesting than anything he
   ever wrote."

9 COWARDIN, SAMUEL P., and MORE, PAUL ELMER. The Study of Eng-
   lish Literature. New York: Henry Holt, pp. 38-39.
   Commentary on "Song To Celia" and "To the Immortall
   Memoirie, and Friendship of that Noble Paire, Sir Lucius
   Cary, and Sir H. Morison."

10 CRAIG, HARDIN. The Enchanged Glass: The Elizabethan Mind in
   Literature. New York: Oxford Univeristy Press, passim.
   Places Jonson's poetry and prose in its cultural frame-
   work showing how it relates to the major intellectual move-
   ments of the time.

11 DOBREE, BONAMY. "Ben Jonson." Spectator 157 (7 August):245-
   46.
   Review of The Poems of Ben Jonson, edited by Bernard H.
   Newdigate. Emphasis on Jonson's translations and borrowings from the ancients. See 1936.23.

12 ECCLES, MARK. "Jonson's Marriage." RES 12, no. 47 (July):
   257-72.
   Biographical speculation based upon new information
   and the reinterpretation of old information. Suggests
   that Jonson married Anne Lewis, 14 November 1594.

13 _____. "'Memorandums' of the Immortal Ben" MLN 51, no. 8
   (December):520-23.
   Provides substantial evidence that the "Memorandums"
   heretofore regarded as authentic are fakes and were
   originally not meant to be seen otherwise. See 1717.1,
   1906.3, and 1925.17.

14 FOX, ARTHUR W. "With Jonson at Hawthornden." In Men and
   Marvels in the 17th Century. New York: Fortuny's, pp.
   13-47.
   Reprint of 1898.4.

15 G., E. B. "Banks, A Ben Jonson Victim." N&Q 171 (14 November):352.

1936

Attempts to identify the subject of Epigram 31, "Banks
the Usurer" by his relationship to "Chuff" of the same
poem. See 1936.5.

16 HANKINS, JOHN E. "Jonson's 'Ode on Morison' and Seneca'a
     Epistulae Morales." MLN 51, no. 8 (December):518-20.
       Reproduces in parallel text stanzas 3-7 of Jonson's
     poem with relevant passages from the ninety-third epistle
     of Seneca's Epistulae Morales.

17 HUDSON, HOYT HOPEWELL. "Bibliographical Note." In Epigrams,
     The Forest, and Underwoods. New York: for the Facsimile
     Text Society by Columbia University Press, n.p.
       Briefly discusses a few of the many bibliographical prob-
     lems surrounding the publication of the Under-Wood or Vol.
     II of the Works, 1640-41.

18 LEAVIS, F. R. "The Line of Wit." In Revaluation: Tradition
     and Development in English Poetry. London: Chatto &
     Windus, pp. 10-36.
       Sees Jonson as a major figure in the tradition of Eng-
     lish poetry. "It took then, Ben Jonson's powerful genius
     to initate the tradition, the common heritage, into which
     a line of later poets could enter, and by which a very
     great Augustan poet was to profit long after civilization
     and literary fashions had been transformed." Reprint in
     1947.8; 1962.11.

19 MURRY, JOHN MIDDLETON. Shakespeare. New York: Harcourt,
     Brace & Co.
       "The issue between Jonson and Shakespeare corresponds
     to the struggle in Jonson's own nature."

20 NEWDIGATE, BERNARD H. "Ben Jonson Query." N&Q 170 (25
     January):65.
       Who is the "Virgin" in "To Sir Thomas, Lord Chancellor"?
     See 1936.4.

21 _____. "The Phoenix and Turtle: Was Lady Bedford the Phoenix?"
     TLS, 24 October, p. 862.
       Describes a MS of Loves Martyr with evidence that Jonson's
     concluding poem was to Lucy, Countess of Bedford.

22 _____. "Jonson Spelling." Observer, 28 June, p. 11.
       A letter defending his editorial judgments to which
     Selincourt (1936.24) took exception.

23 _____, ed. Preface to The Poems of Ben Jonson. Oxford:
     Shakespeare Head Press, pp. vii-xiv.

1936

>   Primarily a discussion of the bibliographical problems
> involved establishing Jonson's text.

24   SELINCOURT, BASIL de. "Ben Jonson's Excellence." Observer,
>   21 June, p. 5.
>   Review of The Poems of Ben Jonson, edited by Bernard
>   H. Newdigate. Some praise for Newdigate but mostly for
>   Jonson. "He is the poet of justice, the just work, the
>   just thought: of justice with all that it implies of
>   penetration, balance, gravity, decision and majesty."
>   See 1936.22, 23.

25   SHILLINGLAW, ARTHUR T. "Hobbes and Jonson." TLS, 18 April,
>   p. 336.
>   Describes a borrowing by Jonson for Discoveries from
>   Fr. Fulgenzio Micanza, the Venetian patriot.

26   WATKINS, W. B. C. Johnson and English Poetry before 1660.
>   Princeton: Princeton University Press, 63-64, 78-80.
>   Johnson knew Ben Jonson's poetry and prose well since
>   he frequently quoted from it. Donne and the metaphysicals
>   most captured his interest but "his appreciation of the
>   lyrics of Jonson and his sons is genuine if limited."

27   WILLIAMSON, GEORGE. "Senecan Style in the Seventeenth Century."
>   PQ 15, no. 4 (October):321-51.
>   Jonson discusses prose style at some length in his Dis-
>   coveries emphasizing brevitas, prespicuitas, simplicitas,
>   venustas, and decentia. Although Jonson does not rigidly
>   follow Seneca, he is nonetheless more influenced by him
>   than any other Latin stylist. "Although Jonson is given
>   to quoting Quintilian, his own practice shows that Senecan
>   doctrine was more persuasive in molding his style."

1937

1   ALEXANDER, HENRY. "Jonson and Johnson." QQ 44, no. 1:13-21.
>   A tercentenary tribute to Jonson outlining the sim-
>   ilarities between his life and character and those of
>   Samuel Johnson's.

2   ANON. "Ben Jonson the Poet: His Hold on Reality." TLS, 25
>   September, p. 691.
>   Argues that Jonson's verse is not subject to general-
>   ities but changes in the course of his career. "As a poet
>   he was neither a born singer nor a consummate artist; but
>   there was a greatness in the man. . . . There is some-

thing in Ben Jonson's forthright pregnant style, his hold
on reality, his scorn of melodious fluency and of verse 'as
smooth as soft cream' which appeals to present taste as it
has not appealed to his countrymen for several generations."

3   BROWN, IVOR. "Too Rare Ben Jonson." Observer, 8 August, p.
11.
     Biographical sketch with brief history of literary rep-
utation. See 1937.23.

4   CHEW, SAMUEL C. The Crescent and the Rose: Islam and England
during the Renaissance. New York: Oxford University Press,
passim.
     Mentions Jonson's contempt for the Koran illustrated in
his poem, "An Execration Upon Vulcan." Reprint in 1965.3.

5   CLARKE, EGERTON. "Ben Jonson's Poetry." Dublin Review 201,
no. 403 (October):325-38.
     Review of The Poems of Ben Jonson, edited by Bernard H.
Newdigate. Considers Jonson a major poet, among the top
ten in English literature. Although his poetry is obvious-
ly from the seventeenth century, it nevertheless has an
energy that radiates beyond the limitations of its age.
As Jonson's reputation as a playwright diminishes, his
standing as a poet rises. See 1936.23.

6   CULMSEE, CARLTON. "Classicism of Ben Jonson." Proceedings
of the Utah Academy of Sciences, Arts, and Letters 14:
67-70.
     Describes unclassical tendencies in Jonson, who may
have either misinterpreted or simply not understood the
true spirit of the greatest classics.

7   ECCLES, MARK. "Jonson and the Spies." RES 13, no. 52 (October):385-97.
     Biographical details particularly as they relate to two
poems: Epigram 59 "On Spies" and Epigram 101 "Inviting a
Friend to Supper." In the latter poem Jonson names at
least one of the spies alluded to in the former.

8   FAIRCHILD, ARTHUR H. R. Shakespeare and the Arts of Design.
Columbia, Mo.: Artcraft Press, passim.
     Discussion of "To Penshurst" in connection with archi-
tecture of the period.

9   HARVEY, PAUL. Oxford Companion to English Literature. Oxford:
Clarendon Press, pp. 418-19.
     Biographical sketch with brief notes on The Forrest and
Under-wood.

1937

10   KELLER, WOLFGANG. "Ben Jonson and Shakespeare." Shakespeare
     Jahrbuch 73 (1937):31-52.
          Discusses parallel aspects of the careers of the two
     writers. Believes that far too much has been made of Jon-
     son's criticism of Shakespeare.

11   KNIGHTS, L. C. Drama and Society in the Age of Jonson. Lon-
     don: Chatto & Windus.346 pp.
          Seeks to define the tradition out of which Jonson's
     values emerged. "The poise and sureness with which Jonson
     confronts the significant developments of his age, strong
     in his knowledge of what are, and what are not, fundamen-
     tal human qualities, will be illustrated in these pages.
     These significant developments--most of them--were aspects
     of the growth of capitalism; and company-promoting, 'pro-
     jecting' and industrial enterprise certainly formed an
     important part of the world which Jonson and his fellows
     observed, the world which gave them their knowledge of
     human nature." Reprinted 1951.7.

12   L., G. G. "Jonson & Seneca." N&Q 173 (20 November):366.
          Finds a Senecan source for "Epode."

13   L., R. E. "Foreign Appreciation of Ben Jonson." N&Q 172
     (9 January):29.
          Requests information of work on Jonson in the United
     States, France, or Germany since 1925.

14   LAWRENCE, W. J. "'Ben' Jonson." Observer, 25 April, p. 10.
          Response to 1937.15. Argues that Jonson obviously
     wanted to be called "Ben" since that name appears on the
     title pages of all the early quartos as well as numerous
     other places.

15   MARTIN, C. "'Ben' Jonson." Observer, 18 April, p. 11.
          Asks why "Ben" rather than "Benjamin"? "Was the name
     habitually abbreviated in his life-time?" See 1937.14.

16   LEISHMAN, J. B. Review of The Poems of Ben Jonson, edited
     by Bernard H. Newdigate. RES 13, no. 52 (October):485-
     88.
          Complains that the notes to the text are incomplete and
     provides some examples of helpful notes on Jonson's poetry.
     See. 1936.23.

17   LUCAS, RICHARD M. "Ben Jonson: Stratford's Broken Reed." In
     Shakespeare's Vital Secret. Keighley: Wadsworth & Co.,
     pp. 200-214.

Reconciles Jonson's "To the Memory of My Beloved . . .
Mr. William Shakespeare," with the theory that the sixth
Earl of Derby was the author of Shakespeare's plays.

*18 McKENNON, W. C. "Critical Theory and Poetic Practice in Ben
       Jonson." Ph.D. dissertation, University of Oregon.
          Cited in Tannenbaum, 1947.10.

19 MATCHETT, WILLIAM H. <u>The Phoenix and the Turtle</u>. London:
       Mouton & Co., passim.
          Jonson's contributions to Chester's <u>Loves Martyr</u> are
       discussed. Assesses Jonson's political views in the early
       1600s and tries to determine how they might be affected
       by his appearance in this volume. Reprinted in 1965.11.

20 NEWDIGATE, BERNARD H., ed. Introduction to <u>The Phoenix and</u>
       <u>the Turtle</u>. Oxford: Basil Blackwell, pp. i-xxiv.
          Believes that Jonson likely had a large part in collect-
       ing the poems by Shakespeare, Marston, Chapman, and others
       for this collection. Jonson's own poem "The Phoenix
       Analysde" may indirectly associate Lucy Harington, Countess
       of Bedford with the Phoenix.

21 _____. "Was Lady Bedford the Phoenix?" <u>TLS</u>, 20 February,
       p. 131.
          Response to 1937.25. Identifies weaknesses in Short's
       argument, concluding that the Countess of Bedford is prob-
       ably the Phoenix. See 1937.20.

22 OSBORN, LOUISE BROWN. <u>The Life, Letters, and Writings of</u>
       <u>John Hoskins</u>. New Haven: Yale University Press, passim.
          Charts the relationship between Jonson and his friend.

23 P., G. D. "Ancestry of Ben Jonson." <u>Observer</u>, 22 August, p.
       7.
          Additional notes on 1937.3. Points out Jonson's possible
       Scottish ancestry and his journey to Scotland.

24 SHILLINGLAW, ARTHUR T. "New Light on <u>Discoveries</u>." <u>Englische</u>
       <u>Studien</u> 71 (June):356-59.
          Jonson used a paragraph from a contemporary letter des-
       cribing Sir Francis Bacon in <u>Discoveries</u>.

25 SHORT, R. W. "Was Lady Bedford the Phoenix?" <u>TLS</u>, 13 Feb-
       ruary, p. 111.
          Response to 1936.20. Argues with external evidence
       that the Countess of Bedford was not intended to be the
       Phoenix. Her family was unfriendly with the Salisburys to
       whom Chester dedicated much of his poetry. See 1937.21.

1937

26 SIMPSON, PERCY. "The Ben Jonson Exhibition." Bodleian Lib-
    rary Quarterly 8, no. 95:405-11.
        A description of the tercentenary commemorative exhibit
    of Jonson material at the Bodley Library.

27 SNODGRASS, A. E. "Rare Ben Jonson." Cornhill Magazine 156
    (August):237-47.
        Wide-ranging tercentenary survey of Jonson's life and
    works.

1938

1   COLLINGWOOD, R. G. The Principles of Art. Oxford: Claren-
    don Press, pp. 22-23.
        Looks at "Hymne" ("Queen and Huntresse") as an example
    of outstanding art in which Jonson constructs patterns of
    imaginative vision.

2   DAICHES, DAVID. Literature and Society. London: Victor
    Gollancz, pp. 104-5.
        Notes that Jonson wrote poetry with ease and common
    sense. Although his verse is "courtly, polished, and grace-
    ful," Jonson eschews Petrarchan conventions. Reprinted
    in 1970.10.

3   FIRTH, CHARLES. "Sir Walter Ralegh's 'History of the World.'"
    In Essays Historical and Literary. Oxford: Clarendon
    Press, pp. 34-60.
        Discusses the possible assistance Jonson may have given
    Ralegh in writing his History.

4   GUINEY, LOUISE IMOGEN. "Ben Jonson." In Recusant Poets. Vol.
    I. New York: Sheed & Ward, pp. 372-82.
        A capsule history of what is known of Jonson's religious
    life along with notes on some of his religious verse.

5   LEISHMAN, J. B. Review of The Phoenix and the Turtle, edited
    by Bernard H. Newdigate. RES 14, no. 55 (July):341-43.
        Raises questions concerning Newdigate's contention that
    Lucy, Countess of Bedford is the Phoenix. See 1937.20.

6   LEVIN, HARRY, ed. Introduction to Ben Jonson: Selected Works.
    The Modern Library. New York: Random House, pp. 3-36.
        Focuses on the graphic quality of Jonson's work. He
    seems a man emersed in London life and able to give the
    reader vivid portraits of his surroundings "of the gloss
    and the clarity and the tactile values that are the tokens
    of the master." Reprinted in 1963.15, 1972.23.

7 _____. "Jonson, Stow, and Drummond." MLN 53, no. 3 (March):
167-69.
A gloss on the syntax of section 18 of Conversations.

8 NETHERCOT, ARTHUR H. Sir William Davenant. Chicago: University
of Chicago Press, pp. 148-51.
Describes Jonson's and Davenant's friendship.

9 NUNGEZER, EDWIN. "Inedited Poems of Daniel." N&Q 175 (10
December):421.
Two poems "The Bodie" and "The Minde" attributed to
Samuel Daniel in the "Supplement" to the Catalogue of
Printed Books in the British Museum were actually written
by Ben Jonson. The poems form sections three and four of
Jonson's elegy, "Eupheme, or The Faire Fame. Left to
Posteritie."

10 PINTO, V. De SOLA. The English Renaissance, 1510-1688. Introductions to English Literature. Vol. 2. Edited by
Bonamy Dobree. Bath: Pitman Press, pp. 288-90.
Sees Jonson as a major figure who began a poetic tradition based largely on Latin models that finally developed
into the art of Dryden.

11 SIMPSON, EVELYN. "Ben Jonson's 'A New Year's Gift'" RES 14,
no. 54 (April):175-78.
This poem dated 1635 and one of the last written by
Jonson, is an adaptation of part to the Main Masque of
Jonson's Pans Anniversarie, presented at court on 17
January, 1620.

12 SIMPSON, PERCY. "Lucy Countess of Bedford." TLS, 8 October,
pp. 643-44.
The Countess is of interst to Jonsonian scholars largely because she acted in five of his masques.

13 TANNENBAUM, SAMUEL A. Ben Jonson: A Concise Bibliography.
New York: Scholars Facsimiles and Reprints, 151 pp.
The first bibliography of Jonson that attempted com-
plete coverage of editions, biography, and criticism.
The organization is less than helpful, many titles are
"creative," but Tannenbaum remains a major contributor to
Jonsonian scholarship.

14 THOMPSON, WALTER, ed. The Sonnets of William Shakespeare and
Henry Wriothesley, Third Earl of Southampton. Oxford:
Henry King & Sons, pp. 67-74.
Jonson's "The Phoenix Analysde" from "Diverse Poetical
Essaies" in The Phoenix and the Turtle holds a clue that

1938

the authors are speaking of the Earl of Southampton and not an unidentified woman.

15   WARD, CHARLES E. "A Jonson Allusion." N&Q 174 (4 June):403.
Notes an allusion to Jonson in "Dr. Wild's Poem or a New Song to an Old Friend from an Old Poet, upon the Hopeful New parliament," printed as a four-page pamphlet around 1680.

16   WHEELER, CHARLES FRANCIS. Classical Mythology in the Plays, Masques, and Poems of Ben Jonson. Princeton: Princeton University Press for the University of Cincinnati, 218 pp.
No one knew mythology better than Jonson, and he used it to animate his work. The main text is an alphabetical listing of Jonson's mythological sources. Reprinted in 1970.44.

17   WILLIAMS, FRANKLIN B., [Jr.]. "The Epigrams of Henry Parrot." Harvard Studies and Notes in Philology and Literature. 20:15-28.
Information on Parrot, to whom Jonson alluded in his poem, "Inviting a Friend to Supper."

1939

1   ALEXANDER, PETER. Shakespeare's Life and Art. London: James Nisbet & Co., pp. 92-93.
Cites Jonson's comment that Shakespeare "was indeed honest and of an open and free nature," and describes the significance of these remarks. Reprinted in 1961.2.

2   BRONOWSKI, JACOB. The Poet's Defence. Cambridge: University Press, pp. 89-98.
Jonson revered Aristotle. He summarizes Poetics in Discoveries, and in his writings there is plentiful evidence of Aristotle's influence. "It was Jonson who made imitation part of English criticism."

3   BUSH, DOUGLAS. Review of Classical Mythology . . . of Ben Jonson, by Charles Francis Wheeler. JEGP 38, no. 2:315.
Adds a few more mythological references for those who might use this "useful book." See 1938.16.

4   EHRSAM, THEODORE G. Review of Ben Jonson: A Concise Bibliography, by Samuel A. Tannenbaum. Library Quarterly 9, no. 1 (January):100-101.

Describes the bibliography and notes its general accuracy in all cases except short articles and reviews. See 1938.13.

5   GRAHAM, C. B. "Allusions to Ben Jonson in Restoration Comedy." RES 15, no. 58 (April):200-204.
    Supplementary material for The Jonson Allusion Book, 1922.4.

6   McEUEN, KATHRYN ANDERSON. Classical Influence Upon the Tribe of Ben. Cedar Rapids, Iowa: Torch Press, 316 pp.
    A full study of the major classical writers: Martial, Juvenal, Persius, Horace, Theocritas, Vergil, Anacreon, and others, who served as models for Jonson and his group. "The most noteworthy influence exerted by the classics upon their [Jonson and his followers] verse is seen in the ease with which they wrote. Jonson's own lyrics show a concision and a restraint, a polish and a care in structure which are not reflected especially in the verse of Herrick and Carew." Reprinted in 1968.8.

7   McPEEK, JAMES A. S. Catullus in Strange and Distant Britain. Harvard Studies in Comparative Literature. Cambridge, Mass.: Harvard University Press, pp. 313-18.
    Catallus's influence on Jonson was of less importance than that of other classical poets; nevertheless, traces of Catullus can be found in a number of Jonson's poems.

8   NEUMANN, JOSHUA H. "Notes on Ben Jonson's English." PMLA 54, no. 3 (September):736-63.
    A discussion of Jonson's diction: foreign words, Latinisms, newly coined words, invectives, etc.

9   RENDALL, GERALD H. Ben Jonson and the First Folio. Editions of Shakespeare's Plays. Colchester: Folcroft Press, 24 pp.
    Argues that Jonson's criticism of Shakespeare gives more evidence of the authenticity of Shakespeare's authorship.

10 SHORT, R. W. "Jonson's Sanguine Rival." RES 15, no. 59 (July):315-17.
    Identifies Michael Drayton as the poet in Epistle 12 in The Forrest. Dates the poem around 1601.

11 SIMPSON, EVELYN. Review of Ben Jonson: Selected Works, edited by Harry Levin. RES 15, no. 60 (October):477-78.
    Appreciation for a new popular edition of Jonson. Some editorial errors are noted. See 1938.6.

1939

12   _____. "Jonson and Donne, A Problem of Authorship." <u>RES</u> 15,
      no. 60 (October):274-82.
          Takes up attribution problems of elegies 38-41 of the
      <u>Under-wood</u>. One of these, "An Elegie. The Expostulation,"
      was published among Donne's poems of 1633. Simpson con-
      cludes that the evidence for Donne's authorship is over-
      whelming. However, she points out that the other poems
      are not attributed to Donne and that there is no good rea-
      son to do so. See also 1926.11 and 1978.4.

13   SIMPSON, PERCY. "Ben Jonson and the Devil Tavern." <u>MLR</u>
      34, no. 3 (July):367-73.
          Discusses the history of the Devil Tavern and the history
      and influence of <u>Leges Convivales</u>, a code drawn up by Jon-
      son for his meetings in the Apollo room of the tavern.

14   _____. "Ben Jonson's Sanguine Rival." <u>RES</u> 15, no. 60 (Octo-
      ber):464-65.
          Response to 1939.10. Maintains that Samuel Daniel is
      more likely the poet referred to in Epistle 12.

15   _____. Review of <u>Classical Mythology . . . of Ben Jonson</u>,
      by Charles Francis Wheeler. <u>MLR</u> 34, no. 3 (July):435-36.
          Welcomes the study as an important contribution to Jon-
      sonian scholarship. Lists a number of errors and inaccur-
      acies. See 1938.16.

16   THOMPSON, ELBERT N. S. "The Octosyllabic Couplet." <u>PQ</u> 18,
      no. 3 (July):257-63.
          A brief history of the octosyllabic couplet, "a metric-
      al form of even more ancient and respected lineage than
      heroic verse," in English literature, and a discussion of
      Jonson's very important place in that history.

17   VINCENT, HOWARD P. "Ben Jonson Allusions." <u>N&Q</u> 177 (8 July):
      26.
          Notes allusions to Jonson in "The Copie of a Letter sent
      from the Roaring Boyes in Elizium: (London, 1641).

18   WARREN, AUSTIN. <u>Richard Crashaw</u>. Baton Rouge: Louisiana
      State University Press, pp. 95-97.
          Discussion of some similarities of Jonson's and Crashaw's
      poetic styles.

19   WINTERS, YVOR. "The Sixteenth Century Lyric in England."
      <u>Poetry</u> 53, no. 5 (February):258-70.
          A general survey of sixteenth-century poetry. Notes
      that Jonson does not inherit the Petrarchan strain passed
      down to him. However, he does have a "dramatic and heroic"

view of life, since he "deals with problems of conduct
arising from relationships between one human being and
another" because these relationships involve "tragic or
other difficulties."

1940

1   BOAS, F. S. <u>Christopher Marlowe</u>. Oxford: Clarendon Press,
     passim.
         Believes that there is an echo of Jonson's experience
     in prison in "Inviting a Friend to Supper."

2   BRODERSEN, G. L. "Jonson and the 'Sons of Ben.'" <u>Manitoba
     Arts Review</u> 2 (December):5-18.
         Comment on Jonson's influence on the lyric and on the
     heroic couplet.

3   BUSH, DOUGLAS. Review of <u>Classical Influence Upon the Tribe
     of Ben</u>, by Kathryn Anderson McEuen. <u>JEGP</u> 39, no. 3:408-9.
         Description of the book as useful and accurate though
     not of compelling interest. The conclusion reached, that
     Jonson and his followers were highly influenced by clas-
     sical writers, could hardly be a surprise to anyone. See
     1939.6.

4   CAWLEY, R[OBERT] R[ALSTON]. <u>Unpathed Waters. Studies in the
     Influence of the Voyages on Elizabethan Literature</u>.
     Princeton: Princeton University Press, passim.
         Theme of the book has bearing on Jonson's poetry.

5   DANIELS, R. B. <u>Some 17th Century Worthies in a Twentieth
     Century Mirror</u>. Chapel Hill: University of North
     Carolian Press, passim.
         References to Jonson's poetry "recapturing the lyric
     spirit of ancient Greece."

6   ECCLES, MARK. Review of <u>Ben Jonson: A Concise Bibliography</u>,
     by Samuel A. Tannenbaum. <u>MLN</u> 55, no. 3 (March):238-39.
         A publication announceent that also notes some omis-
     sions. See 1938.13.

7   FUNKE, OTTO. "Ben Jonson's 'English Grammar.'" <u>Anglia</u>
     64:1117-34.
         A comparison of Ramus's rhetoric and Jonson's <u>English
     Grammar</u> shows that Jonson was closer to Ramus than had
     been recognized by other critics.

8   GILBERT, A[LLAN] H. Review of <u>Classical Mythology . . . of
     Ben Jonson</u>, by Charles Francis Wheeler. <u>PQ</u> 19, no. 1

1940

(January):92-96.
Supplements Wheeler with additional mythological sources
for Jonson. See 1938.16.

9 JONAS, LEAH. "Ben Jonson." In <u>The Divine Science: The Aesthe-
    tic of Some Representative Seventeenth Century Poets</u>. New
    York: Columbia University Press, pp. 16-46.
    Jonson's theory of literature was basically didactic.
    He believed that the poet was to instruct and to scorn
    those who would not follow the instruction. "The true poet
    must be willing to labor for the best interest of mankind
    without reward and without fear of consequences."

10 LEMMI, C. W. Review of <u>Classical Mythology . . . of Ben Jon-
    son</u>, by Charles Francis Wheeler. <u>MLN</u> 55, no. 4 (April):
    310-12.
    A few clarifications and additions to the catalog of
    mythological references. See 1938.16.

11 POROHOVSCHIKOV, PETER S. <u>Shakespeare Unmasked</u>. New York:
    Savoy Book Pub., pp. 239-41, 244-45.
    Believes that Jonson's contradictory statements about
    Shakespeare support the argument that Shakespeare the
    actor was not the author of plays.

12 SHARP, ROBERT LATHROP. <u>From Donne to Dryden</u>. Chapel Hill:
    University of North Carolina Press, pp. 5-12, 76-84.
    Jonson is seen as a critical force counter to the meta-
    physicals. "He shows an un-Elizabethan moderation in say-
    ing that extremes of antiquity and newness are to be
    avoided; he speaks of the value of pure diction, of the
    danger of coining new words, and of the importance of
    accuracy; he warns against hyperbole and mixed metaphors."
    Jonson recognizes the importance of establishing rules
    for poets in the practice of their art.

13 SHORT, R. W. "Ben Jonson in Drayton's Poems." <u>RES</u> 16, no.
    62 (April):149-58.
    Drayton and Jonson were not friends, as had been thought
    the case, but enemies because of their rivalry over Lucy,
    Countess of Bedford. See 1940.15.

14 SIMPSON, PERCY. Review of <u>Classical Influence Upon the Tribe
    of Ben</u>, by Kathryn Anderson McEuen. <u>MLR</u> 35, no. 3 (July):
    389-90.
    Points out some errors and questions a few assumptions,
    but generally supports the high quality of literary scholar-
    ship. See 1939.6.

15 SIMPSON, PERCY, and TILLOTSON, KATHLEEN. "Ben Jonson in
Drayton's Poems." <u>RES</u> 16, no. 63 (July):303-6.
Response to 1940.13. There are no unfavorable references to Jonson in Drayton's poetry nor is there any evidence
that the two poets were rivals for Lucy, Countess of Bedford. Argues that Short's conjectures are a travesty.
They are "a painful example of the way in which literary
history should not be written."

16 WELLS, HENRY W. <u>New Poets from Old: A Study in Literary
Genetics</u>. New York: Columbia University Press, passim.
References to Jonson's influence on the development of
modern poetry.

1941

1 ALLEN, DON CAMERON. Review of <u>Classical Influence Upon the
Tribe of Ben</u>, by Kathryn Anderson McEuen. <u>MLN</u> 56, no. 3
(March):241.
A work of painstaking scholarship, but which tells us
nothing new about Jonson and his circle. See 1939.6.

2 BARTLETT, PHYLLIS BROOKS, ed. <u>The Poems of George Chapman</u>.
New York: Modern Language Association, pp. 471-78.
Reprint of 1634.3.

3 BENTLEY, GERALD EADES. "Seventeenth Century Allusions to
Ben Jonson." <u>HLQ</u> 5, no. 1 (October):65-113.
Lists 152 allusions to Jonson in the seventeenth cen-
tury which before had not been noted.

4 F., R. E. "Chelsea Sands." <u>N&Q</u> 181 (2 August):62.
Query: are there sands around Chelsea as seems to be
suggested in "to Celia"?

5 HARBAGE, ALFRED. <u>Shakespeare's Audience</u>. New York: Columbia University Press, passim.
Jonson's criticism of Shakespeare is not representative
of contemporary views of Shakespeare. Moreover, Jonson
himself finally came to realize the true greatness of
Shakespeare. Reprinted 1969.9.

6 HUNT, CLAY. "The Elizabethan Background of Neo-Classic Polite
Verse." <u>ELH</u> 8, no. 4 (December):273-304.
Neoclassicism is not just a verse technique which one
cultivates to provide poetic form. Rather it is a way of
life--a point of view on the world. Jonson is the first
English poet to develop this point of view that in turn
becomes a positive force behind his work.

1941

7   M., J. F. Untitled. <u>N&Q</u> 181 (16 August):98.
       Response to 1941.4.

8   NEWDIGATE, BERNARD H. <u>Michael Drayton and His Circle</u>. Oxford:
       Shakespeare Head Press, 254 pp.
          Information on some of the individuals on whom Jonson
       wrote epigrams. Also examines the question of Jonson's
       and Drayton's friendship. Reprinted in 1961.12.

9   RANSOM, JOHN CROWE. <u>The New Criticism</u>. Norfolk, Conn.: New
       Directions, pp. 159-75.
          Amplified remarks made by Eliot in 1919.5.

10   SAMPSON, GEORGE. "Ben Jonson." In <u>The Concise Cambridge His-</u>
       <u>tory of English Literature</u>. Cambrdige: Cambridge Univer-
       sity Press, pp. 295-310.
          Summary of critical opinion on Jonson's poems. "In the
       main they are strong, manly, intelligent utterances, less
       read than they should be. But they repel by sheer lack
       of charm."

11   SIMPSON, PERCY. <u>Cambridge Bibliography of English Literature</u>.
       Edited by F. W. Bateson. Vol. 1. New York: Macmillan Co.,
       pp. 613-19.
          Selected bibliography of Jonson's works and criticism.

12   UPSHAW, MARION H. "The Function of the Elizabethan Lyric with
       Reference to the Plays of shakespeare and Ben Jonson."
       Master's thesis, Univeristy of Arizona.
          Lyrics within dramas serve various purposes: "portrayal
       of character, creation of emotional atmosphere, advance-
       ment of dramatic action, satirization, and creation of
       comic effect."

13   WILSON, F. P. "Shakespeare and the Diction of Common Life."
       <u>Proceedings of the British Academy</u> 27:167-98.
          Shakespeare's diction is compared with Jonson's and
       other early seventeenth-century writers.

<u>1942</u>

1   ANON. "Alas Poor Ghost!" <u>TLS</u>, 30 May, p. 271.
          Response to 1942.2. Laments the passing of Salathiel
       Pavy. "Only now that we must forgo it do we realize how
       much the name went to the making of the child we loved."
       See 1942.5 and 1942.6.

2   BENTLEY, GERALD EADES. "A Good Name Lost: Ben Jonson's La-
         ment for S.P." TLS, 30 May, p. 276.
              Evidence that Sollomon Pavy is the name of the boy re-
         ferred to in Jonson's "Epitaph on S. P. a Child of Q. El.
         Chappel" rather than Salathiel Pavy, the name normally
         given by editors beginning with Gifford in 1816. See
         1942.1; 1942.5 and 1942.6.

3   DAVENPORT, A. "The Quarrel of the Satirists." MLR 37, no. 2
         (April):123-30.
              New information on the poets' war and Jonson's role in
         it.

4   N., R. K. "Ben Jonson's 'To Celia.'" Expl 1, no. 3 (Decem-
         ber):Q 19.
              Asks about punctuation in the first line of Jonson's
         song.

5   PERCIVAL, MARGARET. "Salathiel Pavy." TLS, 6 June, p. 283.
              Response to 1942.2. Gifford may have interpreted Sal.
         as Salathiel based upon the appearance of the name in
         Matthew 1. See 1942.1 and 1942.6.

6   WHITE, N. B. "A Good Name Lost." TLS, 13 June, p. 295.
              Short response to 1942.2. The misreading of Salathiel
         came about because of the wording "Sal. a child." See
         1942.1 and 1942.5.

                               1943

1   APP, AUSTIN J. "Old Ben Jonson on 'Grading' Compositions."
         CE 4, no. 5 (February):318-20.
              Commentary on Jonson's advice to teachers in Discoveries.
         Jonson says one must "temper his own powers and descend
         into the others infirmities." Author finds this good for
         the modern teacher.

2   BOAS, R. P. "'To Celia.'" Expl 1, no. 4 (February):item 28.
              Ambiguity in the first line of "To Celia."

3   EAGLE, R. L. "Ben Jonson and Shakespeare." Baconiana 27
         (January):28-35.
              An analysis of "To the Memory of My Beloved . . . Mr.
         William Shakespeare," intended to demonstrate that it
         raises many questions about the authenticity of Shakespeare's
         plays.

1943

4 LEVIN, HARRY. "Ben Jonson's Metempsychosis." PQ 22, no. 2
   (July):231-39.
        The satire of both Jonson and Donne "springs from some
   perception of the disparities between the real and the
   ideal. Hence the satirist's position is always shifting;
   sooner or later he must embrace one extreme or the other.
   Donne, in choosing religion, chose the idealistic extreme.
   Jonson chose realism."

5 PAGE, FREDERICK. "Jonson and Shakespeare." N&Q 184 (30
   January):79.
        Asks why Baconians identify Shakespeare as the subject
   of the epigram "Poet-Ape."

6 PALMER, JOHN. "O Rare Ben Jonson." Everybody's (10 July):11.
        General biographical and critical comment on Jonson.

7 SIMPSON, PERCY. "The Rhyming of Stressed with Unstressed
   Syllables." MLR 38, no. 2 (April):127-29.
        Unusual metrics in early seventeenth-century poets
   including Jonson.

8 TILLYARD, E. M. W. The Elizabethan World Picture. London:
   Chatto & Windus, passim.
        Includes Jonson among those writers "united in holding
   with earnestness, passion, and assurance to the main outlines of the medieval world picture as modified by the
   Tudor regime, although they all knew that the coherence of
   this picture had been threatened."

1944

1 ESDAILE, KATHERINE. "Ben Jonson and the Devil Tavern."
   Essays and Studies by . . . the English Association.
   Vol. 29. Collected by Una Ellis-Fermor. Oxford: Claren-
   don Press, pp. 93-100.
        Historical treatment of "Ben's Club" using contemporary
   poems and letters to piece together a picture of the famous
   Apollo Room.

2 GRIERSON, H[ERBERT] J. C., and SMITH, J. C. A Critical History of English Poetry. London: Oxford University Press,
   pp. 103-6.
        Points out the two sides of Jonson's nature as seen in
   his poetry, and also remarks on the "clean cut and shapely"
   beauty of his verse.

3   PUTNEY, RUFUS [D.]. "What 'Praise to Give?' Jonson vs. Stoll."
    PQ 23, no. 4 (October):307-19.
        Jonson's praise of Shakespeare in "To the Memory of My
    Beloved . . . Mr. William Shakespeare" is evidence that
    Jonson was aware of Shakespeare's worth. Particularly he
    recognized his brilliant innovations in the development of
    dramatic tragedy.

4   ROLLINS, HYDER EDWARD, ed. A New Variorum Edition of Shake-
    speare's Sonnets. Philadelphia: J. B. Lippincott, passim.
        In Conversations Jonson is highly critical of sonnets in
    general, but interestingly, he does not mention Shakespeare
    in particular.

1945

1   ANON. "Shakespeare and Ben Jonson." N&Q 188 (2 June):241-42.
        Review of Shakespeare and Jonson . . . , by Gerald
    Eades Bentley. A general description and summary of Bent-
    ley. See 1945.2.

2   BENTLEY, GERALD EADES. Shakespeare and Jonson; Their Rep-
    utations in the Seventeenth Century Compared. 2 vols.
    Chicago: University of Chicago Press.
        Volume one gives the author's definition of an allusion,
    the method of collecting allusions, tables of the distribu-
    tion of allusions, and some conclusions regarding the com-
    parative popularity of Shakespeare and Jonson. Volume two
    records 59 allusions to Shakespeare and 1079 allusions to
    Jonson which had not been listed by earlier compilers.
    Bentley summarizes: "Jonson's general popularity was great-
    er than Shakespeare's from the beginning of the century to
    1690; Shakespeare's reputation was growing more rapidly
    than Jonson's in the last two decades. Throughout the
    century Jonson was unchallenged in most critical writing
    as the greatest English dramatist, his popularity in crit-
    ical writings being greater than his over-all popularity."

3   BUSH, DOUGLAS. English Literature in the Earlier Seventeenth
    Century, 1600-1660. Oxford History of English Literature.
    Oxford: Clarendon Press, pp. 104-11, 556-58.
        A solid discussion of the critical background of Jonson's
    poetry and an evaluation of his current status among in-
    telligent readers. "In recent decades critical noses have
    been in great indignation at the thought of poetical fra-
    grance, and magic and wonder and mystery, and Jonson has
    risen on the wave of the anti-romantic reaction. . . Our

increasing respect for Jonson's classical art, our unwill-
ingness to call his genius talent, is doubtless a sign of
increasing sanity." A bibliography is included. Revised
in 1962.1.

4   HARBAGE, ALFRED. "Bentley's 'Shakespeare and Ben Jonson.'"
    MLN 60, no. 6 (June):414-17.
        Review of Shakespeare and Jonson . . . , by Gerald Eades
    Bentley. Praise for the wide and careful reading of seven-
    teenth-century books to trace allusions to Jonson and
    Shakespeare. The reviewer questions Bentley's conclusions
    that Jonson was a more popular writer than Shakespeare.
    "Jonson as a truly great writer had some measure of pop-
    ularity as well as literary reputation, and Shakespeare
    some measure of literary reputation as well as popularity,
    but the distinction between them is clear enough in the
    main. As an entertainer of the court, as a colorful per-
    sonality, as a center of a literary circle, as a creator of
    critical issues, and a citizen by naturalization of Academic-
    land, Jonson naturally called forth a greater volume of
    testimony from bookish people than did Shakespeare, who,
    primarily, was only a writer whom people liked." See
    1945.2.

5   JOHNSTON, GEORGE BURKE. Ben Jonson: Poet. New York: Col-
    umbia University Press, 183 pp.
        A comprehensive study of Jonson's poetry which follows
    a rough chronological pattern. Johnston calls for a re-
    evaluation of the poet based not on what we expect but what
    Jonson attempted to do and how successful he was in this.
    Johnston concludes that in his poetry Jonson "found the truth,
    the order, the beauty, and the justice which he could not
    find in his London." Reprinted in 1970.26.

6   McEUEN, KATHRYN A[NDERSON]. "Jonson and Juvenal." RES 21,
    no. 82 (April):92-104.
        Though Jonson was "by nature a satirist," he did not
    write formal classical verse satire. Describes the sa-
    tiric method and purpose Jonson used, which was similar to
    Juvenal.

7   SHARP, ROBERT BOIES. "Jonson's 'Execration' and Chapman's
    'Invective': Their Place in Their Authors' Rivalry."
    SP 42, no. 3 (July):555-63.
        An analysis of the quarrel between Jonson and Chapman
    which culminated in Chapman's "Invective." Believes there
    was no single issue which caused the break between the two
    poets, but the issue which might finally have led Chapman

to write the "Invective" was the "rights" to certain areas
of classical scholarship. Argues that the "Invective" was
written well before Chapman's death and dates it probably
around 1623-24. Chapman's modern editor, P. B. Bartlett,
suggests a similar date; though Herford and Simpson suggest
a date very near Chapman's death.

8   SIMPSON, PERCY. "The Art of Ben Jonson." In Essays and Studies
     of Members of the English Association. Vol. 30. Collected
     by C. H. Wilkinson. Oxford: Clarendon Press, pp. 35-49.
          Discusses Jonson's theories of literature and his con-
     cept of dramatic art.

9   _____. Review of Shakespeare and Jonson . . . , by Gerald Eades
     Bentley. RES 21, no. 84 (October):334-36.
          "A contribution of the utmost value to a clear under-
     standing of the seventeenth-century outlook on letters."
     See 1945.2 and 1946.6.

10   WILSON, F. P. Elizabethan and Jacobean. Oxford: Clarendon
     Press, passim.
          Some of Jonson's best known verse moves beyond the
     Elizabethan mainly in "the perfection of their form, so
     consciously sought and achieved." But other poems are nearer
     Donne's styles.

11   _____. Review of Shakespeare and Jonson . . . , by Gerald Eades
     Bentley. Library, 4th ser. 26, nos. 2 & 3 (September &
     December):199-202.
          Adds four allusions overlooked by Bentley. See 1945.2.

1946

1   ANON. Review of Ben Jonson: Poet, by George Burke Johnston.
     TLS, 11 May, p. 227.
          Brief publication announcement. See 1945.5.

2   ANON. Review of Ben Jonson: Poet, by George Burke Johnston.
     TLS, 18 May, p. 236.
          A description with a paragraph summary of each chapter.
     See 1945.5.

3   BALDWIN, T. Review of Shakespeare and Jonson . . . , by Ger-
     ald Eades Bentley. JEGP 45, no. 2:232-34.
          Although Bentley's conclusions are generally correct,
     there are other matters which ought also to be considered.
     During the seventeenth century Jonson and Shakespeare be-
     came symbols for "conflicting literary dogma. . . . Jon-

1946

> son had become the symbol of learning and Shakespeare of
> nature." Thus it was left to the romantics to lift
> Shakespeare to the position with which we associate him
> today. Baldwin is also suspicious of the application of
> statistics to literary questions. "Statistics deal with
> quantity, whereas in the eternal verities only quality is
> of value." See 1945.2.

4   BENTLEY, GERALD EADES. The Swan of Avon and the Bricklayer
    of Westminster. The Inaugural Lecture of Gerald Eades
    Bentley. Princeton: no. publ., 18 pp.
        Though Shakespeare is often regarded as philosopher and
    poet more than public playwright, it was actually Ben Jon-
    son who disdained public appeal and wrote for posterity.
    This is the "great irony" of the two careers, and it is
    even more ironic that Jonson recognized the timelessness
    of Shakespeare's work.

5   CLAUSEN, WENDELL. "The Beginnings of English Character-Writing
    in the Early Seventeenth Century." PQ 25, no. 1 (January):
    32-45.
        Discusses Jonson's part in the development of character
    writing as a "Literary mediator." Jonson's interest in
    the classics, his important position in London literary
    circles, and his own "vigorous personality" were contrib-
    uting facrors in the development of this subgenre.

6   GREG, W. W. "Shakespeare and Jonson." RES 22, no. 85 (Jan-
    uary):58.
        Response to 1945.9. Argues that Shakespeare was more
    read than Jonson in the seventeenth century.

7   HERRICK, M[ARVIN] T[HEODORE]. The Fusion of Horatian and
    Aristotelian Literary Criticism, 1531-55. Urbana: Uni-
    versity of Illinois Press, pp. 104-8.
        Jonson blended Horace and Aristotle for his own theory
    of poetry.

8   JOHN, LISLE CECIL. "Ben Jonson's Epigram CXIV to Mistress
    Philip Sidney." JEGP 45, no. 2 (April):214-17.
        Biographical information about Mistress Philip Sidney
    that tends to corroborate Jonson's high regard for her.

9   MASSON, DAVID. Life of John Milton. New York: Peter Smith.
    Reprint of 1873.3.

10 MIZENER, ARTHUR. Review of Ben Jonson: Poet, by George
    Burke Johnston. Kenyon Review 8, no. 1 (Winter):170-71.

Finds that one can learn a great deal from this book,
particularly about sources and literary traditions, but
it does not bring us to the kind of understanding of Jonson's poetry one might have hoped for. See 1945.5.

11   SHIPLEY, JOSEPH T., ed. Encyclopedia of Literature. Vol. 1.
New York: Philosophical Library, p. 220.
Identifies Jonson as a poet, playwright, and critic.

12   TALBERT, E[RNEST] W[ILLIAM]. Review of Ben Jonson: Poet, by
George Burke Johnston. MLN 61, no. 3 (March):205-7.
Johnston begins with a strong thesis but clearly fails
to prove it. That the label "classicist" does not always
fit Jonson is an interesting point, but Johnston does not
prove this point with a detailed examination of Jonson's
versification. Finds additional problems with the book.
See 1945.5.

1947

1   ANON. "Ben Jonson's Poems." Review of Ben Jonson: The
Poems . . . , edited by C. H. Herford and Evelyn Simpson.
TLS, 5 July, p. 336.
Reviewer takes the opportunity to reevaluate Jonson's
poetry and the criticism of that poetry. In Jonson "the
lover of Latin and the lover of life were always at odds."
But he was quite capable of writing with great sensitivity
and tenderness. He can move from biting satire to gentle
lyrics to vulgar scatology to open self-effacement. "So
diverse a nature should not be reduced to a formula."
See 1947.5.

2   ATKINS, J. W. H. English Literary Criticism: The Renaissance.
London: Methuen & Co., passim.
Jonson's place in literary criticism during the Renais-
sance is discussed along with aspects of his critical views.

3   EMPSON, WILLIAM. Seven Types of Ambiguity. 2d ed. New York:
New Directions, pp. 242.
Discussion of two lines of "To Celia."

4   GILBERT, A[LLAN] H. "Jonson and Drummond or Gil on the King's
Senses." MLN, 62, no. 1 (January):35-37.
Discusses the similarity between Drummond's "for the
Kinge" and Jonson's song which Patricia sings in Gypsies
Metamorphos'd. See also 1959.10.

1947

5   HERFORD, C. H.; SIMPSON, PERCY; and SIMPSON, EVELYN, eds.
    Ben Jonson: The Poems, The Prose World. Vol. 8. Oxford:
    Clarendon Press, 674 pp.
        A detailed description of textual problems in editing
    Jonson, along with the full text of the poems.

6   HUDSON, HOYT HOPEWELL. The Epigram in the English Renaissance.
    Princeton: Princeton University Press, passim.
        Survey of the development of the epigram along with a
    discussion of those writers most successful with this verse
    form.

7   KIRBY, T[HOMAS] A. "The Triple Tun." MLN 62, no. 3 (March):
    191-92.
        Identifies the tavern referred to in Herrick's poem on
    Jonson.

8   LEAVIS, F. R. Revaluation: Tradition and Development in Eng-
    lish Poetry. New York: George W. Stewart.
        Reprint of 1936.18 and reprinted in 1962.11.

9   STROUD, THEODORE A. "Ben Jonson and Father Thomas Wright."
    ELH 14, no. 4:274-82.
        Presents evidence that Father Thomas Wright was respon-
    sible for Jonson's conversion to Catholicism while Jonson
    was in prison for killing Gabriel Spencer in 1598.

10 TANNENBAUM, SAMUEL A., and TANNENBAUM, DOROTHY R. Supplement
    to A Concise Bibliography of Ben Jonson. New York: pub-
    lished by S. A. Tannenbaum.
        Additions to 1938.13.

11 TOWNSEND, FREDA L. "Ben Jonson's 'Censure' of Rutters 'Shep-
    heard's Holy-Day.'" MP 44, no. 4 (May):238-47.
        Jonson was not as orthodox in his critical theories as
    many writers have maintained. His praise of Rutter's
    Shepheard's Holy-Day "tells us . . . that Jonson's dramatic
    laws were most probably original in their formulation and
    had little to do with ancient prescriptions. No critic of
    Jonson, as law giver or a dramatist, can afford to ignore
    his praise of Rutter's unclassical play."

12 TUVE, ROSEMOND. Elizabethan and Metaphysical Imagery. Chicago:
    University of Chicago Press, passim.
        Jonson's critical views and his rhetorical and stylistic
    practices are discussed.

13 WEBSTER, A. BLYTHE ET AL, eds. "On Ben Jonson." In A Saints-
    bury Miscellany. New York: Oxford Univeristy Press,
    pp. 213-16.

1948

14 WIMSATT, W[ILLIAM] K., Jr. "The Structure of the 'Concrete
    Universal' in Literature." PMLA 62, no. 1 (March):262-80.
        In Discoveries Jonson recognizes the complexity and or-
    ganic quality of poetry.

1948

1 BOAS, F. S. "Edward Howard's Lyrics and Essays." Contemporary Review 174, no. 992 (August):107-11.
       Howard's book Lyrics and Essays was published in 1674.
   In this volume Howard has high praise for Jonson as a
   dramatist and as an arbiter of the language. "He gave our
   English Tongue firmness, greatness, enlarged and improved
   it, without patching of French words to our speech, according to some of our modern Pens."

2 BRADBROOK, M. C. Review of Ben Jonson: The Poems . . . , edited by C. H. Herford, Percy Simpson and Evelyn Simpson.
   MLR 43, no. 2 (April):259-60.
       Praise for Herford and the Simpsons' edition. On Jonson's
   poetry Bradbrook observes that it "has a wider range and
   scope than that of any other Elizabethan." Jonson not
   only writes poetry, but he also gives us a vivid picture
   of his age. See 1947.5.

3 BROOKS, TUCKER. A Literary History of England. Edited by
   Albert C. Baugh. New York: Appleton-Century-Crofts, pp.
   627-31.
       Although one does not easily recognize Jonson's greatness,
   it is there in nearly every line he wrote. He believed
   that "poetry was the criticism of life, and criticism could
   be no easy thing for author or for reader." Jonson could
   be urbane or melodic, but was always influential. Reprinted in 1967.2.

4 CHILD, HAROLD. "The Triumph of Ben Jonson." In Essays and
   Reflections. Edited by S. C. Roberts. Cambridge: University Press, pp. 3-11.
       Reprint of 1936.7.

5 CLARK, DONALD LEMEN. John Milton at St. Paul's School: A
   Study of Ancient Rhetoric in English Renaissance Education.
   New York: Columbia University Press, passim.
       The quarrel between Jonson and Alexander Gill was polit-
   ical as well as literary. Gill wrote a satire on The Magnetic Lady and was opposed to Jonson's alleged writing of
   inflammatory verse on Buckingham. Reprinted in 1964.5.

1948

6   GRAVES, ROBERT. <u>The White Goddess: A Historical Grammar of</u>
    <u>Poetic Myth</u>. New York: Creative Age Press, passim.
        Identifies Jonson and John Skelton as the only two Eng-
    lish poets "who had the necessary learning, poetic talent,
    humanity, dignity, and independence of mind to be Chief
    Poets."

7   GREG, W. W. Review of <u>Ben Jonson: The Poems . . .</u> , edited
    by C. H. Herford, Percy Simpson and Evelyn Simpson. <u>RES</u> 24,
    no. 93 (January):65-66.
        With general praise for the volume, presents a short
    list of textual questions and a much longer list of ques-
    tions regarding the editors' prose style. See 1947.5.

8   HONIG, EDWIN. "Notes on Satire in Swift and Jonson." <u>NMQ</u> 18,
    no. 2 (Summer):155-63.
        Jonson did not often write of love unless the theme was
    "underlined by the realistic detail, the odor of contamin-
    ated flesh." Yet, when he actually wrote of the weakness
    of the human flesh he was formal and detached. Swift, how-
    ever, was much more moved by the bestial and irrational
    qualities of man.

9   KIRBY, THOMAS A. "'The Triple Tun' Again." <u>MLN</u> 63, no. 1
    (January):56-57.
        Additional information 1947.7.

10 WILSON, EDMUND. "A Definitive Edition of Ben Jonson." <u>NY</u> 24
    (6 November):123-27.
        Review of <u>Ben Jonson</u>, edited by C. H. Herford and Percy
    Simpson; and <u>Ben Jonson: The Poems . . .</u> , edited by C.
    H. Herford, Percy Simpson and Evelyn Simpson. Herford and
    Simpson is not a good edition for the ordinary scholarly
    reader, but then Jonson may simply not be a very inter-
    esting writer for most people. Though Jonson was certain-
    ly gifted, he failed to make the most of those gifts.
    "His truculent and anxious personality, as revealed by the
    obsessions that appear in his work as well as what we know
    of his life, presents a curious case, which could reward
    psychological study." See 1925.17 and 1947.5.

11 _____. "Morose Ben Jonson." In <u>The Triple Thinkers: Twelve</u>
    <u>Essays on Literary Subjects</u>. New York: Oxford University
    Press, pp. 213-32.
        Work toward the psychological study suggested in 1948.10.
    "Ben Jonson seems an obvious example of a psychological
    type which has been described by Freud and designated by a
    technical name, <u>anal erotic</u>. . . ." This quality of Jonson's
    personality limited his creative capabilities. Though he

was a man of genius, that genius was never given the freedom
to flower; instead was tightly restricted. As a result Jonson will forever remain a poet of unrealized promise no
matter how many critics call for a reevaluation of his work.
Reprinted in 1963.23.

1949

1 AUBREY, JOHN. "Ben Jonson," and "William Shakespeare." In
   Aubrey's Brief Lives. Edited by Oliver Lawson Dick. London: Secker & Warburg, pp. 177-80, 275-76.
        Publication of 1680.1 and 1680.2.

2 CAREW, THOMAS. "To Ben Jonson. Upon occasion of his Ode of
   defiance annext to his Play of the new Inne." In The Poems
   of Thomas Carew with his Masque Coelum Britannicum. Edited by Rhodes Dunlap. Oxford: Clarendon Press, pp. 64-
   65.
        Reprint of 1640.2.

3 CHUTE, MARCHETTE. Shakespeare of London. New York: Dutton,
   passim.
        Jonson's personal, professional, and critical relation-
   ships with Shakespeare are fully discussed. Concludes "In
   spite of all their differences Jonson loved Shakespeare
   and called him 'my beloved'. . . . The highest praise
   Jonson could give a man was to call him honest; for the
   phrase had high connotations in the Renaissance. . . . It
   was a word which in turn he applied to Shakespeare."

4 DUNCAN, RONALD. Introduction to Poems of Ben Jonson. London:
   Grey Wall Press, pp. 7-17.
        Jonson is a major poet, "the main link in the line from
   Chaucer to Dryden." Besides being influential in the
   development of English poetry, his work is of the highest
   quality. "Jonson is the most graceful and supple of all
   English lyricists."

5 HIGHET, GILBERT. The Classical Tradition. New York: Oxford:
   University Press, pp. 202, 238-39.
        Shakespeare may have gained some of his information about
   the classics through conversations with Jonson. There is
   also a brief discussion of "To the Immortall Memorie, and
   Friendship of that Noble Paire, Sir Lucius Cary and Sir
   H. Morison."

6 LEISHMAN, J. B., ed. The Three Parnassus Plays. London: Ivor
   Nicholson & Watson, 398 pp.
        Reprint of 1886.6.

1949

7   POTTS, L. J.   "Ben Jonson and the Seventeenth Century." In
    English Studies 1949. New Series, vol. 2. Collected by
    Sir Philip Magnus. London: John Murray, pp. 7-24.
        A survey of Jonson's contemporaries and the intellectual
    climate in which they lived and worked. Commentary on the
    traditional points of argument in Jonsonian biography and
    criticism.

8   SAINTSBURY, GEORGE. "Ben Jonson: his equipment." In A
    History of Criticism. Vol. 2. London: William Blackwood,
    pp. 197-209.
        Reprint of 1902.6.

9   WILSON, J[OHN] DOVER. "Ben Jonson and Julius Caesar." ShS 2
    (1949):36-43.
        Modern critics have probably made too much of Jonson's
    criticism of Shakespeare. However, it would appear that
    Jonson "failed to understand Shakespeare," and there is
    evidence of "the unconscious realization by a proud spirit
    of another's superiority."

1950

1   BREDVOLD, LOUIS I. "The Rise of English Classicism: Study in
    Methodology." CL 2, no. 3 (Summer):253-68.
        An extended comparison of the French and English devel-
    opment of classicism. Jonson is a key figure in the study
    because he made a very original and a very English con-
    tribution to the rise of classicism. "With all his human-
    istic learning and his demand for order and control in
    art, Jonson remains as English as John Bull."

2   CRAIG, HARDIN. "Ben Jonson as a Poet," In A History of Eng-
    lish Literature. New York: Oxford University Press, pp.
    293-94.
        Short survey of the poetry listing the most important
    titles. For all his classicism there is in Jonson a great
    sense of humanity which emerges in his poetry. Reprinted
    in 1962.4.

3   GRAESSE, JEAN GEORGE THEODORE. "Ben Jonson." In Tresor de
    Livres Rares et Precieux. Vol. 3. New York: S. Hacker,
    pp. 476-77.
        Reprint of 1859-69.1.

4   H., E. Review of Ben Jonson. Vols. 1-10. NMQ 22, no. 4
    (Winter):469-71.
        The ten volumes of Jonson's works produced thus far are
    a self-perpetuating production of minutia related to Jon-

son's canon. It has all been done in a painstaking and
careful manner; however, there is very little if any real
appreciation for Jonson amidst all the annotation.

5 JOHNSTON, GEORGE BURKE. "Scott and Jonson." N&Q 195, no. 24
   (25 November):521-22.
      Indicates how well Scott read Jonson by pointing out a
   number of allusions in Scott to him.

6 PELTZ, CATHARINE W. "Thomas Campion, An Elizabethan Neo-Clas-
   sicist." MLQ 11, no. 1 (March):3-6.
      Campion prepared the way for Jonson and the development
   of neoclassicism. "Jonson's role was that of conscious
   builder previous to whom a few sporadic experiments had
   been made as to the possibility of establishing an English lyric based securely upon classic foundations."

7 SHAPIRO, I. A. "The 'Mermaid Club.'" MLR 45, no. 1 (January):
   6-17.
      The famous literary club never really existed in the
   form we have come to believe. Beaumont's verse letter to
   Jonson describing meetings at the Mermaid is of a later
   date than is normally assumed. See 1951.11.

8 WALLERSTEIN, RUTH [C.]. Studies in Seventeenth-Century Poetic.
   Madison: University of Wisconsin Press, passim.
      Jonson's elegiac verse is integrated into the evolution-
   ary treatment of seventeenth-century poetry.

9 WEAVER, BENNETT. "Twenty Unpublished Letters of Elizabeth
   Barrett to Hugh Stuart Boyd." PMLA 65, no. 4 (June):397-418.
      Recalling Jonson's epitaph "On Sir John Roe," Elizabeth
   Barrett remarks, "I scarcely ever read anything which seemed
   to me at once so simple and so noble."

1951

1 BACHRACH, A. G. H. "Sir Constantyn Huygens and Ben Jonson."
   Neophil 35:120-29.
      Huygens is most remembered as the Dutch translator of
   Donne; however, he also translated some of Jonson and was
   strongly influenced by him. Juygens was a man of letters
   in his own right, and one can find echoes of Jonson in
   his works.

*2 COOK, E. "The Tribe of Ben." Master's thesis, Cambridge
   University.
      Cited in Brock and Welsh, 1974.9.

1951

*3   ENCK, JOHN J. "Ben Jonson's Imagery." Ph.D. dissertation, Harvard University.
       Cited in Brock and Welsh, 1974.9.

4   EVANS, G. BLAKEMORE, ed. General Introduction to <u>The Plays and Poems of William Cartwright</u>. Madison: University of Wisconsin Press, pp. 3-80.
       "Jonson's influence can best be seen in the classical polish, neatness, and impersonal tone of much of Cartwright's verse. . . ."

5   ING, CATHERINE. <u>Elizabethan Lyrics</u>. London: Chatto & Windus, pp. 118-31. Focuses on "Song" ("Slow, slow, fresh fount") its musical setting and qualities.

6   JOHNSTON, GEORGE BURKE. "Ben Jonson of Gresham College." <u>TLS</u>, 28 December, p. 837.
       Further observations on 1951.12. Those items Jonson rewrote which had been destroyed in his fire could have been used in his lectures on rhetoric. The items destroyed which would not have been useful in his lectures were never rewritten.

7   KNIGHTS, L. C. <u>Drama and Society in the Age of Jonson</u>. London: Chatto & Windus, 346 pp.
       Reprint of 1937.11.

8   LEISHMAN, J. B. <u>The Monarch of Wit: An Analytical and Comparative Study of the Poetry of John Donne</u>. London: Hutchinson University Library, pp. 14-17.
       Discusses the similarities of Donne and Jonson. "They both took the short poem more seriously than typical Elizabethan poet . . . each wrote what he valued most for a fit audience though few." Both poets developed relatively new styles which incorporated among other things realistic and satirical verse. Reprinted 1966.10.

9   SHAPIRO, I. A. "'The Mermaid Club' A Rejoinder." <u>MLR</u> 46, no. 1 (January):59-63.
       A response to 1951.11. Believes Simpson over reacted to his article. The Mermaid Club did exist but not in the "mythologized" way the nineteenth-century scholars led us to believe.

10   SIMPSON, PERCY. "Francis Beaumont's Verse-letter to Ben Jonson: 'The Sun, which doth the greatest comfort bring. . . .'" <u>MLR</u> 46, nos. 3 & 4 (July and October):435-36.

1952

Brief comment on Beaumont's tribute to Jonson. Does not question the attribution of the poem.

11 _____. "'The Mermaid Club' An Answer." MLR 46, no. 1 (January):58-59.

Challenges Shapiro's argument in 1950.7. The existence of the Mermaid Club is well documented, and there is reasonable support for our understanding of what went on there.

12 SISSON, C. J. "Ben Jonson of Gresham College." TLS, 21 September, p. 604.

Jonson may have been a professor of rhetoric at Gresham College in the early 1620s. If this were the case, Discoveries may well be lecture notes rather than a commonplace book. The incomplete English Grammar may have had the same purpose. See also 1951.6.

13 WALKER, RALPH S. "Literary Criticism in Jonson's Conversations with Drummond." English 8, no. 47 (Summer):222-27.

Cautions against placing too much trust in Drummond's Conversations. We must consider carefully Drummond's lack of humor and his inability to perceive some of Jonson's critical remarks. Conversations must be studied against the backdrop of Discoveries. Revised in 1953.14.

14 WHITE, HELEN C.; WALLERSTEIN, RUTH C.; and QUINTANA, RICARDO, eds. Seventeenth Century Verse and Prose. Vol. 1. New York: Macmillan, pp. 122-24.

Jonson was both a Christian and literary humanist. "In the second sense that he wished to use the ideals and the forms of classical literature as models to discipline the artlessness of his time and the exuberance which seemed to diffuse rather than to concentrate and intensify the realization of idea as beauty, and to throw away the hardwon gains of aesthetic reasons."

15 WRONKER, STANLEY S. "Pope and Ben Jonson." N&Q 196, no. 23 (10 November):495-96.

An echo of Jonson's "To the Memory of My Beloved . . . Mr. William Shakespeare," in Pope's Epistle II of An Essay on Man.

1952

1 ALLEN, FRANK. "Drink to Me Only . . ." N&Q 197, no. 8 (April):161.

1952

A retired physics professor thinks "smells" and "swear"
are offensive and suggests new wording for line fifteen
of "To Celia." See 1952.12.

2   ANON. "Momentum." <u>TLS</u>, 10 October, p. 661.
        Review of <u>Ben Jonson: Commentary . . .</u> , edited by C.
     H. Herford, Percy Simpson, and Evelyn Simpson. A final trib-
     ·ute to Mr. and Mrs. Simpson and the late C. H. Herford for
     this "epic piece of English scholarship." See 1952.7.

3   BRYANT, J. A., Jr. "The Significance of Ben Jonson's First
        Requirement for Tragedy: 'Truth of Argument.'" <u>SP</u> 49
        no. 2 (April):195-213.
        A wide-ranging essay discussing Jonson's critical views
     as they apply to tragedy. Discussion of <u>Discoveries</u> as
     well as Jonson's part in Ralegh's <u>History of the World</u>.
     Bryant concludes that the accepted view of Jonson's criti-
     cal attitude toward tragedy needs substantial revision.

4   BUSH, DOUGLAS. <u>English Poetry: The Main Currents from</u>
        <u>Chaucer to the Present</u>. New York: Oxford University
        Press, pp. 52-53.
        Points out the advantages and disadvantages of Jonson's
     neoclassicism. The "intellectual and emotional rationality
     and control lucid and logical symmetry" are balanced against
     "the conscious manipulation of fancy and word and rhythm
     by the skilled artificer."

5   FULLER, THOMAS. <u>The Worthies of England</u>. Edited by John Free-
        man. London: George Allen & Unwin, pp. 382-83.
        Reprint of 1662.1.

6   HARBAGE, ALFRED. <u>Shakespeare and the Rival Traditions</u>. New
        York: Macmillan Co., passim.
        General comparison of the careers of Jonson and Shake-
     speare.

7   HERFORD, C. H.; SIMPSON, PERCY; and SIMPSON, EVELYN, eds.
        <u>Ben Jonson: Commentary, Jonson's Literary Record, Sup-</u>
        <u>plementary Notes Index</u>. Oxford: Clarendon Press, 668 pp.
        A compilation of substantive statements on Jonson during
     the seventeenth century and by major literary figures, for
     example, Charles Churchill, Alfred Lord Tennyson, and
     Thomas Carlyle, through the nineteenth century.

8   KLIEGMAN, BENJAMIN. "A 'Jonson-Shakespeare' Portrait." <u>ShN</u>
        2, no. 7 (November):35.
        Discusses the authenticity of the portrait attributed
     to Karel van Mander of Jonson and Shakespeare playing chess.

9   McELWEE, WILLIAM. The Murder of Sir Thomas Overbury. New
       York: Oxford University Press, pp. 41-42.
          Short discussion of "To Sir Thomas Overbury."

10   MUTSCHMANN, H., and WENTERSDORF, K. Shakespeare and Cathol-
       icism. New York: Sheed & Ward, pp. 124-30.
          Emphasizes Jonson's association with Catholicism, which
       was strongest during the time he and Shakespeare were closest
       friends.

11   OGBURN, DOROTHY, and OGBURN, CHARLTON. The Star of England.
       New York: Coward-McCann, passim.
          Disciples of J. Thomas Looney (1920.3), the authors find
       ample evidence in Jonson to buttress the anti-Stratfordian
       case.

12   SEVERS, J. BURKE. "Drink to Me Only . . ." N&Q 197, no. 12
       (June):262.
          Response to 1952.1. The line which Mr. Allen would
       emend is climactic in the poem, and the wording reflects
       that climactic tone.

13   THOMSON, PATRICIA. "The Literature of Patronage, 1580-1630."
       ELC 2 no. 3 (July):267-84.
          "To Penshurst" is in the genre of patronage poetry;
       however, saying so does not mean that the poem is artific-
       ial or patronizing. On the contrary, Jonson's poem is
       honest and independent.

14   WALKER, RALPH S. "Ben Jonson's Discoveries: A New Analysis."
       E&S, 5:32-51.
          Justifies the organization of Discoveries into a coher-
       ent collection of various writings and not just a haphazard
       collection of unrelated excerpts. Most important, it con-
       tains "a body of consistent critical thought, the study of
       which is essential to the understanding of Jonson's mind
       and art, and which constitutes it a work of major signif-
       icance in the history of English criticism. Revised
       1953.14.

                                  1953

1   ANON. Review of Ben Jonson of Westminster, by Marchette
       Chute. CJ 49, no. 3 (December):139.
          Announces the "attractive biography" of a great clas-
       sicist. See 1953.6.

1953

2   BRADBROOK, M. C. Review of <u>Ben Jonson: Commentary</u> . . . ,
     by C. H. Herford, Percy Simpson and Evelyn Simpson. <u>MLN</u>
     48, no. 4 (October):460.
          Announcement and short description. See 1952.7.

3   BUXTON, JOHN. "The Poets' Hall called Apollo." <u>MLR</u> 48, no.
     1 (January):52-54.
          Presents evidence that Jonson's <u>Leges Convivales</u>, a code
     of rules for the Apollo Room of the Devil Tavern, were
     written earlier than 1624 as had been previously believed,
     perhaps as early as 1619.

4   CHEW, SAMUEL C. "O Rare Ben." <u>New York Herald Tribune Book</u>
     <u>Review</u>, 1 February, p. 14.
          Review of <u>Ben Jonson: Commentary</u> . . . , edited by C.
     H. Herford, Percy Simpson, and Evelyn Simpson. A tribute
     to the Simpsons and the late C. H. Herford on the publica-
     tion of this final volume. See 1952.7.

5   _____. Review of <u>Ben Jonson of Westminster</u>, by Marchette
     Chute. <u>New York Herald Tribune Book Review</u>, 18 October,
     p. 1.
          Finds this biography brings to life the dry facts of the
     subject's life by surrounding them with the color and pag-
     entry of Renaissance London. See 1953.6.

6   CHUTE, MARCHETTE. <u>Ben Jonson of Westminster</u>. New York: E.
     P. Dutton & Co., 380 pp.
          Critical biography of Jonson. There is a strong emphasis
     on background material to give more color to Jonson's life,
     but there is also sound criticism. A general discussion of
     the poetry emphasizes Jonson's own attitude toward his work
     while surveying the variety of poetic styles Jonson adapt-
     ed.

7   DAVIE, DONALD. <u>Purity of Diction in English Verse</u>. New York:
     Oxford University Press, pp. 199-202.
          In <u>Discoveries</u> Jonson sought a middle ground in poetry
     between too much strength and too much ease.

8   GREG, W. W. Review of <u>Ben Jonson: Commentary</u> . . . , edited
     by C. H. Herford, Percy Simpson, and Evelyn Simpson. <u>RES</u>,
     4, no. 15 (July):285.
          A brief tribute to the editors for seeing this fifty-
     year project through to its conclusion. A short description
     of Vol. 11. See 1952.7.

9   HARBAGE, ALFRED. Review of <u>Ben Jonson of Westminster</u>, by
     Marchette Chute. <u>New York Times Book Review</u>, 18 October,
     p. 3.

1954

Miss Chute is better on background than on Jonson and weakest on literary criticism. She is far too much an apologist for Jonson. Like Dryden, she should allow us to admire Jonson without loving him. See 1953.6.

10   KRUTCH, JOSEPH WOOD. Review of Ben Jonson of Westminster, by Marchette Chute. SatR (17 October):13-14.
        An excellent interpretation of Jonson though there is more that could be said and different interpretations of the same facts that could be given. See 1953.6.

11   O'CONOR, NORREYS JEPHSON. Review of Ben Jonson of Westminster, by Marchette Chute. ArQ, no. 1 (Spring):89-90.
        An excellent biography which "makes an understandable mosaic from the various parts, at the same time keeping cross strains of thought and feeling clearly in view and in proper perspective." Miss Chute "wears her scholarship with a difference, perhaps because she never forgets that people in past times were as lively, adventurous, and passionate as are men and women today." See 1953.6.

12   PROUTY, CHARLES TYLER. "Two Elizabethans." YR 43, no. 3 (March):471-73.
        Review of Ben Jonson of Westminster, by Marchette Chute. The background is painted in vivid colors, but the figure of Jonson himself never quite emerges. See 1953.6.

13   SIMPSON, PERCY. "A Westminster Schoolboy and Ben Jonson." TLS, 27 November, p. 761.
        Prints a newly discovered elegy on Ben Jonson by Gyles Oldisworth, who complains that the authorities have money for everything but a proper monument for Jonson.

14   WALKER, RALPH S., ed. Ben Jonson's Timber or Discoveries. Syracuse, N.Y.: Syracuse University Press.
        Revised versions of 1934.21; 1951.13; and 1952.14.

15   WITHINGTON, ELEANOR. "Nicholas Brist and Jonson's Commendation of Joseph Rutter." N&Q 198, no. 4 (April):152-53.
        An explication of the last twelve lines of Jonson's commendatory poem to Joseph Rutter's Shepheard's Holy-Day. See 1954.8.

1954

1   ANON. "The World of Ben Jonson." TLS, 31 December, p. 851.
        Review of Ben Jonson's Westminster, by Marchette Chute.

1954

Although Miss Chute has unvocered nothing new about Jonson, she has sifted carefully and arranged the facts accurately for her biography. See 1953.6.

2 BLANSHARD, RUFUS A. "Thomas Carew and the Cavlier Poets." Transactions of the Wisconsin Academy of Sciences Arts and Letters 43 (1954):97-105.
Reviews Jonson's influence on Carew and others. "Jonson's careful attention to form and decorum, his distaste for tortured and obscure displays of wit, his solid classical learning, his control of tone and idea, set a critical and practical standard comparable to Dryden's in its authority."

3 BUXTON, JOHN. Sir Philip Sidney and the English Renaissance. London: Macmillan, 283 pp.
See 1964.4.

*4 CUBETA, PAUL M. "A Critical Study of Ben Jonson's Non-Dramatic Poetry." Ph.D. dissertation, Yale University.
Cited in Brock and Welsh, 1974.9.

5 EVANS, ROBERT OWEN. "The Theory and Practice of Poetic Elision from Chaucer to Milton with Special Emphasis on Milton." Ph.D. dissertation, University of Florida.
Jonson is studied along with a number of other poets who made extensive use of elision in their verse.

6 HEMPHILL, GEORGE. "Jonson's 'Fit of Rime against Rime.'" Expl 12, no. 7 (May), item 50.
Argues for a broad definition of the word "rime." "All conventions of verse, particularly the modern ones."

7 HOLDEN, WILLIAM P. Anti-Puritan Satire, 1572-1642. Yale Studies in English, vol. 126. New Haven: Yale University Press.
Remarks on Jonson's anti-Puritan epigrams.

8 JOHNSTON, GEORGE BURKE. "'An Epistle Medicant' by Ben Jonson." N&Q 199, no. 11 (November):471.
A gloss for "want" in Jonson's epistle. Believes the word should be emended "wants" meaning "moles as military engineers or pioneers, digging trenches and undermining the fortifications of the 'Bed-rid Wit.'"

9 _____, ed. Introduction to Poems of Ben Jonson. Muses Library. Cambridge, Mass.: Harvard University Press, pp. xxiii-xlv.
A survey of Jonson's most important poems concludes, "The poems as a whole do not have the stature of the great

comedies; but to borrow Ben's image, lilies have their
beauties as well as oaks, and to stretch it further, much
may be said for onions and thistles." Reprinted in 1962.10.

10 MAIN, C. F. "Two Items in the Jonson Apocrypha." N&Q 199,
no. 6 (June):243-45.
Argues that "Epitaph on an Honest Lawyer" and "On the
Countess Dowager of Pembroke" should be attributed to
Jonson.

11 RØSTVIG, MAREN-SOFIE. The Happy Man: Studies in the Metamor-
phoses of a Classical Ideal, 1600-1700. Oxford: Oxford
University Press, passim.
The popularity of the beatus ille theme in seventeenth-
century poetry is apparent in Jonson's "To Penshurst" as
well as several other of his poems.

12 SCHIRMER, WALTER F. Geschichte der englische und amerikanis-
chen literatur. Vol. 1. Tubingen: Max Niemeyer Verlag,
pp. 316-18.
Jonson's lyric purity contrasted sharply with his contemporaries and influential younger writers such as Herrick and Carew.

13 TILLYARD, E. M. W. The English Epic and Its Background. Lon-
don: Chatto & Windus, passim.
Jonson's critical remarks on the epic are traced to
Aristotle and Heinsius.

14 WARD, A. C. "Ben Jonson." In Illustrated History of English Literature. Vol. 2. New York: Longmans, Green &
Co., pp. 1-8.
Points out the great differences between the scurrility
of Jonson's plays and the astonishing beauty of his lyric
poetry.

1955

1 ANON. "Ben Jonson The Poet." TLS 6 May, p. 236.
Review of Poems of Ben Jonson, edited by George Burke
Johnston. Jonson's poetry is roughly on a par with Herrick's. It is his drama or the lyrics from the plays
which give Jonson his reputation as a major literary figure. Moreover in this edition Johnston's preoccupation
with "archaeology" as opposed to "poetry" is tiresome.
The reviewer harkens back to the "cheerful, if slapdash
doctrine of Sir Arthur Quiller-Couch and Professor Saintsbury, that it is the poetry that counts. . . ." See 1954.8.

1955

2   BLANSHARD, RUFUS A. "Carew and Jonson." <u>SP</u> 52, no. 2 (April): 195-211.

A generic study of Jonson's influence on Carew. Although Carew never acknowledges a debt to Jonson as he does to Donne, and although there are fewer borrowings from Jonson than Donne, Jonson's influence may be seen in the similar types of occasional poems the two write and in the similar ways each handles these types.

3   BRYCE, J. C. Review of <u>Ben Jonson's Timber or Discoveries</u>, edited by Ralph S. Walker. <u>Aberdeen Univ. Review</u> 36, no. 113 (Autumn):189-90.

Generally agrees with Walker's rearrangement and reorganization of Jonson's text into a more coherent and useful book. See 1953.14.

*4   ENGLISH, HUBERT M., Jr. "Prosody and Meaning in Ben Jonson's Poems." Ph.D. dissertation, Yale University.

Cited in Brock and Welsh, 1974.9.

*5   GREENSLADE, B. D. "The Falkland Circle: A Study in Tradition from Jonson to Halifax." Ph.D. dissertation, London, University College.

Cited in Guffey, 1968.5.

6   HEUER, HERMANN. Review of <u>Ben Jonson of Westminster</u>, by Marchette Chute. <u>SJH</u> 91:317-18.

Brief publication announcement noting the nonscholarly, popular, somewhat romanticized quality of the book. See 1953.6.

7   JOHNSTON, GEORGE BURKE. "Ben Jonson's Poems." <u>TLS</u>, 10 June, p. 317.

Restrained response to 1955.1 pointing out some factual errors in the review.

8   _____. "Jonson's 'Perseus Upon Pegasus.'" <u>RES</u>, 6, no. 21 (January):65-67.

A gloss on line seven of "An Epigram to William, Earl of Newcastle," which takes issue with Herford and the Simpsons' note on the line. See 1955.14.

9   MAXWELL, J. C. "Ben Jonson's Poems." <u>TLS</u>, 3 June, p. 310.

Review of <u>Poems of Ben Jonson</u>, edited by George Burke Johnston. Criticizes Johnston for his conservative editing and reluctance to emend what appears to be errors in the earlier editions. Maxwell refers to this style of editing as "Foliolatry." See 1954.9.

10   McLEOD, A. L.   Review of Poems of Ben Jonson, edited by George
     Burke Johnston.   Books Abroad 29, no. 4 (Autumn):473.
          Announcement of "perhaps the best single-volume edition
     of Jonson's poems."   See 1954.9.

11   MORRISON, MARY.   "A Possible Source for Ben Jonson's 'Execra-
     tion Upon Vulcan.'"   RLC 29 (1955):249-50.
          The French humanist Nicolas Bourbon may have provided
     the starting point for Jonson's poem.   In Nugae published
     1533 Bourbon has a poem describing the loss of many of his
     books and manuscripts in a fire.

12   POIRIER, MICHEL.   Review of Poems of Ben Jonson, edited by
     George Burke Johnston.   EA 8, no. 4 (October-December):
     339-40.
          A short publication announcement and description.   See
     1954.9.

13   _____.   Review of Ben Jonson of Westminster, by Marchette
     Chute.   EA 8, no. 4 (October-December):339-40.
          Brief though favorable review.   See 1953.6.

14   REEVES, JOHN D.   "Perseus and the Flying Horse in Peele and
     Heywood."   RES 6, no. 24 (October):397-99.
          Additional comment on 1955.8 centering on Jonson's con-
     fusion of Perseus and Bellerophon.

15   RYAN, PAT, Jr.   Review of Poems of Ben Jonson, edited by
     George Burke Johnston.   QJS 42, no. 1 (February):100.
          "A splendid new text" which will hopefully increase
     Jonson's popularity among the general reading public.
     See 1954.9.

16   SIRLUCK, ERNEST.   "Shakespeare and Jonson Among the Pamphleteers
     of the First Civil War: Some Unreported Seventeenth-
     Century Allusions."   MP 53, no. 2 (November):88-99.
          Cites a number of allusions to Jonson and Shakespeare
     which had previously gone unnoticed.   Sirluck notes that
     "what is quite clear . . . is that Puritan Pamphleteers,
     writing almost exclusively for their own party, counted on
     a rather detailed knowledge of Shakespeare's and Jonson's
     plays and continued to do so long after the theaters were
     closed."

17   STARNES, DeWITT T., and TALBERT, ERNEST WILLIAM.   "Ben Jonson
     and the Dictionaries." In Classical Myth and Legend in
     Renaissance Dictionaries.   Chapel Hill: University of North
     Carolina Press, pp. 135-212.

1955

> A discussion of the manner in which Jonson utilized dic-
> tionary information on mythology in his poems and plays
> with special emphasis on the masques.

18   STEWART, J. I. M. "By Pindar's Fire." New Statesman and
       Nation, 2d ser. 49 (22 January):110-11.
       Review of Poems of Ben Jonson, edited by George Burke
       Johnston. "A useful minor edition." Stewart is not com-
       pletely happy with the biography in the introduction. See
       1954.9.

19   THAYER, C. G. Review of Ben Jonson's Timber or Discoveries,
       edited by Ralph W. Walker. Books Abroad 29, no. 1 (Win-
       ter):100.
       Announcement of a new and convenient text. See 1953.14.

20   WALTON, GEOFFREY. Metaphysical to Augustan: Studies in Tone
       and Sensibility in the Seventeenth Century. London: Bowes,
       passim.
       Defines Jonson's place in the history of poetry between
       the metaphysical wit and the "social poise" of Restoration
       wit. Explores different areas in Jonson's poetry bring-
       ing the reader's attention to poems he might not otherwise
       have noted. Walton concludes that Jonson's poetry "even
       more than his plays, links seventeenth century culture
       and the polite civilization of the Augustans to the better
       features of the medieval social order and to the half
       religious ideal of Courtesy." Reprinted in 1962.19; 1974.33.

1956

1   BARNHART, CLARENCE, ed. "Ben Jonson." In The New Century
      Handbook of English Literature. New York: Appleton-Cen-
      tury-Crofts, pp. 634-35.
      Life and works article with predictable comparison to
      Shakespeare.

2   BENHAM, ALLEN R. "Horace and His Ars Poetica in English: A
      Bibliography." Classical Weekly 49, no. 1 (17 October):
      1-5.
      Jonson's translation was the third in English, though
      numerous others followed.

3   BRADBROOK, F. W. "Ben Jonson's Poetry." In From Donne to
      Marvell. The Pelican Guide to English Literature. Vol. 3.
      Edited by Boris Ford. Baltimore: Penguin Books, pp. 131-
      41.

A survey of Jonson's poetry noting the variety of verse, his care and accuracy in composition, his careful reflection and criticism of poetry, and, of course, the interesting influence of the classics.

4   BROWN, CALVIN S., ed. The Reader's Companion to World Litera-
    ture. New York: Dryden Press.
        "Even in an age when every hack playwright could turn
    out good lyrics, Jonson was outstanding; and his younger
    contemporaries, the Cavlier Poets, modeled their verses
    on his. . . ."

5   BUCHAN, HANNAH. Review of Poems of Ben Jonson, edited by
    George Burke Johnston. RES 7, no. 26 (April):214-15.
        Favorable note on both Jonson's poems and Johnston's
    edition. See 1954.9.

6   BULLETT, GERALD. "'Drink to Me Only . . . '" TLS, 1 June,
    p. 329.
        Suggests that a printer's error altered the meaning of
    "To Celia," for it appears that the poet would not change
    Jove's necture for Celia's. See 1956.10 and 1956.14.

7   CHURCHILL, CHARLES. Poetical Works. Edited by Douglas Grant.
    Oxford: Clarendon Press.
        Reprint of 1761.1.

8   DAICHES, DAVID. "Ben Jonson." In Critical Approaches to
    Literature. Englewood Cliffs, N. J.: Prentice Hall, pp.
    176-82.
        Emphasizes the practical nature of Jonson's criticism,
    which although different from "the way we use the term
    when we refer to the evaluation of individual works . . . ,
    derives from the same habit of mind as that which turns
    most readily to the assessment of works of literature and
    is less happy in philosophical discussion of its nature."

9   EVANS, A. J. Shakespeare's Magic Circle. Westport, Conn.:
    Associated Booksellers, pp. 76-78.
        Believes that "Poet-ape" was written with Shakespeare,
    the actor, in mind, and it certainly had nothing to do
    with the man who wrote the poems and plays we normally
    associate with Shakespeare.

10 GEORGE, DANIEL. "'Drink to me only . . .'" TLS, 8 June,
    p. 345.
        Response to 1956.6. Calling attention to another ambig-
    uity in the poem, wonders if Celia were wearing perfume.
    See 1956.14.

1956

11 HERRICK, ROBERT. <u>The Poetical Works of Robert Herrick</u>, edited
    by L. C. Martin. Oxford: Clarendon Press.
      Reprint of 1648.2.

12 HEUER, HERMANN. Review of <u>Poems of Ben Jonson</u>, edited by
    George Burke Johnston. <u>SJH</u> 92 (1956):364.
      Publication notice with brief description of Johnston's
    edition. See 1954.9.

13 HIBBARD, G. R. "The Country House Poem of the Seventeenth
    Century." <u>JWCI</u> 19:159-74.
      Traces the history and significance of the country house
    poem from Jonson's "To Penshurst" and "Sir Robert Wroth"
    through Carew's "To Saxham" and "To my Friend G. N. from
    Wrest" and Herrick's "A Country-life: to his brother Mr.
    Thomas Herrick" and "A Panegyrick to Sir Lewis Pemberton,"
    concluding with Marvell's "Upon Appleton House." Hibbard
    discusses the construction of homes and the way in which
    the home reflected certain values. Jonson's poems also
    reflect this idea and become a pattern of other country
    house poems of the early seventeenth century.

14 HORSMAN, E. A. "'Drink to me only . . .'" <u>TLS</u>, 8 June, p.
    345.
      Response to 1956.6. "Change" should be read in its
    seventeenth-century context as "exchange," meaning the
    poet would not exchange Celia's necture for Jove's. See
    1956.10.

15 JAYNE, SEARS R. <u>Library Catalogues of the English Renaissance.</u>
    Berkeley: University of California Press, passim.
      See the index for items of Jonsonian interest.

*16 LANGVARDT, ARTHUR LeROY. "The Verse Epigram in England during
    the Sixteenth and Early Seventeenth Centuries." Ph.D. dis-
    sertation, Univeristy of Colorado.
      Cited in Brock and Welsh, 1974.9.

1957

1 CALDIERO, FRANK. "Ben Jonson's Course in Freshman English."
    <u>CE</u> 19, no. 1 (October):7-11.
      Cites Jonson's comments on style in <u>Discoveries</u> as a
    basis for teaching freshman English and humanistic values.
    Jonson recommends reading the best authors, listening to
    the best speakers, and lots of practice.

2 GERRITSEN, JOHAN. Review of <u>Ben Jonson: Commentary . . .</u> ,
    edited by C. H. Herford, Percy Simpson and Evelyn Simpson.
    <u>ES</u> 38:120-26.
       A detailed study of some of the textual problems in
    Herford and the Simpsons' edition. See 1952.7.

3 HOLMES, CHARLES S., FUSSELL, EDWIN et al, eds. "Ben Jonson."
    In <u>Major Critics</u>. New York: Alfred A. Knopf, pp.71-87.
       Jonson is not a pedant venerating the past for its own
    sake. Instead he used the wisdom of the ancients to under-
    stand better the literary problems of the present.

4 JOHN, LISLE CECIL. "Ben Jonson's 'To Sir William Sidney, on
    his Birthday,'" <u>MLR</u> 52, no. 2 (April):168-76.
       Extensive commentary on the life of Sir William Sidney,
    who died at the age of 22, one year after Jonson wrote his
    poem. Jonson's poem should be read as an admonition to
    Sir William to live up to his distinguished name.

5 LEGOUIS, EMILE [HYACINTHE]. <u>A History of English Literature</u>.
    New York: Macmillan Co., pp. 3340-43.
       Revision of 1926.7. Reprint of 1935.14.

6 McGINNIS, PAUL J. "Ben Jonson's 'Discoveries.'" <u>N&Q</u> 202,
    no. 4 (April):162-63.
       Traces borrowings in <u>Discoveries</u> from Juan Luis Vives
    and Seneca.

7 MILES, JOSEPHIN. <u>Eras and Modes in English Poetry</u>. Berkeley:
    University of California Press, passim.
       Traces Jonson's position in the tradition of English
    poetry from Skelton to Yeats.

8 MOLONEY, MICHAEL F. "The Prosody of Milton's <u>Epitaph</u>, <u>L'Allegro</u>
    and <u>Il Penseroso</u>." <u>MLN</u> 72, no. 3 (March):174-78.
       A comparative study of the metrics of Jonson's epitaphs
    with those in "L'Allegro" and "Il Penseroso."

9 MUSGROVE, SYDNEY. <u>Shakespeare and Jonson</u>. The Macmillan
    Brown Lectures. Auckland University College Bulletin, no.
    51, English Series, no. 9. Auckland: Auckland University
    College, 55 pp.
       Identifies two phases of Jonson's criticism of Shake-
    speare. The first phase "was reported badly, perhaps with
    some malice, but certainly without full comprehension, by
    the Scottish poet Drummond of Hawthornden. . . . The sec-
    ond phase is taken from the memorial poem which Jonson
    contributed to the first folio of 1623."

1957

10   OSBORN, JAMES M. "Ben Jonson and the Eccentric Lord Stanhope."
     TLS, 4 January, p. 16.
        A description of Lord Charles Stanhope's marginal nota-
     tions in his 1640 edition of Jonson's Works.

11   P., R. "Jonson's 'To John Donne.'" Expl 16, no. 3 (December):
     25.
        Query on the meaning of the poem with particular refer-
     ence to line 5 "a knowing," line 6 reference of "which,"
     and the construction of line 7. See 1958.3.

12   RACE, SYDNEY. "Harleian MS 6395 and its Editor." N&Q 202, no.
     2 (February):77-79.
        Information on anecdotes about Jonson.

*13 STICKNEY, RUTH FRANCES. "Formal Verse Satire from Lodge to
     Jonson with Particular Reference to the Imitation of
     Classical Models." Ph.D. dissertation, University of
     Minnesota.
        Cited in Brock and Welsh, 1974.9.

*14 TRIMPI, WILLIAM WESLEY, Jr. "The Classical Plain Style and
     Ben Jonson's Poems." Ph.D. dissertation, Harvard Univer-
     sity.
        Cited in Trimpi, 1962.17.

15   VAN DEUSEN, MARSHALL. "Criticism and Ben Jonson's 'To Celia.'"
     EIC 7, no. 1 (January):95-103.
        Discusses various interpretations of "To Celia" among
     the Stanford University faculty.

*16 WESTON, E. "The Poetry of Ben Jonson." Ph.D. dissertation,
     University of Nottingham.
        Cited in Brock and Welsh, 1974.9.

17   WILSON, JOHN DOVER. "Shakespeare's 'Small Latin'--How Much?"
     ShS 10:12-26.
        A thorough exploration of the accuracy of Jonson's obser-
     vation.

18   WIMSATT, WILLIAM K., Jr., and BROOKS, CLEANTH. "English Neo-
     Classicism: Jonson and Dryden." In Literary Criticism:
     A Short History. New York: Alfred A. Knopf, pp. 174-95.
        Emphasis on the tradition and style of Jonson's satire.
     "Jonson wrote a kind of native classicism which it has
     been difficult for any audience since the mid- 18th cen-
     tury really to enjoy--obscene yet moralizing, caustic,
     thorny, vulgar, immediate, Londonian and topical (and so
     now obscure). It was Roman satiric technique applied to
     London vice, and a solid instance of the Augustan principle
     of imitation or recreating of the classical model."

1   BARISH, JONAS A. "Baroque Prose in the Theatre: Ben Jonson."
     PMLA 73, no. 3 (June):184-95.
          An examination of Jonson's prose style, some character-
     istics of which, such as asymmetrical qualities and avoid-
     ance of the mellifluous, are found in his poetry as well.

2   BENTLEY, GERALD EADES. Review of Shakespeare and Jonson, by
     Sydney Musgrove. SQ 9, no. 4 (Autumn):575.
          Finds lectures to be an interesting and persuasive pres-
     entation. See 1957.9.

3   COMBELLACK, FREDERICK M. "Jonson's 'To John Donne.'" Expl 17,
     no. 1 (October):6.
          Response to 1957.11. Paraphrase of the poem focusing
     on the meaning of "wit." See 1966.19.

4   CUBETA, PAUL M. "'A Celebration of Charis': An Evaluation of
     Jonsonian Poetic Strategy." ELH 25, no. 3 (September):
     163-80.
          Jonson combines the mode of classical poetry with the
     manner of sixteenth- and seventeenth-century contemporary
     verse.

*5   HAWORTH, W. "Ben Jonson's Criticism: A Study of its Place
     in the Development of English Literary Criticism in the
     Sixteenth and Seventeenth Centuries, up to 1650." Ph.D.
     dissertation, Manchester University.
          Cited in Brock and Welsh, 1974.9.

6   HOWARTH, HERBERT. "Falkland and Duppa's Jonsonus Virbius."
     Expl 17, no. 2 (November), item 11.
          Title of the memorial volume on Jonson emphasizes the
     chastity of Jonson's muse.

7   JOHNSTON, GEORGE BURKE. "An Apocryphal Jonsonian Epigram."
     N&Q 203, no. 12 (December):542-44.
          Prints a poem ascribed to Jonson and written on the fly
     leaf of a copy of the 1640 Works. Johnston does not
     believe the poem is actually by Jonson.

8   ROSKY, WILLIAM. "Imagination in the English Renaissance:
     Psychology and Poetic." SRen 5 (1958):49-73.
          Commentary on the reading and writing of poetry in the
     late English Renaissance. Although there was suspicion
     about imaginative writing, critics such as Sidney and Jon-
     son, looking back to Aristotle, contended that a greater
     realism could be achieved through imagination.

1958

9 STEADMAN, JOHN M. "'Perseus upon Pegasus' and 'Ovid Moralized.'"
   <u>RES</u> 9, no. 36 (November):407-10.
         Further notes on Jonson's allusion in "An Epigram to
   William, Earle of Newcastle."

10 WATSON, GEORGE. "Ramus, Miss Tuve, and the New Petromachia."
   <u>MP</u> 55, no. 4 (May):259-62.
         Argues against the wide literary influence of Ramus,
   but admits that there are plausible reasons to suggest
   that Jonson did feel some effects of Ramus influence.

<u>1959</u>

1 BAMBOROUGH, J. B. <u>Ben Jonson</u>. Writers and their Works, no.
   112. London: Longman, Green & Co., 43 pp.
         General study of Jonson's life, reputation, and works.
   One is likely not to find Jonson completely satisfactory
   as a poet. "While Jonson's use of words is always precise,
   vigorous and meaningful, he almost always brings into play
   only their immediate denotatory or 'dictionary' significance,
   and only rarely calls up their complete range of suggestion,
   evocation or emotive power."

2 _____. Review of <u>Shakespeare and Jonson</u>, by Sydney Musgrove.
   <u>RES</u> 10, no. 39 (August):308.
         Finds an interesting and different point of view on
   Shakespeare and Jonson; however, to make his point Musgrove's comparisons are sometimes "overstrained." See
   1957.9.

3 BROWN, A. D. FITTON. "Drink to Me, Celia." <u>MLR</u> 54, no. 4
   (October):554-57.
         Attempts to discover what edition of Philostratus's
   <u>Epistles</u> Jonson was using when he wrote his famous song.

*4 COHEN, GERALD. "A Comparative Evaluation of the Pastoral
   Tradition in English and French Literature in the Early
   Seventeenth Century." Ph.D. dissertation, University of
   Washington.
         Cited in Brock and Welsh, 1974.9.

5 COPE, JACKSON, I. "Jonson's Reading of Spenser: The Genesis
   of a Poem." <u>EM</u> 10:61-66.
         Jonson's "Epistle to Elizabeth, Countesse of Rutland"
   is a reworking of Spenser's <u>The Ruines of Time</u>.

6 DANIEL, GEORGE. <u>The Selected Poems of George Daniel of Beswick
   1616-1657</u>. Edited by Thomas B. Stroup. Lexington: University of Kentucky Press, pp. 28-30.

1959

Reprint of 1646.1 (selected) and 1952.7.

7   EVERETT, BARBARA. "Ben Jonson's 'A Vision of Beauty.'" CritQ
     1, no. 3 (Autumn):238-44.
         Lyric beauty and clarity are the characteristics of this
     poem which also has traces of Jonson's satire.

8   GERRITSEN, JOHAN. "Stansby and Jonson Produce a Folio: A Pre-
     liminary Account." ES 40:52-55.
         Through an examination of Jonson's First Folio, con-
     cludes that the volume was set and printed in 1615 and 1616,
     not two years earlier with a major interruption as suggested
     by Herford and Simpson.

9   KERNAN, ALVIN. The Cankered Muse: Satire of the English
     Renaissance. Yale Studies in English, vol. 142. New Haven:
     Yale University Press, passim.
         Jonson's satiric techniques varied and were influential
     on eighteenth-century writers.

10   MAIN, C. F. "Ben Jonson and an Unknown Poet on the King's
     Senses." MLN 74, no. 5 (May):389-93.
         A further comment on 1947.4. Believes that Drummond did
     not write "For the Kinge" as Gilbert suggested. Instead,
     Jonson's song in Gypisies Metamorphos'd was probably the
     basis on which the libel "For the Kinge" was written though
     its author is unknown.

11   MASON, H. A. Humanism and Poetry in the Early Tudor Period.
     London: Routledge & Kegan Paul, pp. 255-89.
         "When the classics are his commanders, Jonson is a
     pendant: when they serve as guides, Jonson is capable of
     surpassing them."

12   McGINNIS, PAUL J. "Ben Jonson on Savile's Tacitus." CJ 55,
     no. 3 (December):120-21.
         Discusses Jonson's epigram, "To Sir Henrie Savile."
     Savile was the translator of Tacitus's Histories wherein
     Jonson was able to find a philosophy of history which ac-
     corded with his own.

13   MURRAY, W. A. "What was the Soul of the Apple?" RES 10,
     no. 38 (May):141-55.
         Jonson's remark to Drummond regarding Donne's purpose of
     the conceit in Metempsychosis has essentially misled critics
     for many years.

14   TAYLOR, DICK, Jr. "Clarendon and Ben Jonson as Witnesses for
     the Earl of Pembroke's Character." In Studies in the English

1959

Renaissance Drama. Edited by Josephine W. Bennett, Oscar
Cargill, and Vernon Hall, Jr. New York: New York University Press, pp. 322-44.
   Jonson's testimony on the Earl of Pembroke's character
found in The Gypsies Metamorphosed is very significant
because of Jonson's "long and immediate knowledge of court
affairs and his own sturdy integrity."

1960

1   BAMBOROUGH, J. B. "The Early Life of Ben Jonson." TLS, 8
      April, p. 225.
         New information on Jonson when he was a bricklayer.

2   BERRY, HERBERT, and TIMINGS, E. K. "Spenser's Pension." RES
      11, no. 43 (August):254-259.
         Traces the history of Spenser's pension payments and
      concludes that Jonson's remark to Drummond that Spenser
      died of starvation is false.

3   CHUTE, MARCHETTE. Two Gentle Men: The Lives of George Herbert
      and Robert Herrick. London: Secker & Warburg, pp. 184-91.
         Herrick appears not to have actually been "sealed of the
      tribe of Ben," but he greatly admired Jonson. Herrick was
      influenced more by Jonson's learning than his poetry;
      hence, Herrick tended to follow classical models, particu-
      larly Horace, in writing his own poetry.

4   DAICHES, DAVID. "Poetry after Spenser: The Jonsonian and
      Metaphysical Traditions." In A Critical History of English
      Literature. New York: Ronald Press, pp. 346-89.
         Both Jonson's and Donne's poems were reactions to Spenser,
      though they went in different directions. "Jonson, with
      his sense of decorum, clarity, proportion, and classical
      form, brought to lyric poetry both a craftmanship and a
      tone which owed much to classical poets of Rome. . .and
      at the same time never seemed far removed from colloquial
      English and from the tough realism of the commonsense
      approach."

5   DONNER, H. W. Review of Humanism and Poetry in the Early
      Tudor Period, by H. A. Mason. RES 11, no. 43 (August):
      317-19.
         Brief remarks on Mason's treatment of Vives and Jonson.
      See 1959.11.

6   ELLRODT, ROBERT. Lew Poètes Metaphysiques Anglais. Seconde
      Partie. Paris: Librairie José Corti, passim.
         References to Jonson's role in the development of seven-
      teenth-century poetry and criticism.

7   FIELER, FRANK B. "The Impact of Bacon and the New Science
      Upon Jonson's Critical Thought in 'Timber.'" RenP, pp.
      84.92.

Even though everything Jonson says in Discoveries had
been said by someone before, it is nevertheless an original
work because of "his reasoned selection. He took no one
as a dictator, but questioned everyone, taking those beliefs
of other writers which he himself could defend." He followed Bacon in the general break with classical authority.
His concern with literal truth in poetry predates Thomas
Hobbes.

8   GUIDI, AUGUSTO, ed. Lirica Elisabettiana. Collani di Lettera-
      ture Moderne, no. 12. Naples: Edizioni Scientifiche Itlaiane,
      pp. 160-70.
         A short selection of poetry with critical remarks noting
      Jonson's neoclassicism.

9   HENINGER, S. K., Jr. A Handbook of Renaissance Meteorology,
      with Particular Reference to Elizabethan and Jacobean Lit-
      erature. Durham, N.C.: Duke University Press, 281 pp.
         Renaissance explanations of weather phenomena. Chapter
      three of Part II deals specifically with Jonson.

10 JONES, EMRYS. Review of Humanism and Poetry in the Early
      Tudor Period, by H. A. Mason. EIC 10:329-34.
         Criticizes Mason for being "arbitrary in his presentation."
      See 1959.11.

11 JUNGNELL, TORE. "Notes on the Language of Ben Jonson." SMS.
      1:86-110.
         Grammatical and syntactical phenomena found in Jonson's
      Works 1616 including the use of definite and indefinite
      articles, nouns, adjectives, possessive pronouns, etc.

12 MADDISON, CAROL. Apollo and the Nine: A History of the Ode.
      Baltimore: Johns Hopkins Press, pp. 296-304.
         Reviews Jonson's contribution to the history and devel-
      opment of the English ode along with the influence of the
      ode on Jonson's other poetry.

13 MILES, JOSEPHINE. Renaissance, Eighteenth Century, and Mod-
      ern Language in English Poetry. A Tabular View. Berkeley:
      University of California Press, passim.
         Jonson's use of nouns and verbs is analyzed.

14 MURRAY, W. A. "Ben Jonson and Dr. Mayerne." TLS, 2 September,
      p. 561.
         A parallel in Discoveries with a medical pamphlet print-
      ed in 1603.

1960

15 OLDHAM, JOHN. <u>Poems of John Oldham</u>. Edited by Bonamy Dobrée.
    Carbondale: Southern Illinois University Press.
        Reprint of 1683.1.

16 REDDING, DAVID C. "A Note on Jonson Attribution." <u>N&Q</u> 205,
    no. 2 (February):52-53.
        A poem, "In a fish came a dish," attributed to Jonson
    but which Herford and Simpson thought was by Shadwell,
    existed long before Shadwell was writing.

17 SPENCER, HAZELTON. "Ben Jonson." In <u>British Literature</u>. Vol.
    1. 2d ed. Boston: D. C. Heath, pp. 437-46.
        Describes the difference between Jonson and Donne and
    notes that although we may consider the latter a better
    poet, Jonson had more influence on subsequent generations.
    (Earlier editions not seen.)

                            <u>1961</u>

1   ALDEN, RAYMOND MacDONALD. <u>The Rise of Formal Satire in Eng-
    land</u>. University of Pennsylvania Series in Philology,
    Literature and Archaeology, vol. 7, no. 2. Hamden, Conn.:
    Archon Books.
        Reprint of 1899.1.

2   ALEXANDER, PETER. <u>Shakespeare's Life and Art</u>. New York: New
    York University Press.
        Reprint of 1939.1.

3   BAMBOROUGH, J. B. "Joyce and Jonson." <u>REL</u> 2, no. 4 (October):
    45-50.
        Jonson is one of four authors whose complete works Joyce
    read. This essay examines evidence of Jonson's influence
    on Joyce.

4   BLUMENTHAL, WALTER HART. <u>Paging Mr. Shakespeare: A Critical
    Challenge</u>. New York: University Publishers, passim.
        Numerous references to Jonson as Shakespeare's most
    important contemporary.

5   CLUBB, ROBERT L. "The Paradox of Ben Jonson's 'A Fit of Rime
    Against Rime.'" <u>CLAJ</u> 5, no. 2 (December):145-47.
        Jonson's poem appears paradoxical since he used rime in
    his own poetry; however, he is actually ridiculing the
    "inferior contemporary way of riming," while he "pays defer-
    ence to the permanent and superior classical ideal of un-
    rhymed quantitative verse."

                            178

1961

6   DOUGLASS, JAMES W.   "'To Penshurst'." Christian Scholar 44,
    no. 2 (Summer):133-38.
        Takes an "I to thou" approach to the poem rather than
    a "we to a thing" approach. "To Penshurst" is about a
    state of being rather than the description of something.

7   HOLLANDER, JOHN.   Introduction to Ben Jonson. New York: Dell,
    pp. 1-15.
        Surveys Jonson's poetry and emphasizes the ease with
    which his verse could be set to music.

8   _____. The Untuning of the Sky. Princeton, N. J.: Princeton
    University Press, passim.
        Jonson is one of a number of poets whose verse was gov-
    erned by its musical modality.

9   HOWARTH, HERBERT.   "Shakespeare's Gentleness." ShS 14:90-97.
        In line 56 of his "To the Memory of My Beloved . . . Mr.
    William Shakespeare," Jonson says "My gentle Shakespeare."
    Discusses the definition of "gentle" and attempts to deter-
    mine if Shakespeare's character conforms to this definition.

10 KAUFMANN, R. J.   "Under the Seal of Ben." In Richard Brome:
    Caroline Playwright. New York: Columbia University
    Press, pp. 35-46.
        Describes Jonson's friendship with Brome, of which
    "unfortunately we know too little."

11 MAY, LOUIS F.   "Jonson's Epitaph on Solomon Pavy." Expl 20,
    no. 2 (September), item 16.
        "The rhetorical pattern of exaggeration attributes the
    accomplishments of an old man to a precocious boy and thus
    fuses a youth-maturity polarity into something of a para-
    dox."

12 NEWDIGATE, BERNARD H.   Michael Drayton and His Circle. Oxford:
    Shakespeare Head Press, passim.
        Reprint of 1941.8.

13 OSGOOD, CHARLES G[ROSVENOR].   "Epithalamion and Prothalamion:
    'and theyr eccho ring.'" MLN 76, no. 3 (March):205-8.
        Jonson's epithalamions show a strong influence of Spen-
    ser's metrical style.

14 SAINTSBURY, GEORGE.   A History of English Prosody.   3 vols.
    New York: Russell & Russell.
        Reprint of 1908.10.

179

1961

15 SCHELLING, FELIX E. "Ben Jonson and the Classical School."
    In Essential Articles: For the Study of English Augustan
    Backgrounds. Edited by Bernard H. Schelling. Hamden, Conn.:
    Shoe String Press, pp. 173-97.
        Reprint of 1898.8.

16 WALLERSTEIN, RUTH C. "The Development of the Rhetoric and
    Metre of the Heroic Couplet, Especially in 1625-1645."
    In Essential Articles: For the Study of English Augustan
    Backgrounds. Edited by Bernard H. Schilling. Hamden, Conn.:
    Shoe String Press, pp. 198-250.
        Reprint of 1935.34.

17 WILLIAMSON, GEORGE. Seventeenth Century Contexts. Chicago:
    University of Chicago Press.
        Reprint of 1935.37.

18 _____. The Proper Wit of Poetry. Chicago: University of
    Chicago Press, passim.
        Jonson has a significant role in the evolution of seven-
    teenth-century wit and the discriminations which its var-
    ious paths would take.

                            1962

1   ALLISON, ALEXANDER WARD. Toward an Augustan Poetic: Edmund
    Waller's "Reform" of English Poetry. Lexington: University
    of Kentucky Press, pp.4-11.
        Discussion of Jonson's early occasional verse.

2   BUSH, DOUGLAS. English Literature in the Earlier Seventeenth
    Century 1600-1660. Oxford History of English Literature.
    Oxford: Clarendon Press.
        Revision of 1945.3. Includes new information on Jonson
    discovered since 1945, but most important completely revis-
    es the selected bibliography of criticism on Jonson.

3   COURTHOPE, W. J. A History of English Poetry. Vols. 3 & 4.
    New York: Russell & Russell.
        Reprint of 1910.2.

4   CRAIG, HARDIN. The Literature of the English Renaissance:
    1485-1600. A History of English Literature. Vol. 2. New
    York: Collier Books.
        Reprint of 1950.2.

5   DAVIS, B. E. C. Edmund Spenser: A Critical Study. New York:
    Russell & Russell.
        Reprint of 1933.5.

6   GIBSON, H. N. The Shakespeare Claimants. New York: Barnes
      & Noble, passim.
         Jonson's writings and recorded words on Shakespeare
      are used to refute the charges of anti-Stratfordians.

7   HARDISON, O. B., Jr. The Enduring Moment: A Study of the
      Idea of Praise in Renaissance Literary Theory and Practice.
      Chapel Hill: University of North Carolina Press, passim.
         Discussions of Jonson's style in his elegies and his
      poetry of praise. "Both as rationalist and neoclassicist
      Jonson suspected the extravagant claims that earlier hum-
      anists had made for poetry as well as the extravagant
      poetry that had resulted from the attempts to live up to
      these claims."

8   HART, JEFFREY. "Ben Jonson's Good Society." ModA 7, no. 1
      (Winter):61-68.
         "To Penshurst" is the beginning of a subgenre of poems
      which "are concerned with the collision between the estab-
      lished and the insurgent, between tradition and novelty,
      between habit and critical consciousness. . . ." Provides
      a thorough explication of "To Penshurst."

9   HUNTER, WILLIAM B. [Jr.]. Review of Ben Jonson, by John
      Hollander. SCN 20, nos.1 & 2 (Spring-Summer):11.
         Describes the shortcomings of the introduction and text.
      See 1961.7.

10 JOHNSTON, GEORGE B[URKE]. Poems of Ben Jonson. Muses Library.
      Cambridge, Mass.: Harvard University Press.
         Paperback reprint of 1954.9.

11 LEAVIS, F. R. "The Line of Wit." In Seventeenth-Century Eng-
      lish Poetry: Modern Essays in Criticism. Edited by
      William R. Keast. New York: Oxford University Press,
      pp. 31-49.
         Reprint of 1936.18 and 1947.8.

12 McKENZIE, JAMES. "Jonson's 'Elizabeth, L. H.'" N&Q 207, no.
      6 (June):210.
         Elizabeth, Lady Hunsdon, a patroness of poets, may be
      the subject of Jonson's poem.

13 MOORMAN, F. W. Robert Herrick: A Biography and Critical
      Study. New York: Russell & Russell.
         Reprint of 1910.7.

14 PUTNEY, RUFUS [D.]. "Jonson's Poetic Comedy." PQ 41, no. 1
      (January):188-204.

1962

>   Discusses Jonson's methods of achieving a comic reaction
> in his poetry through stylistic and metrical alterations.

15   RACKIN, PHYLLIS. "Poetry without Paradox: Jonson's 'Hymne'
        to Cynthia." Criticism 4, no. 3 (Summer):186-96.
            An explication of "Queen and Huntress" not on new crit-
        ical principles of paradox, irony, ambiguity, or tension--none
        of which seem to apply to the poem--but on the basis of the
        Renaissance principle of decorum as described by Rosemond
        Tuve in her book, Elizabethan and Metaphysical Imagery.
        See 1947.12.

16   STEESE, PETER. "Jonson's A Song." Expl 21, no. 4 (December),
        item 31.
            "Despite the harmony and balance [of the poem] Jonson
        achieves through his use of an Aristotelian framework, he
        fails to work through this form to achieve a true expression
        of romantic passion."

17   TRIMPI. WESLEY [Jr.]. Ben Jonson's Poems: A Study of the
        Plain Style. Stanford, Calif.: Stanford University
        Press, 302 pp.
            Discoveries is used to bring the reader to a critical
        understanding of Jonson's poetry. Jonson's prose criticism
        presents "a consistent exposition of a stylistic position,"
        which is illustrated in the poem. This position is based
        upon classical models and classical prescriptions, but Jon-
        son is not slavishly imitative. He builds on a tradition
        rather than being enthralled by it.

18   _____. "Jonson and the Neo-Latin Authorities for the Plain
        Style." PMLA 77, no. 1 (March):21-26.
            Jonson was a major influence in the anti-Ciceronian
        movement in prose and the anti-Petrarchan movement in
        poetry. "Jonson's Discoveries is particularly valuable as
        a statement of the neo-Latin influence on the plain style,
        since it describes a rhetorical position which he consis-
        tently practiced in his writing.

19   WALTON, GEOFFREY. "The Tone of Ben Jonson's Poetry." In
        Seventeenth-Century English Poetry: Modern Essays in
        Criticism. Edited by William R. Keast. New York: Oxford:
        University Press, pp. 193-214.
            Reprint of 1955.20. Reprinted in 1974.33.

1963

1   ANON. "Studies in Ben." TLS, 2 August, p. 594.
    Review of Ben Jonson's Poems: A Study . . . , by Wesley
    Trimpi, Jr. Calls work the most detailed and elaborate
    treatment ever given Jonson's poetry. The commentary on
    style illuminates Jonson's verse. See 1962.17.

2   BABB, HOWARD S. "The 'Epitaph on Elizabeth, L. H.' and Ben
    Jonson's Style." JEGP 63, no. 4:738-44.
    Provides a full explication of the poem and concludes
    with general comments on Jonson's style drawn from the poem.
    "His compression of meaning goes hand in hand with a spare-
    ness of style here, with the naked dignity of Jonson's
    language."

3   BEAURLINE, LESTER A. "Euphues, Arcadia, and the Plain Style."
    VQR 39, no. 2 (Spring):341-44.
    Review of Ben Jonson's Poems: A Study . . . , by Wesley
    Trimpi, Jr., whose "mechanical use of historical evidence
    . . . produces some disappointing results." See 1962.17.

4   CUBETA, PAUL M. "A Jonsonian Ideal: 'To Penshurst.'" PQ 42,
    no. 1 (January):14-24.
    A full explication of "To Penshurst." Compares it to
    "To Sir Robert Wroth" and Martial's epigrams. Finds Jonson
    "succeeded in molding the ethical and the aesthetic into a
    harmony revealed in the structure of the verse."

5   _____. "Ben Jonson's Religious Lyrics." JEGP 62, no. 1
    (January):96-110.
    A survey of Jonson's limited but interesting religious
    verse. "Jonson's attitudes are like Herbert's, moderate in
    pitch. One finds none of the violently dramatic power felt
    in Donne. . . . Jonson never manifests any sustained doubts
    about the possibility of his ultimate salvation. His re-
    ligious poems may open with the plaintive cry of the de-
    spairing sinner, but each closes with his confidence firmly
    restored."

6   DAY, MARTIN S. "Ben Jonson and Other Contemporaries of Shake-
    speare." In History of English Literature to 1660. New
    York: Doubleday, pp. 330-37.
    Jonson was opposed to the Spenserian style. Instead
    "he brought to English verse the chiseled craftsmanship and
    tone of Roman antiquity." Jonson's prose is also very im-
    portant though it is largely paraphrased from the ancients.

1963

*7   DESSEN, ALAN CHARLES. "Ben Jonson and the "Estates' Morality
     Tradition." Ph.D. dissertation, John Hopkins University.
     Cited in Brock and Welsh, 1974.9.

8   DUNN, ESTHER CLOUDMAN. Ben Jonson's Art: Elizabethan Life
     and Literature as Reflected Therein. New York: Russell &
     Russell, 159 pp.
     Reprint of 1925.12.

9   ELIOT, T. S. "Ben Jonson." In Ben Jonson: A Collection of
     Critical Essays. Edited by Jonas A. Barish. Englewood
     Cliffs, N.J.: Prentice Hall, pp. 14-23.
     Reprint of 1919.5.

10   FRIED, WILLIAM. Review of The Complete Poetry of Ben Jonson,
     by William B. Hunter, Jr. SCN 21, nos. 1 & s (Spring and Sum-
     mer):13.
     A brief notice commending the publishers for printing a
     handsome and scholarly edition of Jonson in paperback. See
     1963.12.

11   HARDISON, O. B., Jr., ed. "Ben Jonson." In English Literary
     Criticism. The Renaissance. New York: Appleton-Century-
     Crofts, pp. 269-92.
     "Despite its [Discoveries'] fragmentary nature, it is a
     manifesto of the movement which was to triumph after the
     Restoration and one of the most significant literary doc-
     uments of its time."

12   HUNTER, WILLIAM B.[Jr.]. Introduction to The Complete Poetry
     of Ben Jonson. New York: New York University Press,
     pp. vii-ix.
     Short outline of Jonson's life with a note on the text
     and a comment on the musical settings for some of Jonson's
     lyrics.

13   KLEIN, D. "Ben Jonson." In The Elizabethan Dramatists as
     Critics. New York: Philosophical Library, pp. 307-410.
     "Jonson's views on the subject of poetic creation con-
     trast sharply with those of Shakespeare. Shakespeare em-
     phasized the inspirational aspects of the process; Jonson
     emphasized the deliberative. The difference in attitude is
     the difference between the romantic and the classic."

14   LAWRENCE, RALPH. Review of Ben Jonson's Poems: A Study . . . ,
     by Wesley Trimpi, Jr. English 14:246.
     Brief description of a welcomed study of Jonson's poetry.
     See 1962.17.

15   LEVIN, HARRY. "An Introduction to Ben Jonson." In <u>Ben Jonson:</u>
     <u>A Collection of Critical Essays</u>. Edited by Jonas A. Barish.
     Englewood Cliffs, N.J.: Prentice Hall, pp. 40-59.
          Reprint of 1938.6; 1972.23.

16   MACLEAN, HUGH. Review of <u>Ben Jonson's Poems: A Study</u> . . . ,
     by Wesley Trimpi, Jr. <u>UTQ</u> 33, no. 1 (October):89-97.
          A description of the study and its implications. "How
     fortunate we are to have this good book all students of
     Jonson's poetry will fully realize." See 1962.17.

17   PINTO, V. De S[OLA]. Review of <u>Ben Jonson's Poems: A Study</u>
     <u>. . . .</u>, by Wesley Trimpi, Jr. <u>CQ</u> 5, no. 2 (Summer):180-
     81.
          "Trimpi's book is ponderous, crammed with a variety of
     not very well digested learning and extremely hard to
     read." See 1962.17.

18   REDWINE, JAMES DANIEL, Jr. "Ben Jonson's Criticism of the
     Drama." Ph.D. dissertation, Princeton University.
          Contains excerpts from all of Jonson's works which re-
     flect upon his view of drama along with an analysis of these
     excerpts. See also 1970.30.

19   SCOTT, SIR WALTER. <u>The Life of Dryden</u>. Edited by Bernard
     Kreissman. Lincoln: University of Nebraska Press.
          Reprint of 1834.1.

20   SPINGARN, J. E. <u>A History of Literary Criticism in the</u>
     <u>Renaissance.</u> Introduction by Bernard Weinberg. New York:
     Harcourt, Brace & World.
          Reprint of 1899.7.

21   STEIN, ARNOLD. "Plain Style, Plain Criticism, Plain Dealing,
     and Ben Jonson." <u>ELH</u> 30, no. 3 (September):306-16.
          Review of <u>Ben Jonson's Poems: A Study</u> . . . , by
     Wesley Trimpi, Jr. "The basic charge to be made against
     the scholarship of this book is that it practices an eclec-
     tic dogmatism. It disparages rhetoric in poetry and does not
     hear its own rhetoric. The degree of critical self-aware-
     ness is limited." See 1962.17.

*22 WADA, UICHI. <u>Ben Jonson.</u> Tokyo: Kenkyusha.
          Cited in Brock and Welsh, 1974.9.

23   WISON, EDMUND. "Morose Ben Jonson." In <u>Ben Jonson: A Collec-</u>
     <u>tion of Critical Essays</u>. Edited by Jonas A. Barish. Engle-
     wood Cliffs, N.J.: Prentice Hall, pp. 60-74.
          Reprint of 1948.11.

1963

24   WINSTANLEY, WILLIAM. The Lives of the most Famous English
       Poets. Introduction by William Riley Parker. Gainesville,
       Fla.: Scholars' Facsimiles and Reprints.
       Reprint of 1687.1.

                               1964

1   BARISH, JONAS A. Review of Ben Jonson's Poems: A Study . . . ,
       by Wesley Trimpi, Jr. MP 61, no. 3 (February):240-43.
       "A preliminary triumph of Trimpi's is to restore Jon-
       son's Timber or Discoveries to its rightful status as a
       major critical document." The discussion of the poetry
       is extremely helpful though Trimpi's own style tends toward
       "unrelieved didacticism." See 1962.17.

2   BARR, C. B. L. "More Books from Ben Jonson's Library." BC
       13, no. 3 (Autumn):346-48.
       A list of books found with Jonson's signature partially
       obliterated.

3   BUXTON, JOHN. Review of Ben Jonson's Poems: A Study . . . ,
       by Wesley Trimpi, Jr. Archiv 201, no. 3 (August):
       216-18.
       The most interesting part of this book is Trimpi's met-
       rical analysis which "shows Jonson achieved a subtlety of
       movement which is wholly poetic 'by the controlled variation
       of the syntactical against the rhythmical unit of the verse
       line,' and especially by caesural variation--the means used
       with such mastery by Milton in his blank verse."
       See 1962.17.

4   _____. Sir Philip Sidney and the English Renaissance. 2d ed.
       London: Macmillan, pp. 227-29.
       Describes Jonson's association with Lucy, Countess of
       Bedford. New edition of 1954.3.

5   CLARK, DONALD LEMEN. John Milton at St. Paul's School: A
       Study of Ancient Rhetoric in English Renaissance Education.
       Hamden, Conn.: Archon Books.
       Reprint of 1948.5.

6   ENCK, JOHN J. Review of Ben Jonson's Poems: A Study . . . ,
       by Wesley Trimpi, Jr. MLR 59, no. 1 (January):106.
       While most of the book is "undeniably correct," readers
       will find stretches "dull and repetitous." See 1962.17.

7   FRAJND, MARTA. "Teorijshi stavovi Bena Dzonsona." FP 1-2:
       231-45.

1964

Jonson insisted on the supremacy of matter over form.
He was unhappy with the current direction of literature
and therefore called for a return to the "clarity and severity of the ancients." There are two major drawbacks to
Jonson's literary criticism. First, it was borrowed. Second, it reveals a "certain shortsightedness in considering
the scope of art."

8   GOLDING, SANFORD. Review of <u>Ben Jonson's Poems: A Study . . .</u> ,
    by Wesley Trimpi, Jr. JEGP 63, no. 1:166-68.
    Provides the general groundwork for a really complete
    study of the individual poems. The focus of this book is
    on "the critical precepts and the tradition behind Jonson's
    style of writing." Major criticism is that Trimpi does not
    explicate enough poems. See 1962.17.

9   HOWARTH, R. G. <u>A Pot of Gillyflowers: Studies and Notes</u>.
    Cape Town: privately printed, passim.
    Brief commentary on Jonson.

10 HUNT, MARY LELAND. <u>Thomas Decker</u>. New York: Russell & Russell.
    Reprint of 1911.3.

11 HUSSEY, MAURICE, ed. Introduction to <u>Jonson and the Cavaliers</u>.
    Poetry Bookshelf. London: Heinemann, pp. 1-18.
    The "Tribe of Ben" can only be defined historically and
    socially. There was not a consistent clearly identifiable
    stylistic character. It became "a nodal point of poetry
    in the reigns of James I and Charles I and an influence
    afterwards upon critical opinion for years to come."

12 JOHNSON, SAMUEL. <u>Poems</u>. Edited by E. L. McAdam, Jr. New
    Haven: Yale University Press.
    Reprint of 1747.1.

*13 JONES, ROBERT CHARLES. "Well-Made Men and Men-Making Poets:
    Ben Jonson and the Problem of the Poet as a Teacher of
    Men." Ph.D. dissertation, Harvard University.
    Cited in Brock and Welsh, 1974.9.

14 KENNER, HUGH, ed. Introduction to <u>Seventeenth Century Poetry</u>:
    <u>The Schools of Donne and Jonson</u>. New York: Holt, Rinehart
    & Winston, pp. xi-xxxii.
    Compares Jonson to Ezra Pound. Each had "enormous didac-
    tic zeal, intent on a public literary career and on re-
    claiming the dignity due to poets: great eclectics, great
    classicizers, great transposers of past modes; students of
    vernacular energy; informal scholars; polymaths; irascible
    Jonson, Pound."

1964

15 MACLEAN, HUGH. "Ben Jonson's Poems: Notes on the Ordered
    Society." In Essays in English Literature from the Ren-
    aissance to the Victorian Age. Presented to A. S. P.
    Woodhouse, 1964. Toronto: University of Toronto Press,
    pp. 43-68.
        Although Jonson's poems do not set forth a fully devel-
    oped theory of society, they nevertheless explore three
    recurrent themes: "the virtue of friendship between good
    men . . . the relationship that ought ideally to obtain
    between prince and poet . . . and the social attitudes and
    actions befitting a 'ruling class.'"

16 MOODY, WILLIAM V[AUGHN], and LOVETT, ROBERT M. A History of
    English Literature. New York: Scribners.
        Reprint of 1902.5.

17 NOSWORTHY, J. M. "Marlowe's Ovid and Davies's Epigrams--A
    Postscript." RES 15, no. 60 (November):397-98.
        Jonson may have transcribed for the printer Marlowe's
    translation of Ovid.

18 PARTRIDGE, E[DWARD] B. Review of Ben Jonson's Poems: A
    Study . . . , by Wesley Trimpi, Jr. RN 17, no. 4 (Winter):
    348-50.
        The long defense of Jonson's style might not have been
    necessary before taking up the poetry. In addition,
    Trimpi belabors his thesis while discussing the poetry.
    See 1962.17.

19 REES, JOAN. Samuel Daniel: A Critical and Biographical Study.
    Liverpool: Liverpool University Press, passim.
        Jonson and Daniel were not friends, though both suffered
    temporarily for having been accused of writing seditious
    comments in their plays.

20 RICHMOND, H. M. The School of Love: The Evolution of the
    Stuart Love Lyric. Princeton, N.J.: Princeton University
    Press, passim.
        Sets forth Jonson's contribution to the development of
    the Stuart love lyric and the way in which he built upon
    ancient and contemporary continental models.

21 SYLVESTER, WILLIAM. "Jonson's 'Come, My Celia' and Catullus'
    'Carmen V.'" Expl 22, no. 5 (January), item 35.
        A discussion of Jonson's source for this poem.

22 WILLIAMS, GEORGE W. Review of Ben Jonson's Poems: A Study
    . . . , by Wesley Trimpi, Jr. SAQ 63, no. 1:116-17.
        "An important contribution to criticism of seventeenth
    century poetry and prose." See 1962.17.

1965

23   WINZELER, CHARLOTTE. "Curse upon God: Classical and Eliza-
      bethan Thought Blended." BYUS 5, no. 2 (Winter):87-94.
         An explication of "An Execration Upon Vulcan." The
      poem, though light and playful, is a blending of classical
      and seventeenth-century thought into an outstanding critique
      of literature.

1965

1   BARKER, J. R. "A Pendant to Drummond of Hawthornden's Conver-
     sations." RES 16, no. 63 (August):284-88.
        Describes marginal annotations in Drummond's copy of
     Jonson's Works 1616 which tend to corroborate the accuracy
     of Sibbald's transcription of Drummond's MS of Conversations.

2   BASKERVILLE, CHARLES REED. The Elizabethan Jig. New York:
     Dover Publications.
        Reprint of 1929.2.

3   CHEW, SAMUEL C. The Crescent and the Rose: Islam and England
     during the Renaissance. New York: Octagon Books.
        Reprint of 1937.4.

4   EVANS, WILL McCLUNG. Ben Jonson and Elizabethan Music. New
     York: De Capo Press.
        Reprint of 1929.5.

5   FROST, DAVID. "Shakespeare in the Seventeenth Century." SQ
     16, no. 1 (Winter):81-89.
        Challenges the conclusions Bently reached in 1945.2.

6   HARRIS, VICTOR, and HUSAIN, ITRAT, eds. English Prose 1600-
     1660. New York: Holt, Rinehart & Winston, pp. 309-11.
        Although most of Jonson's prose is borrowed from other
     writers, he nevertheless emerges as "a man as independent
     as he is vigorous in his judgment."

7   HARRISON, JOHN SMITH. Platonism in English Poetry of the
     Sixteenth and Seventeenth Centuries. New York: Russell &
     Russell.
        Reprint of 1903.5.

8   HUTCHISON, BARBARA. "Ben Jonson's 'Let Me Be What I Am': An
     Apology in Disguise." ELN 2, no. 3 (March):185-90.
        Reads the poem not as a misogynistic diatribe, but as
     a "monument to Jonson's integrity, his steadfast refusal
     to be seduced by appearances or by the vagaries of fashion."

1965

9   Le COMTE, EDWARD. <u>Grace to a Witty Sinner: A Life of Donne</u>.
    New York: Walker & Co., passim.
      Commentary on Jonson's poems on Donne and his remarks
    about Donne.

10   LEMAY, J. A. LEO. "Jonson and Milton: Two Influences in
    Oakes's Elegie." <u>NEQ</u> 38, no. 1 (March):90-92.
      Shows a parallel between Jonson's "Epitaph of Elizabeth,
    L. H." and Urian Oakes's poem "An Elegie upon the Death
    of the Reverend Mr. Thomas Shepard . . . ," which was writ-
    ten in 1677 and has been acclaimed as one of the most sig-
    nificant poems in Colonial American literature.

11   MATCHETT, WILLIAM H. <u>The Phoenix and the Turtle</u>. The Hague:
    Mouton.
      Reprint of 1937.18.

12   MEYNELL, ALICE. <u>The Wares of Autolycus: Selected Literary
    Essays of Alice Meynell</u>. Edited by P. M. Fraser. London:
    Oxford University Press.
      Reprint of 1897.5.

13   O'CONNOR, DANIEL. "Jonson's 'A Hymne to God the Father.'"
    <u>N&Q</u> 210, no. 9 (September):279-80·
      Gives evidence for an earlier date of the poem than
    1635 which Herford and Simpson use. Part of Jonson's poem
    appears in 1627, <u>A Collection of Private Devotions</u> by John
    Cousin.

14   RAJAN, B., and GEORGE, A. G. "Ben Jonson." In <u>Makers of Lit-
    erary Criticism</u>. Vol. 1. New York: Asia Publishing House,
    pp. 140-71.
      Commentary on Jonson's criticism with a selection drawn
    largely from <u>Discoveries</u>.

15   SCHMIDTCHEN, PAUL W. "O Rare Ben Jonson." <u>Hobbies</u> 69, no. 12
    (February):106.
      Description of the <u>Works</u>, 1616, for amateur book collec-
    tors.

16   TAINE, H. A. <u>The History of English Literature</u>. Vol. 2. New
    York: Frederick Ungar Publishing Co.
      Reprint of 1883.3.

17   THOMPSON, FRANCIS. <u>A Renegade Poet and other Essays</u>. New
    York: Books for Libraries.
      Reprint of 1910.11.

18   THORNDIKE, ASHLEY H.   The Influence of Beaumont and Fletcher
     on Shakespeare. New York: Russell & Russell.
         Reprint of 1901.4.

19   UPHAM, ALFRED HORATIO.   The French Influence in English Lit-
     erature. New York: Octagon Books, passim.
         Reprint of 1908.12.

20   WHITE, HAROLD OGDEN.   Plagiarism and Imitation during the
     English Renaissance. New York: Octagon Books.
         Reprint of 1935.36.

                            1966

1   BABINGTON, BRUCE.   "Ben Jonson's Poetry of the Surface."
         Words: Wai-Te-Ata Studies in Literature, no. 2 (December):
         66-81.
             Jonson's poems have a clarity which leads to a basic
         usefulness. Clarity is "an image of the ordered life,"
         thus the poem becomes a reflection of that life.

2   BEAURLINE, LESTER A.   "The Selective Principle in Jonson's
         Shorter Poems." Criticism 8, no. 1 (Winter):64-74.
             We can learn much about Jonson's art by examing the
         alternatives he might have chosen. Comparison of "On
         My First Son" with the account of his son's death which
         Jonson gave Drummond. Revised 1974.5.

3   BERGMAN, JOSEPH A.   "Shakespeare's 'Purge' of Jonson, Once
         Again." Emporia State Research Studies 15:27-33.
             A review of the possible places where Shakespeare deliv-
         ered his purge of Jonson. Bergman votes for Hamlet.

4   BROADUS, EDMUND KEMPER.   The Laureatship: A Study of the Office
     of Poet Laureate in England. Freeport, N.Y.: Books for
     Libraries.
         Reprint of 1921.3.

5   [BRYDGES, Sir SAMUEL EGERTON, bart.] Censura Literaria. Vol.
         1. New York: AMS Press.
         Reprint of 1805.1.

6   HAYASHI, TETSUMARO.   "Ben Jonson and William Shakespeare:
         Their Relationship and Mutual Criticism." EWR 3, no. 1
         (Winter):23-47.
             Jonson's criticism of Shakespeare and the latter's vague
         or sometimes camouflaged rejoinders "seem to indicate the
         spirit of the Renaissance and the conflict between two

1966

contradictory forces: namely, conflict between thesis and
antithesis and their continual resolution or synthesis in
and Hegelian sense."

7   JOHNSON, CAROL. "Ben Jonson: The Conduct of Reason." In
    Reason's Double Agents. Chapel Hill: University of
    North Carolian Press, pp. 55-64.
         Looks "beyond the plainness and the urbanity" of Jon-
    son's verse for "that subtle correspondence of means and
    content. . . ." Johnson concludes that Jonson "found expres-
    sion for unerring certainties at all times rate, not forced,
    but subtilized by craft."

8   JOHNSON, NELL ECKERT. "Jonson's Ovidian Elegies with Partic-
    ular Attention to the 'Underwood' xxix- 'The Expostulation'
    Controversy." Ph.D. dissertation, University of Colorado.
         A discussion of the erotic elegy with a consideration
    of the attribution of "The Expostulation" thought to be by
    Donne or Jonson.

9   LEISHMAN, J. B. The Art of Marvell's Poetry. London: Hutch-
    inson, passim.
         Consideration of Jonson's influence on Marvell.

10 ____. The Monarch of Wit. New York: Harper Torchbooks,
    Harper & Row.
         Paperback reprint of 1951.8.

11 MAIDMENT, JAMES. Introduction to Sir Thomas Overburies Vis-
    ion, by Richard Niccols. New York: Johnson Reprint Corp.,
    pp. 19-26.
         Reprint of 1873.2.

12 PARTRIDGE, A. C., ed. Introduction to The Tribe of Ben: Pre-
    Augustan Classical Verse in English. Columbia: University
    of South Carolina Press, pp. 12-20.
         Points out common qualties of Jonson's and Donne's verse:
    "masculinity, integrity, command of pungent epigram and a
    preference for natural rhythms of speech. . . . The tone of
    both is urbane, and their songs are unmelodious. If Jon-
    son's can more easily be set to music, it is because they
    are simpler in rhythm and vocabulary."

13 PUTNEY, RUFUS D. "'This So Subtle Sport': Some Aspects of
    Jonson's Epigrams." UCSLL 10 (February):37-56.
         A defense of Jonson's subject matter and style. Putney
    takes issue with Eliot's criticism of Jonson arguing that
    there is a richness and beauty in Jonson that many readers
    overlook because they have been put off by the coarseness
    of some of his poetry.

14 REXROTH, KENNETH. "The Works of Ben Jonson." SatR 49 (17
    December):25.
        Jonson was, unlike most creative writers, a scholar.
    In addition, "he was scholarly in a way that no literary
    scholars are today--literary scholarship mattered at the
    beginning of the seventeenth-century; it was harder work.
    Jonson knew much more about erudite matters than scholars
    know today. And then of course he was not an academician
    but a creative artist, a bohemian intellectual, and a man
    who was largely self-educated."

15 ROLLIN, ROGER R. Robert Herrick. New York: Twayne Publish-
    ers, pp. 177-82.
        Though Herrick modeled his craft on Jonson's poetry and
    criticism, he did not slavishly follow Jonson. "The poet,
    in short must be open to instruction, but he must be his
    own man. Whatever he takes from his literary predeces-
    sors . . . he must re-create so that something new is made
    from something old."

16 SHAFER, ROBERT. The English Ode to 1660: An Essay in Literary
    History. New York: Gordian Press.
        Reprint of 1918.7.

17 STEENSMA, ROBERT C. "Ben Jonson: A Checklist of Editions,
    Biography and Criticism." RORD 9:29-46.
        Unannotated checklist of Jonsonian editions and criticism
    1947-1964.

18 TUCKER, MARTIN, ed. Moulton's Library of Literary Criticism.
    Vol. 1. New York: Frederick Ungar Pub.
        Abridgment of 1901.3.

19 WIERSMA, STANLEY M. "Jonson's To John Donne." Expl 25, no. 1
    (September), item 4.
        Response to 1958.3. Though essentially correct, Combel-
    lack has missed the "ironic ambiguity" in the poem.

                              1967

 1 BERTHELOT, JOSEPH A. Michael Drayton. New York: Twayne
    Publishers, pp. 143-44.
        Short discussion of "The Vision of Ben Jonson, on the
    Muses of his Friend M. Drayton."

 2 BROOKE, TUCKER. A Literary History of England. Edited by Al-
    bert C. Baugh. New York: Appleton-Century-Crofts.
        Reprint of 1948.3.

1967

3   BUXTON, JOHN. A Tradition of Poetry. New York: St. Martin's
        Press, passim.
            Compares Jonson's verse to that of other poets of the
        English Renaissance.

4   CHRISTOPHER, GEORGIA B. "A Study of the Jonsonian Pastoral,
        and Apocalyptic Strains in Silex Scintillans." Ph.D.
        dissertation, Yale University.
            Vaughan was heavily influenced by Jonson's often sen-
        suous lyrics.

5   COLERIDGE, SAMUEL TAYLOR. The Literary Remains of Samuel
        Taylor Coleridge. Collected and edited by Henry Nelson
        Coleridge. New York: AMS Press.
            Reprint of 1836.2.

6   DRAPER, JOHN W. The Funeral Elegy, and the Rise of English
        Romanticism. New York: Octagon Books.
            Reprint of 1929.4.

7   DUNLAP, RHODES. "The Allegorical Interpretation of Renais-
        sance Literature." PMLA 82, no. 1 (March):39–43.
            Jonson uses allegory in much of his writing, but he often
        became impatient with those who would over interpret him.
        "'Application,' he [Jonson] complains, 'is now growne a
        trade with many; and there are, that professe to have a
        key for the decyphering of every thing: but let wise and
        noble persons take heed how they be too credulous, or give
        leave to these invading interpreters'--interpreters whom
        Jonson elsewhere calls 'those common Torturers, that bring
        all wit to the Rack: whose Noses are ever like Swine
        spoyling and rooting up the Muses Gardens.'"

8   ERSKINE, JOHN. The Elizabethan Lyric. New York: Macmillan Co.
            Reprint of 1903.3.

9   HURD, RICHARD. The Works of Richard Hurd. Vol. 2. New York:
        AMS Press.
            Reprint of 1811.1.

10   JONES, ROBERT C. "The Satirist's Retirement in Jonson's
        'Apologetical Dialogue.'" ELH 34, no. 4 (December):447–67.
            Jonson's satire often suffers from an ambivalent attitude
        on the poet's part. On the one hand he wants to claim that
        his art is too lofty to affect the object of his satire,
        but on the other hand he wants to "transform the world
        through his art."

11 KITCHIN, GEORGE. <u>A Survey of Burlesque and Parody in English</u>.
        New York: Russell & Russell.
            Reprint of 1931.14.

12 McCUTCHEON, ELIZABETH. "Jonson's 'To Penshurst,' 36." <u>Expl</u>
        25, no. 6 (February), item 52.
            Discusses the use of the word "officiously."

13 MUIR, KENNETH. <u>Introduction to Elizabethan Literature</u>. New
        York: Random House, passim.
            Comparison of Jonson to such contemporaries as Marlowe,
        Nash, and Lodge.

14 NANIA, ANTHONY J. "Ben Jonson: A Checklist of Editions,
        Biography, and Criticism 1947-1964: Addenda." <u>RORD</u> 10:32.
            Supplement to 1966.15.

15 PALMER, JOHN. <u>Ben Jonson</u>. Port Washington, N.Y.: Kennikat
        Press.
            Reprint of 1934.16.

16 PAPAJEWSKI, HELMUT. "Ben Jonson Laudatio Auf Shakespeare:
        Kategorien des literatischen Urteils in der Renaissance."
        <u>Poetica</u> 1, no. 4 (October):483-507.
            An explication of Jonson's "To the Memory of my Beloved
        . . . Mr. William Shakespeare" showing how the assessment
        fits into Jonson's other stated critical views and how the
        poem compares to other dedicatory poems of the age.

17 RUDENSTINE, NEIL L. <u>Sidney's Poetic Development</u>. Cambridge,
        Mass.: Harvard University Press, pp. 147-48.
            Explanation for Sidney's more romantic style as opposed
        to Jonson's plain neoclassic mode.

18 SKELTON, ROBIN. "The Masterpoet and the Multiple Tradition;
        the Poetry of Ben Jonson." <u>Style</u> 1, no. 3 (Fall):225-46.
            The public and social aspects of Jonson's poetry apply
        to him as a teacher of poetry. "Writing in the middle
        of the creative confusions of a literary and artistic Ren-
        aissance, he attempted to establish the poet's role in the
        new society."

19 TAYLER, EDWARD W., ed. "Ben Jonson." In <u>Literary Criticism</u>
        <u>of Seventeenth-Century England</u>. New York: Knopf, pp.
        74-144.
            Introductory comments to Jonson's criticism.

20 WINTERS, YVOR. <u>Forms of Discovery: Critical and Historical</u>
        <u>Essays on the Forms of the Short Poem in English</u>. Chicago:
        Allan Swallow, passim.
            "If the reader with fixed habits could wrench his at-
        tention to the major poems [of Jonson] long enough to ap-
        preciate them, this act would not only put him in posses-

sion of one of the two greatest bodies of short poems com-
posed in the English Renaissance but would aid him to
understand a number of other great poets as well."

1968

1   BENNETT, JOSEPHINE WATERS. "Benson's Alleged Piracy of
    Shakespeare's Sonnets and of some of Jonson's Works." SB
    21:235-48.
        A discussion of the controversy between Walkley and
    Benson over the rights to publish Jonson's poetry and of
    Benson's publication of some of Jonson's poems with Shake-
    speare's sonnets.

2   CHERNAIK, WARREN L. The Poetry of Limitation: Study of
    Edmund Waller. New Haven: Yale University Press, passim.
        There is much of Jonson's influence in Waller's poetry,
    which "like Jonson's is characterized by classical restraint;
    both poets are highly conscious of writing in a tradition,
    and both believe strongly in economy. Waller follows the
    Cavalier poets in general in giving poetry a social context,
    and Jonson in particular in making it essentially public."

3   CIBBER, THEOPHILUS, comp. The Lives of the Poets of Great
    Britain and Ireland. Vol. 1. Hildescheim: Georg Olms
    Verlagsbuchhandlung.
        Reprint of 1753.2.

4   GARDINER, JUDITH K. "Craftmanship in Context: Ben Jonson's
    Poetry." Ph.D. dissertation, Columbia University.
        The intention is "to assess Jonson's non-dramatic work
    as a whole in the context of his other areas of endeavor.
    In particular, this essay aims to extend the present under-
    standing of Jonson's non-dramatic poetry in two directions:
    toward a more accurate particularity and toward more help-
    ful generalization."

5   GUFFEY, GEORGE ROBERT, comp. "Ben Jonson." In Supplements
    to Elizabethan Bibliographies. London: Nether Press, 53
    pp.
        Unannotated listing of items on Jonson since 1947.

6   HOUCK, J. K. "An Unidentified Borrowing in Jonson's 'Discov-
    eries.'" N&Q 213, no. 10 (October):267-68.
        Borrowing from Quintilian.

7   LEE, SIDNEY [L.]. The French Renaissance in England. New
    York: Octagon Books.
        Reprint of 1910.6.

8   McEUEN, KATHRYN ANDERSON. <u>Classical Influence Upon the Tribe</u>
       <u>of Ben</u>. New York: Octagon Books.
          Reprint of 1939.6.

9   McGUIRE, PHILIP CARROLL. "'The Soul in Paraphrase': A Study
       of the Devotional Poems of Jonson, Donne, and Herbert."
       Ph.D. dissertation, Stanford University.
          Jonson's classical plain style was particularly suited
       for his religious verse which was supposed to be brief,
       clear, and humane.

10 MOLESWORTH, CHARLES. "Property and Virtue: The Genre of the
       Country-House Poem in the Seventeenth Century." <u>Genre</u> 1,
       no. 2 (April):141-57.
          The country-house poem, which is "such a fruitful mar-
       riage of history and poetry, is most appropriate to a cen-
       tury in which these two 'disciplines' were so closely allied."
       Jonson's use of the country-house is emblematic. Virtue
       may be demonstrated through the passage of time and his-
       tory records and makes important "the life of memory."

11 MURRIN, MICHAEL. "Poetry as Literary Criticism." <u>MP</u> 65, no.
       3 (February):202-7.
          Several poets made critical poetic observations on Jon-
       son, while Jonson captured at least an element of critical
       consensus when he wrote that pictures and poetry "both in-
       vent, faine, and devise many things, and accomodate all
       they invent to use, and service of Nature."

12 PARFITT, G[EORGE] A. E. "The Poetry of Thomas Carew." <u>RMS</u> 12:
       56-67.
          In attempting to define Carew's genius, Parfitt both
       compares and contrasts Jonson and Carew. He concludes that
       Carew was helpfully influenced by both Donne and Jonson,
       but in no case was he able to reach the true greatness
       of either poet.

13 _____. "The Poetry of Ben Jonson." <u>EIC</u> 18, no. 1 (January):
       18-31.
          A reassessment of Jonson. Challenges a prevailing
       view that Jonson wrote with no inspiration. The impulse
       of his poetry moves from "values to experience, for his
       <u>a priori</u> belief in certain ethical tenets governs his selec-
       tion, analysis, and expression of material." Concludes
       that the impulse is didactic and the chief features of
       his best verse are "energy, assurance and rhythmical alert-
       ness."

1968

14   PARSONS, D. S. J.   "The Odes of Drayton and Jonson." QQ 75,
     no. 4 (Winter):675-84.
          Although other English poets wrote odes before, "it
     remained for Drayton and Jonson not only to capture the
     spirit of the ode but to master its intrinsic classical
     requirements." Finally, however, Jonson's "personal warmth
     and stoic strength of mind" were better applied in other
     poetic forms than the ode.

15   PETERSON, RICHARD S.   "The Praise of Virtue: Ben Jonson's
     Poems." Ph.D dissertation, University of California,
     Berkeley.

          Jonson's poetry of praise is complimentary in its intent,
     and is certainly beyond that of hired panegyrist or flatter-
     er.

16   SPINGARN, J. E., ed. Critical Essays of the Seventeenth Cen-
     tury. Vol. 1. Bloomington: Indiana University Press.
          Reprint of 1908.11.

17   VICKERS, BRIAN. Francis Bacon and Renaissance Prose. Cam-
     bridge: University Press, pp. 135-36.
          Analysis of Jonson's praise of Bacon in Discoveries.

18   WILLIAMS, RAYMOND. "Pastoral and Counter-Pastoral." CritQ
     10, no. 3 (Autumn):277-90.
          The pastoral image of the quiet, peaceful, and harmon-
     ious life is carried forward in poems on country estates.
     Yet these poems make certain discriminations. It is not
     just a matter of country being compared to city, but of
     country being compared to corrupted country--to aspects of
     the country which the city has invaded. "The forces of
     pride, greed and calculation are evidently active among
     landowners as well as among city merchants and courtiers.
     What is being celebrated is then perhaps an idea of rural
     society, as against the pressures of a new age; and the
     image of this idea is the house in which Jonson has been
     entertained." Revision 1969.24.

19   WILSON, GAYLE EDWARD. "Jonson's Use of the Bible and the
     Great Chain of Being in 'To Penshurst.'" SEL 8, no. 1
     (Winter):77-89.
          "To Penshurst" is an optimistic expression, which pro-
     vides man with a plan for a good and happy life. "They must
     imitate in small the divine law manifested by the Great
     Chain of Being, that governs the universe. The only way
     in which man can achieve this end, Jonson makes clear, is
     to practice the ethical standards based on the religious
     Truth contained in the Old and New Testaments."

20 WYNDHAM, GEORGE. Essays in Romantic Literature. Edited by
      Charles Whimbley. Essay Index Reprint Series. New York:
      Books for Libraries Press.
          Reprint of 1919.11.

21 ZWICKER, STEVEN N. "Dryden's Borrowing from Ben Jonson's
      'Panegyre.'" N&Q 213, no. 3 (March):105-6.
          Line 162 is the concluding line of the "Prologue to
      John Banks" in Dryden's The Unhappy Favorite.

<u>1969</u>

1 BAYFIELD, M. A. A Study of Shakespeare's Versification. New
      York: MS Press.
          Reprint of 1920.1.

2 BOYD, JOHN DOUGLAS. "T. S. Eliot as Critic and Rhetorician:
      The Essay on Jonson." Criticism 11, no. 2 (Spring):167-82.
          Analysis of the validity of Eliot's remarks on Jonson.
      Concentrates on logic and rhetoric rather than contrasting
      critical opinions. Provides a very close reading of key
      sentences in Eliot's essay.

3 BROOKS, HAROLD F. "'A Satyricall Shrub.'" TLS, 11 December,
      p. 1426.
          A poem listed as possibly by Rochester is largely lifted
      from Jonson.

4 C., R. "Scribimus indocti doctique epigrammata passim." In
      Times' Whistle. Edited by J. M. Cowper. New York: Green-
      wood Press, pp. 132-33.
          Reprint of 1871.1; 1922.4; 1615.1.

5 CALDER, DANIEL J. "The Meaning of 'Imitation' in Jonson's
      Discoveries." NM 70, no. 3 (September):435-40.
          Takes issue with 1947.2. Argues that Jonson largely
      accepts Aristotle's mimetic theory of imitation.

6 CHAPMAN, MILDRED S. "Ben Jonson and the Court." Ph.D. dis-
      sertation, Louisiana State University.
          The relationship Jonson enjoyed with the court and its
      influence on his career.

7 DOUGHTIE, EDWARD. "Ferrabosco and Jonson's 'The Houre-glasse.'"
      RQ 22, no. 2 (Summer):148-50.
          Based on textual evidence, argues that Jonson and Fer-
      rabosco collaborated on music and text for "The Houre-
      glasse."

1969

8 FIKE, FRANCIS. "Ben Jonson's 'On My First Sonne.'" <u>Gordon
   Review</u> 11:205-20.
   An explication of the poem which, according to the author,
   has not been properly explicated before. Concludes that
   in the poem are all the standard elements of an elegy:
   praise of the departed, demonstrable loss, lamentation, consolation, and moral exhortation.

9 HARBAGE, ALFRED. <u>Shakespeare's Audience</u>. New York: Columbia University Press.
   Reprint of 1941.5.

10 HILBERRY, CLARENCE BEVERLY. <u>Ben Jonson's Ethics in Relation to
    Stoic and Humanistic Ethical Thought</u>. Folcroft, Pa.: Fol-
    croft Press.
    Reprint of 1933.8.

11 INGLIS, FRED. "Jonson the Master: Stones Well Squared." In
    <u>The Elizabethan Poets: The Making of English Poetry from
    Wyatt to Ben Jonson</u>. London: Evans Brothers, pp. 127-56.
    Takes up Jonson and his contemporaries who practiced
    the plain style.

12 LANG, ANDREW. <u>History of English Literature</u>. New York: AMS
    Press.
    Reprint of 1921.9.

13 LAWRENCE, W. J. <u>Those Nut-Cracking Elizabethans: Studies of
    the Early Theatre and Drama</u>. New York: Haskell House
    Publishers.
    Reprint of 1935.12.

14 Le COMTE, EDWARD. <u>The Notorious Lady Essex</u>. New York: Dial
    Press, passim.
    Remarks on Jonson's masques during the wedding celebra-
    tion of Francis Howard and Robert Carr and his epithalamion
    for them.

15 MASSON, DAVID. <u>Drummond of Hawthornden</u>. New York: Greenwood
    Press.
    Reprint of 1873.5.

16 MURPHY, G. N., and SLATTERY, WILLIAM C. "Meaning and Structure
    in Jonson's 'Epitaph on Elizabeth, L. H.'" <u>ReAL</u>, 2 no.
    1:1-3.
    Suggests a new reading for the poem.

17 NICHOLS, J. G. <u>The Poetry of Ben Jonson</u>. New York: Barnes
    & Noble, 177 pp.

1969

A thorough discussion of the various subjects, forms, and styles. Acknowledges that Jonson can never always be liked by everyone and does not construct excessive apologies for the poet. Jonson was a complex man of many temperaments and his poetry reflects this. Through all however, he deserves if not our love at least our admiration.

18   PARFITT, G[EORGE] A. E. "Ethical Thought and Ben Jonson's Poetry." SEL 9, no. 1 (Winter):123-34.
The distinctive feature of Jonson's ethical view is that it is based in society rather than religion. Moveover, Jonson's ethical perceptions and prescriptions are consistent throughout his career. "The kind of concentrated insight into aspects of humanity which is Jonson's enduring merit as a poet spring directly from the central position of ethical views in his verse." Reprinted in 1974.24.

19   PIPER, WILLIAM BOWMAN. The Heroic Couplet. Cleveland: Case Western Reserve University Press, passim.
Describes the individual qualities of the Jonsonian couplet and traces its influence on later poets.

20   _____. "The Inception of the Closed Heroic Couplet." MP 66, no. 4 (May):306-21.
Jonson's prominent role in the development of the heroic couplet is described, but Piper points out that Jonson did not slavishly imitate his classical models. "Jonson, even when prompted by the sharply closed distich and the sharply indicated detachment of Martial, followed the natural shape of his thought, rather than a strictly epigrammatic form of organization and its correspondent indications of epigrammatic poise."

21   SCOTT, MARY AUGUSTA. Elizabethan Translations from the Italian. Bibliography & Reference series 280; Essays in Literature & Criticism 32. New York: Burt Franklin Press. Reprint of 1916.9.

22   SPANOS, WILLIAM V. "The Real Toad in the Jonsonian Garden: Resonance in the Nondramatic Poetry." JEGP 68, no. 1 (January):1-23.
Acknowledges the useful work done by Walker and Johnston but argues that describing classical influences does not fully explain the attraction of Jonson's verse. One sees in Jonson the classical qualities of simplicity, clarity, economy or brevity, order, and wholeness, but these are animated by "ethical resonances" which enliven what might otherwise be a static imitation. "The aesthetic pleasure,"

201

1969

Spanos suggests, "derives from the resonance generated by
the fusion of the opposites."

23   SWINBURNE, ALGERNON CHARLES. A Study of Ben Jonson. Lincoln:
University of Nebraska Press.
Reprint of 1889.7.

24   WILLIAMS, RAYMOND. The Country and the City. London: Chatto
& Windus, passim.
Revision of 1968.18. In addition there are references
to Jonson's country poetry throughout the book to emphasize
the theme that all was not peace and beauty in the rural
setting.

25   WYKES, DAVID. "Ben Jonson's 'Chast Booke'--The Epigrames."
RMS 13:76-87.
Discusses the style, structure, and subject matter of
the epigrames with particular emphasis on Jonson's use of
names. Challenges T. K. Whipple's earlier contention that
Jonson "makes no pretence to the reformer's zeal." Wykes
argues, "Jonson may not be a zealot, but here, as almost
everywhere else, he is concerned with morals and society."

1970

1   ANON. Review of Ben Jonson, by J. B. Bamborough. TLS, 16
October, p. 1187.
Paraphrases the thesis of the book: that Jonson tried to
rise above his station in life and his vocation as a hack
playwright by bringing art and purity to his age. See
1970.5.

2   ANON. Review of The Heirs of Donne and Jonson, by Joseph H.
Summers. YR 60, no. 2 (December):vi-vii.
Regards the book as an unpretentious survey of early
seventeenth-century English poetry which avoids "new-
fangledness and critical excesses." See 1970.37.

3   BACHE, WILLIAM B. "Verbal Complexity in 'On My First Son.'"
CEA 32, no. 4 (January):12.
An explication focusing on "The obvious, basic tension
in the poem . . . between the felt response to the son's
death and the deliberate verbal skill of the poet."

4   BALD, R. C. John Donne: A Life. Oxford: Clarendon Press,
passim.
Jonson's epigrams to Donne are among the evidence of the
two poets' long-standing friendship.

5   BAMBOROUGH, J. B. <u>Ben Jonson</u>. London: Hutchinson University
     Library, 191 pp.
         Jonson's poetry is superficial. He is greatly restrict-
     ed by the classical tradition which gives his verse an
     artificial, unreal quality which today we have difficulty
     appreciating. Obviously not an apology for Jonson and
     heavily influenced by Eliot's essay.

6   BARISH, JONAS A. "Jonson's Dramatic Prose." In <u>Literary Eng-
     lish Since Shakespeare</u>. Edited by George Watson. Oxford:
     Oxford University Press.
         Discusses all of Jonson's prose. In comparison to
     Bacon Jonson's prose had a "gnarled and knotted texture."

7   BLAKENEY, EDWARD HENRY, ed. <u>Horace on the Art of Poetry:</u>
     <u>Latin Text, English Prose Translation, Introduction, Notes,</u>
     <u>with Ben Jonson's English Verse Rendering</u>. New York: Books
     for Libraries Press.
         Reprint of 1928.8.

*8   BROCK, D. HEYWARD. "Poet and Society: A Critical Study of
     Ben Jonson's Concept of Society in the Light of Classical
     and Christian Ideals." Ph.D. dissertation, University of
     Kansas.
         Cited in Brock and Welsh, 1974.9.

9   CHETWOOD, WILLIAM RUFUS. <u>Memoirs of the Life and Writings of</u>
     <u>Ben Jonson, Esq</u>. New York: Garland Publishing Co.
     Reprint of 1756.1.

10   DAICHES, DAVID. <u>Literature and Society</u>. New York: Haskell
     House.
         Reprint of 1938.2.

11   DOWLING, LINDA C. "Ben Jonson, His Learned Hand and True
     Promethean Art: A Study of the Non-Dramatic Poetry."
     Ph.D. dissertation, Brown University.
         A study of the social nature of Jonson's poetry which
     is most clearly seen in the epigrams but is also found in
     his more private verse.

12   FARMER, NORMAN K., Jr. "A Theory of Genre for Seventeenth-
     Century Poetry." <u>Genre</u> 3, no. 4 (December):293-317.
         Formulates a more descriptive theory of genre for seven-
     teenth-century poetry than the more common divisions of
     metaphysical, Spenserian, and Cavalier. Establishes a
     continuum scale from referential to nonreferential and
     from extramural to intramural and then places the various
     types of poems: elegies, epigrams, verse epistles, lyrics,
     etc., along this scale.

1970

13 FIELD, MICHAEL JAY. "Alternate Design: A Study of the Inter-
    action of Theme and Structure in Ben Jonson's Poetry."
    Ph.D. dissertation, Cornell University.
        Study centers on two poems: "On the Famous Voyage" and
    "To the Immortal Memorie and Friendship of that Noble Paire,
    Sir Lucius Cary, and Sir H. Morison" to show how "form,
    meaning, and moral judgment are inextricably intertwined
    in many of Jonson's poems."

14 FOSTER, JOHN WILSON. "A Redefinition of Topographical Poetry."
    JEGP 69, no. 3 (July):394-406.
        Compares Denham's "Coopers Hill" and "Pope's Windsor
    Forest" to Jonson's "To Penshurst." "Jonson's boyant sense
    of the concrete, his intensive description, permits no
    marriage in the poem between morality and pictorial design.
    The eulogizing and moralizing (upon the virtues of chastity,
    fruitfulness, and nobility) are designed, it seems to me,
    merely to supply a conventional raison d'etre for what is at
    center simply a spirited and jubilant expression of feeling."

15 FREEHAFER, JOHN. "Leonard Digges, Ben Jonson, and the Begin-
    ning of Shakespeare Idolatry." SQ 21, no. 1 (Winter):63-
    75.
        Diggs also wrote an early elegy on Shakespeare which was
    not published until after his death in 1635. This elegy
    attempts to correct or answer what Diggs thought were ac-
    cusations or slurs within Jonson's "On the Memory, of My
    Beloved . . . Mr. William Shakespeare."

16 GIANAKARIS, CONSTANTINE J. "The Humanism of Ben Jonson."
    CLAJ 14, no. 2 (December):115-26.
        A survey of Jonson's humanistic background and its most
    probable and most influential sources. "A steady humanis-
    tic 'faith' was produced in him [Jonson] insisting that an
    ultimate harmony was possible--not necessarily probable--if
    man would permit his reason to rule."

17 GILL, ROMA. Review of Ben Jonson's Poems: A Study . . . , by
    Wesley Trimpi, Jr. ES 51, no. 3 (June):254-56.
        A helpful but not totally satisfactory study. Few and
    unsubstantial comparisons of Jonson to other seventeenth-
    century poets. Undue reliance on a statistical study of
    caesural pauses. But there is much "industrious research
    and clear sighted critical comments." See 1962.17.

18 GRANSDEN, K. W., ed. Introduction to Tudor Verse Satire.
    London: Athlone Press, pp. 1-29.
        In a survey essay Jonson is noted for his significant
    role in the development of various modes of satire.

1970

19 GREENE, THOMAS M. "Ben Jonson and the Centered Self." <u>SEL</u>
   10, no. 2 (Spring):325-48.
        Discusses the image of circularity in Jonson's works.
   "Most of the works of Jonson's large canon--including the
   tradedies and comedies, verse and prose--can be categor-
   ized broadly in their relation to an implicit or explicit
   center. That is to say one can describe an image or
   character or situation as durable, as center-oriented and
   centripetal . . . or one can describe them as moving free,
   as disoriented and centrifugal, in quest of transformation."
   There is room within this circle for an exuberant curiosity,
   but there is a firmness at the center which makes for an
   ethical continuity.

20 GREENWOOD, G[EORGE] G. <u>The Shakespeare Problem Restated</u>.
   Westport, Conn.: Greenwood Press.
        Reprint of 1908.6.

21 HAHAMOVITCH, LILLIAN. "An Approach to the Non-Dramatic Poetry
   of Ben Jonson." Ph.D. dissertation, University of Miami.
        Historical approach to Jonson based upon his eclectic
   concept of imitation. Judgment is based upon Jonson's
   success in dealing with specific forms.

22 HELD, GEORGE. "Jonson's Pindaric on Friendship." <u>CP</u> 3, no.
   1 (Spring):29-41.
        An explication of "To the Immortall Memorie, and Friend-
   ship of that Noble Paire, Sir Lucius Cary, and Sir H. Morison." Poem is unified and uses the Pindaric ode form to
   inhance the theme of immortality through friendship.

23 HOLLWAY, MORAG. "Jonson's 'Proper Strain.'" <u>CR</u> 13:51-67.
        Jonson's response to his environment through his
   poetry. Specific emphasis on "To Penshurst," "To Sir Robert Wroth," and "To the Immortall Memorie, and Friendship
   of . . . Sir Lucius Cary and Sir H. Morison."

24 JACOB, GILES. "Ben Jonson." In <u>An Historical Account of the
   Lives and Writings of Our Most Considerable English Poets</u>.
   New York: Garland Publishing, pp. 272-75.
        Reprint of 1720.1.

25 _____. "Ben Jonson." In <u>The Poetical Register</u>. New York:
   Garland Publishing, pp. 146-52.
        Reprint of 1719.1.

26 JOHNSTON, GEORGE BURKE. <u>Ben Jonson: Poet</u>. New York: Octa-
   gon Books.
        Reprint of 1945.5.

1970

27   KAY, W. DAVID. "The Shaping of Ben Jonson's Career: A Re-
      examination of Facts and Problems." <u>MP</u> 67, no. 3 (Feb-
      ruary):224-37.
          Jonson attempted to show a shape or growth to his career
      as a poet. "Like Milton, though perhaps in a more super-
      ficial way, Jonson was manifesting his belief that the poet
      'ought himself to be a true poem.'"

28   MAGNUS, LAURIE. <u>A Dictionary of European Literature</u>. New
      York: Johnson Reprint Corp.
          Reprint of 1926.8.

29   NEWTON, RICHARD C. "Foundations of Ben Jonson's Poetic Style:
      <u>Epigrammes</u> and <u>The Forrest</u>." Ph.D. dissertation, Univer-
      sity of California, Berkeley.
          Describes the basic stylistic elements of Jonson's poetry
      and importance of these elements to Jonson in defining his
      concept of the poet.

30   REDWINE, JAMES D[ANIEL], Jr. ed. <u>Ben Jonson's Literary Crit-
      icism</u>. Regents Critics Series. Lincoln: University of
      Nebraska Press, 260 pp.
          Organizes Jonson's criticism under eight headings: the
      art of criticism, the functions of a poet and critic, com-
      ical satire, comedy, tragedy, masque, contemporary poets
      and playwrights, and contemporary actors and audiences.
      See also 1963.18.

31   RIVERS, ISABEL. "The Poetry of Conservatism, 1600-1745: Jon-
      son, Dryden, and Pope." Ph.D. dissertation, Columbia
      University.
          Relates the poets' views of their public function which
      often were contrasted with the changing political realities.
      Of Jonson, Mrs. Rivers points out "temperament, personal
      ethics, and sense of poetic function pulled him in dif-
      ferent directions." See also 1978.30.

32   ROLLIN, ROGER R. Review of <u>The Poetry of Ben Jonson</u>, by J.
      G. Nichols. <u>SCN</u> 28, no. 3 (Autumn):50.
          "A reasonably reliable guide to Jonson's poetry for the
      student who is not yet ready for Trimpi." Rollin suggests
      that it is about time to quit trying to make Jonson into
      a better poet than he is. He is competent but not great.
      See 1969.17.

33   SCHOENBAUM, SAMUEL. "Shakespeare and Jonson: Fact and Myth."
      In <u>The Elizabethan Theatre</u>. Vol. w. Edited by David Gal-
      loway. Hamden, Conn.: Archon Books, pp. 1-19.

A systematic account of the stories and anecdotes about
Jonson and Shakespeare. The author sifts the fact from the
fancy.

34 _____. "Shakespeare vs. Jonson." In Shakespeare's Lives. Oxford: Clarendon Press, pp. 92-97.
Similar but not identical to 1970.33.

35 SAINTSBURY, GEORGE. A History of Elizabethan Literature. New
York: Russell & Russell.
Reprint of 1887.4.

36 SHADOIAN, JACK. "'Inviting a Friend to Supper': Aspects of
Jonson's Craft and Personality." CP 3, no. 2 (Fall):29-35.
There is considerable complexity within this poem which
brings out several of Jonson's central qualities: his
classicism, decorum, and moral commitment.

37 SUMMERS, JOSEPH H. The Heirs of Donne and Jonson. New York:
Oxford University Press, passim.
"Jonson attempted one of the most difficult things a
poet can conceive in any age: to present an ideal of the
mean, of rational control and fulfilled public function, so
that it seizes the imagination of the reader and stirs his
emotions. The clarity, the learning, and the labour were
necessary for the successful communication of such an ideal;
they also reflected it."

38 _____. "The Heritage of Donne and Jonson." UTQ 39, no. 2
(January):107-26.
Similar to Chapter 1, 1970.32. Discusses the similarities of Jonson and Donne as opposed to seeing the two as
starting opposite schools of poetry.

39 SYMONDS, JOHN ADDINGTON. Ben Jonson. New York: AMS Press.
Reprint of 1888.4.

40 TUFTE, VIRGINIA. "Jonson & Donne." In The Poetry of Marriage.
Los Angeles: Tinnon-Brown, pp. 207-29.
Jonson's epithalamia are "deliberate exercises in crafts-
manship" while Donne's though less conventional also reflect
classical traditions.

41 VAN DEN BERG, SARA STREICH. "The Poet in Society: A Study of
Ben Jonson's Poetry." Ph.D. dissertation, Yale University.
Discusses the variety of modes in which Jonson confronts
and evaluates society in his poetry. "His responses to the
world necessitate a variety of personae, or rhetorical
self-projections, which serve to clarify his position in
each poem."

1970

42   VELIE, ALAN R. Review of <u>Ben Jonson's Literary Criticism</u>,
        edited by James D. Redwine, Jr. <u>SCN</u> 28, no. 3 (Fall):50-51.
        "An excellent job in culling, arranging, and discussing
        Jonson's critical writings . . . the book is lively and
        useful." See 1970.30.

43   WEIDHORN, MANFRED. <u>Richard Lovelace</u>. New York: Twayne Pub-
        lishers, pp. 145-47.
        "When at his best he [Lovelace] evinces something of
        the Jonsonian coolness and polish. Like Jonson, he trans-
        lated from Catullus and the later poets of antiquity. . . ."

44   WHEELER, CHARLES FRANCIS. <u>Classical Mythology in the Plays</u>,
        <u>Masques, and Poems of Ben Jonson</u>. Port Washington, N.Y.:
        Kennikat Press.
        Reprint of 1938.16.

45   WHIPPLE, T. K. <u>Martial and the English Epigram from Sir Thom-
        as Wyatt to Ben Jonson</u>. New York: Phaeton Press.
        Reprint of 1925.33.

46   WILDING, MICHAEL. "Jonson, Sin, and Milton." <u>N&Q</u> 215, no. 7
        (November):415.
        An echo of Jonson in Milton.

47   WINNY, JAMES. "The Significance of Ben Jonson." In <u>A Preface
        to Donne</u>. London: Longman, pp. 101-11.
        Jonson's significance was felt more in his influence as
        a literary dictator than in his actual writing.

                                1971

1   ANON. Review of <u>The Heirs of Donne and Jonson</u>, by Joseph H.
        Summers. <u>Contemporary Review</u> 218 (April):224.
        Describes the book as a refreshing and new view of early
        seventeenth-century poetry which "should provide much stim-
        ulating reassessment." See 1970.37.

2   BORROFF, MARIE. "The Triumph of Charis: Through Swards, Not
        Swords." <u>ELN</u> 8, no. 4 (June):257-59.
        Suggests that Charis passes through green fields and
        seas in her triumph rather than swords and seas.

3   BRADLEY, JESSE FRANKLIN, and ADAMS, JOSEPH QUINCY, [Jr.]. <u>The
        Jonson Allusion-Book</u>. New York: Russell & Russell.
        Reprint of 1922.4.

1971

4   CAWLEY, ROBERT RALSTON. <u>Henry Peacham: His Contribution to</u>
      <u>English Poetry</u>. University Park: Pennsylvania State
      University Press, pp. 70-79.
          Peacham's and Jonson's use of the elegy.

5   CHALFANT, FRAN C. "Ben Jonson's London: The Plays, the
      Masques, and the Poems." Ph.D. dissertation, University
      of North Carolina.
          Collection of all London place names found in Jonson
      with commentary on their significance. See also 1978.4.

6   CHALMERS, GEORGE. <u>A Supplemental Apology for the Believers in</u>
      <u>the Shakespeare-Papers</u>. New York: Augustus M. Kelley.
          Reprint of 1799.1.

7   EVANS, MAURICE. Review of <u>The Poetry of Ben Jonson</u>, by J. G.
      Nichols. <u>RQ</u> 24, no. 2 (Summer):277-78.
          As a book of practical criticism on Jonson, this is ex-
      cellent; however, commentary on the Jacobean background is
      simplified and unsatisfactory. See 1969.17.

8   GRUNDY, JOAN. Review of <u>The Poetry of Ben Jonson</u>, by J. G.
      Nichols. <u>YES</u> 1:248-49.
          "A lively and well-written" reconsideration of the poetry.
      There are some problems in that Nichols is too apologetic
      and he relies too heavily on other critics. See 1969.17.

9   HUNTLEY, FRANK L. Review of <u>Ben Jonson</u>, by J. B. Bamborough.
      <u>RQ</u> 24, no. 2 (Summer):275-76.
          A fair and responsible book weighing Jonson's weaknesses
      against his strengths. "Perhaps the greatest weakness of
      the book is the absence of critical analysis of form wheth-
      er it be of a genre or a particular plot or poem. Para-
      phrase, historical summary, and a noting of separate 'beau-
      ties' take its place." See 1970.5.

10   KAY, W. DAVID. "The Christian Wisdom of Ben Jonson's 'On My
      First Sonne.'" <u>SEL</u> 11, no. 1 (Winter):125-36.
          Compares the poem to some of Martial's epigrams in which
      similar thoughts on grief and loss are expressed but then
      shows how Jonson skillfully weaves Christian elements into
      his Latin models.

11   LANGBAINE, GERARD. <u>An Account of the English Dramatic Poets</u>.
      New York: Burt Franklin.
          Reprint of 1691.1.

1971

12 LIVINGSTON, MARY L. "The Art of Jonson's Poetry." Ph.D. dis-
      sertation, Washington University.
          An analysis of Jonson's poetry in the light of Renaissance
      theories of poetry and rhetoric. The study concentrates on
      diction, metaphor, and didacticism.

13 MILLS, LLOYD L. "Ben Jonson's Poetry: A caveat and Two Inter-
      pretations." NLauR 1, no. 1:30-34.
          An explication of "On My First Son."

14 MINER, EARL. The Cavalier Mode from Jonson to Cotton. Prince-
      ton, N.J.: Princeton University Press, 347 pp.
          A thorough treatment of Jonson and his followers. Notes
      that Jonson "alone put the good man at the center of his
      poetry and made us believe that he was such for all of his
      follies. . . . It was his conviction of the centrality of
      the good life to poetry that won him the unparalleled re-
      spect of his contemporaries."

15 PARFITT, GEORGE A. E. "Compromise Classicism: Language and
      Rhythm in Ben Jonson's Poetry." SEL 11, no. 1 (Winter):
      109-23.
          Jonson's classicism has been greatly misunderstood by
      previous Jonsonian scholars and critics. It is in the
      peculiarities of Jonson's style which have heretofore not
      been recognized that the reader will find the real nature
      of Jonson's classicism.

16 PEBWORTH, TED-LARRY. "Jonson's Timber and the Essay Tradition."
      Essays in Honor of Esmond Linworth Marilla. Edited by
      Thomas Austin Kirby and William John Olive. Baton Rouge:
      Louisiana State University Press, pp. 115-26.
          Discoveries shows a movement of the essay tradition
      away from Bacon and back to the pattern of Montaigne and
      Cornwallis.

17 RAHM, LINDA K. "The Poet-Lover and Shakespeare's Sonnets."
      Ph.D. dissertation, Cornell University.
          "A Celebration of Charis" is discussed in an appendix
      "showing how the author's dual stance enables him to make
      a profoundly moral comment on the artist's role in society."

18 RATHMELL, J. C. A. "Jonson, Lord Lisle, and Penshurst." ELR
      1, no. 3 (Autumn):250-60.
          A survey of Lord Lisle's correspondence along with com-
      mentary on the historical situation and the poetic ideal.
      Lisle, the owner of Penshurst, prided himself on his hos-
      pitality, but during the years Jonson is most likely to

have written the poem, he was in a desperate financial situation. Jonson advises Lisle to place his values on more
enduring virtues than wealth.

19 SUCKLING, SIR JOHN. The Works of Sir John Suckling. Edited
by Thomas Clayton and L. Baurline. Oxford: Clarendon
Press.
Reprint of 1646.2.

20 TABACHNICK, STEPHEN E. "Jonson's 'Epitaph on Elizabeth, L.
H.'" Expl 29, no. 9 (May), item 77.
From a close reading of the poem suggests that Elizabeth died pregnant with an illegitimate child. The identity
of Elizabeth has, of course, never been determined.

21 WALSH, WILLIAM. "Swains of Solyma, Advise." Review of The
Heirs of Donne and Jonson, by Joseph H. Summers. Encounter
37, no. 6 (December):61.
Book is more in the British tradition of scholarship.
"Mr. Summers' temperate, conscientiously qualified state-
mentis as admirable as the assumptions and aims informing
his criticism are humane and pointed." See 1970.37.

22 WARD, A. W. "Ben Jonson." In The English Poets. Vol. 2.
Edited by Thomas Humphrey Ward. Freeport, N.Y.: Books for
Libraries Press, pp. 1-7.
Reprint of 1880.1.

23 WEINBERGER, G. J. "Jonson's Mock-Economiastic 'Celebration
of Charis.'" Genre 4, no. 4 (December):305-28.
"A Celebration of Charis in Ten Lyric Pieces" is a
"mockencomium" describing the ideal by placing against
it the real which is weak and corrupt. "By concentrating
on the potential of these ideals, and by revealing the
ways in which Charis fails to live up to them, is in
fact a false Laudatio in that she is not praised at all."

1972

1 ANON. "Ben Jonson, and Mr. Baker." In Visits from the Shades.
Preface by Arthur Freeman. New York: Garland Press,
pp. 38-48.
Reprint of 1704.1.

2 ARDEN, JOHN. "An Embarrassment of the Tidy Mind." Gambit 6,
no. 22:30-36.
Jonson does not fit into a literary critic's prefabric-
ated categories. However, he is a major link between Shakespeare and Milton.

1972

3   BROOKS, SARAH WARNER. <u>English Poetry and Poets</u>. Freeport,
       N.Y.: Books for Libraries Press.
          Reprint of 1890.5.

4   BRYANT, J. A., Jr. <u>The Compassionate Satirist: Ben Jonson and
       His Imperfect World</u>. Athens: University of Georgia Press,
       204 pp.
          Deals largely with drama but takes up the question of
       satire and poetry and the "alleged incompatibility between
       the two. . . . At the root of the difficulty was Jonson's
       own flat assertion about the impossibility of anyone's
       becoming a good poet without first being a good man. . . .
       Jonson surely knew that all poets are men and that some
       very good poets from time to time have lived extremely
       messy lives."

5   CONGREVE, WILLIAM. <u>Amendments of Mr. Collier's False and
       Imperfect Citations</u>. New York: Garland Press.
          Reprint of 1698.1.

6   DAVIS, TOM. "Ben Jonson's Ode to Himself: An Early Version."
       <u>PQ</u> 51, no. 2 (April):410-21.
          A textual study of early manuscript versions of Jonson's
       "Ode to Himself" ("Come leave the loathed stage") compar-
       ing them to the first printed version. Davis speculates
       on reasons for the major differences in the different states
       of the poem.

7   DEWITT, SUSAN V. "Ben Jonson and the English Verse Letter."
       Ph.D. dissertation, University of Washington.
          Treats the verse letter as a form of poetry rather than
       a separate genre. For Jonson the verse letter becomes
       "an act of self-discovery in the presence of a friend."

8   D'ISRAELI, ISAAC. <u>Curiosities of Literature</u>. New York:
       Garland Publishing.
          Reprint of 1793.2.

9   EARL, ROBERT S. "Ben Jonson's Epigrammes: A Study in Con-
       vention." Ph.D. dissertation, Rutgers University.
          Jonson used a broad definition for the epigram for "he
       saw the epigram as a literary form rather than as a means
       of moral reform or a joke book."

10 FISHER, WILLIAM N. "Occupatio in Sixteenth and Seventeenth-
       Century Verse." <u>TSLL</u> 14, no. 2 (Summer):203-22.
          Describes Jonson's use of occupatio, a rhetorical device,
       in selected poems.

11   FRENCH, ROBERTS W. "On Teaching Irrelevant Poetry." CEA
          34, no. 3 (March):20-21.
          "Hymn to Diana." is a beautiful poem which represents
      the extreme artistic accomplishment of which man is capable.
      At the opposite extreme of art is war and destruction. If
      it were not for the beauty man is capable of creating,
      surely we would despair completely when we see the ugliness
      about us.

12   GREENBLATT, DANIEL. "Ben Jonson's Prosody." RLSt 3:77-92.
          Jonson's prosody falls between two extremes; the artis-
      tic covering or coating of intellect and emotions, and the
      actual substance of the poem itself with thought and ideas
      injected to provide a sense of purpose.

13   GREENSTEIN, CAROLYN. "The Poet and the King: Solux Rex et
          Poeta Non Quotannis Nascitur." Ph.D. dissertation, Colum-
          bia University.
          Discussion of the relationship between James I and his
      poet, Ben Jonson.

14   GWYNN, STEPHEN LUCIUS. The Masters of English Literature.
          Freeport, N.Y.: Books for Libraries Press.
          Reprint of 1904.4.

15   HOLUM, KAREN M. "The Epigram: Semantic Basis for the Pointed
          Ending." Linguistics 94 (15 December):21-36.
          Detailed semantic analysis of twenty epigrams by Jonson
      showing how the construction of the epigram aids in pro-
      ducing its total effect.

16   HONIG, EDWIN. "Examples of Poetic Diction in Ben Jonson."
          Costerus 3:121-62.
          Distinguishes certain of the "striking characteristics"
      of Jonson's poetry, "the variety and limitations of its
      devices, and the type of imagination at work in an extreme-
      ly conscious craftsman of the poetic art."

17   HOWARD-HILL, T.H. "Towards a Jonson Concordance: A Dis-
          cussion of Texts and Problems." RORD 15-16:17-32.
          A complete concordance of Jonson's Works should be
      based on a better edition than Herford and Simpson which
      Howard-Hill briefly shows to be sufficiently defective as
      to also cause the concordance based on it to be defective.

18   HUMEZ, JEAN M. "The Manners of Epigram: A Study of the Ep-
          igram Volumes of Martial, Harington, and Jonson." Ph.D.
          dissertation, Yale University.

1972

> Argues for a logical organization to the Epigrams partly
> on the model of Martial's Book XI.

19 HUSSEY, MAURICE. "Ben Jonson." In The World of Shakespeare and
    His Comtemporaries: A Visual Approach. Studio Books. New
    York: Viking, pp. 109-21.
    An illustrated essay on the life and times of Jonson.

20 ITZKOWITZ, MARTIN E. Review of "Ben Jonson and the Craft of
    Poetry," by James D. Simmonds. SCN 30, nos. 3 & 4 (Fall/
    Winter):57.
    Briefly discusses Chapter II, "Ben Jonson and the Craft
    of Poetry" and Chapter III, "The Well Ordered Poem."
    Vaughan follows Jonson's poetic principles of order, con-
    trol, and clarity. See 1972.35.

21 JORDAN, RICHARD D. "An Interview with Ben Jonson, Composi-
    tion Teacher." CCC 23, no. 3 (October):277-78.
    An ingenious interview with questions by the author and
    answers taken from Jonson's Discoveries.

22 KELLIHER, HILTON. "Anecdotes of Jonson and Cleveland." N&Q
    217 (May):172-73.
    A mid-seventeenth-century anecdote on Jonson's journey
    to Scotland.

23 LEVIN, HARRY. "An Introduction to Ben Jonson." In Grounds for
    Comparison. Harvard Studies in Comparative Literature.
    Cambridge, Mass.: Harvard University Press. pp. 183-206.
    Reprint of 1938.6; 1963.15.

24 LINKLATER, ERIC. Ben Jonson and King James: Biography and
    Portrait. Port Washington, N.Y.: Kennikat Press.
    Reprint of 1931.17.

25 MAROTTI, ARTHUR F. "All About Jonson's Poetry." ELH 39,
    no. 2 (June):208-37.
    A discussion of all of Jonson's poetry, dramatic and
    nondramatic, in an effort to reconcile the complexities
    and contradictions of his art. There are two main im-
    pulses in the poetry linked by the character of the poet.

26 McFARLAND, RONALD E. "Jonson's Epigrams XI ('On Some-thing
    That Walkes Some-where')." Expl 31, no. 4 (December),
    item 26.
    Reads the poem as a much more interesting and complex
    court poem than the usual flattery one expects. See
    1973.26 and 1975.4.

27   McKENZIE, D. F. "The Printer of the Third Volume of Jonson's
     Workes (1640)." SB 25:177-78.
          Presents evidence that John Dawson Junior was the print-
     er of the 1640 Folio edition of Jonson's Workes.

28   McPHERSON, DAVID, ed. Ben Jonson: Selected Works. New York:
     Holt, Rinehart & Winston, pp. 301-5.
          Discusses the strong classical influence on Jonson point-
     ing out that this determines not only verse form and style,
     but subject and theme as well. "His main concern is with
     the proper relationship between the poet and society." He
     should be studied because of his "outstanding quality as
     a poet in his mastery of the plain style."

*29 MILLER, RICHARD. "Diverse Unity: Ben Jonson's Epigrammes."
     Ph.D. dissertation, Columbia University.
          Cited in Brock and Welsh, 1974.9.

30   MILLENKOTT, VIRGINIA R. Review of The Cavalier Mode from
     Jonson to Cotton, by Earl Miner. SCN 30, no. 2 (Summer):
     36-38.
          Supports Miner's thesis that Cavalier poetry is more
     profound and complex than its current reputation would lead
     one to believe. See 1971.14.

31   MOLESWORTH, CHARLES. 'To Penshurst' and Jonson's Historical
     Imagination." Clio (Univ. of Wisconsin) 1, no. 2 (Feb-
     ruary):5-13.
          The country-house poem embodies society, nature, and
     most of all, history. "What Jonson had done then, is to
     offer his country-house poem not only as panegyric, but
     as a celebration of history itself."

32   MURPHY, AVON JACK. "The Critical Elegy of Earlier Seventeenth-
     Century England." Genre 5, no. 1 (March):75-97.
          Presents a case for the literary elegy as a form of
     criticism in the early seventeenth century. Defines major
     themes in the critical elegy: comparison of writers, death
     of literature, immortality in verse, etc. Through close
     reading we may learn something about the writer, but these
     elegies were seldom critical in the modern sense of the
     term.

33   OATES, MARY I. "Ben Jonson's Cary-Morison Ode: A Critical
     Edition with Introduction and Commentary." Ph.D. disser-
     tation, Princeton University.
          A new edition of the poem based upon manuscript sources
     not available to the Simpsons for their edition. An extended
     introduction on the background and influences of the poem.

1972

34   RICHARDSON, DAVID ANTHONY. "Decorum and Diction in the English
      Renaissance." Ph.D. dissertation, University of North
      Carolina.
          Jonson's poetry "represents English neoclassical success
      with the plain style. His occasional verse demonstrates
      that both decorum and the plain style were flexible ideals,
      for they distingusihed sharply between language suited to
      praise and that appropriate for blame.

35   SIMMONDS, JAMES D. "Ben Jonson and the Craft of Poetry." In
      Masques of God: Form and Theme in the Poetry of Henry
      Vaughan. Pittsburgh: University of Pittsburgh Press,
      pp. 22-41.
          Vaughan followed Jonson in the belief "that the end of
      poetry lies not in reflexive satisfaction of the writer or
      a coterie but in its effect on a wider public. They follow
      the maxim that the end of poetry is delightful teaching.
      Its purpose is the persuasive communication of knowledge
      that is useful in the broadest sense, of the eloquent expres-
      sion of intellectually and morally sound ideas."

36   SOFIELD, DAVID R. "English Building Poems, 1600-1680." Ph.D.
      dissertation, Stanford University.
          A study of "Stuart architectural verse, the conventions
      that helped shaped it, and the limits of those conventions.

37   SOUTHALL, RAYMOND. "Understanding Jonson." EIC 22, no. 1
      (January):83-91.
          Review of Ben Jonson, by J. B. Bamborough. Takes issue
      with Bamborough's rather low judgment of Jonson's poetry.
      Jonson's classicism is based "in a specific sense of human
      sociability, in a preoccupation with the art of being
      human." See 1970.5.

38   STEBBING, WILLIAM. Sir Walter Ralegh. New York: Lemma.
          Reprint of 1899.8.

39   TAAFFE, JAMES G. Abraham Cowley. New York: Twayne Publishers,
      pp. 22-23.
          Both Jonson and Cowley had a similar attraction to Hor-
      ace.

40   THOMSON, JAMES. Biographical and Critical Studies. Freeport,
      N.Y.: Books for Libraries Press.
          Reprint of 1896.6.

41   WHIPPLE, EDWIN P. The Literature of the Age of Elizabeth.
      Freeport, N.Y.: Books for Libraries Press.
          Reprint of 1891.2.

1973

1   ANON. Review of "Ben Jonson and the Nature of Aristocracy,"
     by Isabel Rivers. TLS, 16 February, p. 187.
         "Not a book for the lazy-minded." Mrs. Rivers has
     pointed to the inconsistent sometimes actually opposed
     social, ethical, and moral values that Jonson embraced but
     that caused turmoil in his own consciousness. See 1973.30.

2   BAZERMAN, CHARLES. Review of "An Introduction to Ben Jonson,"
     by Harry Levin. Nation 216 (5 February):184-86.
         Levin's observations on Jonson attempted to establish
     for the reader the proper way in which to approach Jonson.
     See 1972.23.

3   BRADY, FRANK; PALMER, JOHN; and PRICE, MARTIN. Literary
     Theory and Structure. New Haven: Yale University Press,
     passim.
         Numerous references to Jonson. See pp. 382-84 for an
     explication of "Epitaph on Elizabeth, L.H."

4   CALLINESCU, MATEI. Review of "An Introduction to Ben Jonson,"
     by Harry Levin. YCGL 22:82-86.
         Levin's criticism is an eclectic gathering of what is
     most suitable for the occasion. See 1972.23.

5   CARICATO, FRANK S. "John Donne and the Epigram Tradition."
     Ph.D. dissertation, Fordham University-
         Describes Jonson's role in the history of the epigram
     in Renaissance English literature.

6   DAVIS, WALTER R. "Jonson's 'An Ode' (Under-Wood 28)." Expl
     31, no. 9 (May), item 70.
         Poem is addressed to a young man who has won a young
     lady through a duel.

7   DONALDSON, IAN. "Jonson's Ode to Sir Lucius Cary and Sir
     H. Morison." SLI 6, no. 1 (April):139-52.
         Explication and reevaluation of this poem, which has
     traditionally been represented in anthologies by just one
     stanza ("It is not growing like a tree . . ."). Donaldson
     believes that the poem must be read in its proper context
     to be truly appreciated.

8   FELLOWES, PETER. "Jonson's 'Epigrams CIII' ('To Mary Lady
     Wroth')." Expl 31, no. 5 (January), item 36.
         Describes the central paradox of the poem. See 1975.7.

1973

9   FORD, H. L. <u>Collation of the Ben Jonson Folios, 1616-31-1640</u>.
     Haskell House Publishers.
          Reprint of 1932.7.

10   FOWLER, ALASTAIR. "The 'Better Marks' of Jonson's 'To Pens-
     hurst.'" <u>RES</u> 24, no. 95 (August):266-82.
          The architectural background for this poem is more im-
     portant than has previously been assumed. "To Penhurst"'s
     complexity is concealed by an easy style. Nevertheless, the
     poem is "rich with allusion, delicate suggestion and com-
     plex wit."

11   GARDINER, JUDITH K. "Line Counts, Word Counts, and Two Jon-
     son Epistles." <u>Style</u> 7, no. 1 (Winter):30-38.
          An objective examination of the empirical effects of
     Jonson's plain style in "To Penshurst" and "To Sir
     Robert Wroth."

12   _____. "'To Heaven.'" <u>CP</u> 6, no. 2 (Fall):26-36.
          An explication taking up the traditional materials
     found in penitential poems and analyzing the manner in
     which Jonson has altered or used in his own way these
     standard elements.

13   GASTON, PAUL L. "Commendation and Approbation: Recent Ben
     Jonson Scholarship." <u>PLL</u> 9, no. 3 (Fall):432-49.
          Short discussions of 1969.17 and 1962.17.

14   GRAY, ARTHUR. <u>How Shakespeare "Purged" Jonson: A Problem
     Solved</u>. New York: AMS Press.
          Reprint of 1928.13.

15   GREENBLATT, DANIEL L. "Generative Metrics and the Authorship
     of 'The Expostulation.'" <u>Centrum</u> 1, no. 2 (Fall):87-104.
          Through a statistical analysis of the metrics in "The
     Expostulation" a conclusion is drawn that John Donne most
     likely did not write the poem. At the same time there is
     no reason to think that Jonson did not write it, though
     it cannot be conclusively proven that he did.

16   HEYWOOD, THOMAS. <u>The Hierarchie of the Blessed Angells</u>. New
     York: Da Capo Press.
          Reprint of 1635.1.

17   JONES-DAVIES, MARIE-THÉRÈSE. <u>Ben Jonson</u>. Paris: Editions
     Seghers, 191 pp.
          See particularly Chapter 3 "Le Poète." Jonson's neo-
     Platonic elements are described. The importance of clas-
     sicism as an influence on Jonson is emphasized. Several
     poems are discussed in relation to these factors.

1973

18 KERRIGAN, WILLIAM. "Ben Jonson Full of Shame and Scorn."
    SLI 6, no. 1 (April):199-217.
        An explication of Jonson's "To Heaven," which reveals a
    different side of Jonson than critics usually present.
    This paper is devoted to the Stoic and melancholy Jonson
    as opposed to the public or social figure we usually see.

19 KNIGHTS, L. C. "Ben Jonson: Public Attitudes and Social
    Poetry." In A Celebration of Ben Jonson. Edited by William
    Blissett, Julian Patrick, and R. W. Van Fossen. Toronto:
    University of Toronto Press, pp. 167-87.
        The social context of patronage for Jonson's poems is
    far removed from our democratic society. Thus we should not
    ask of Jonson's poems something for which they were not
    intended. But the poems do have a great sense of vitality
    "that is common in all good poetry of whatever kind."

*20 KOSSICK, SHIRLEY. "Ben Jonson: Some aspects of his Life and
    Work." UES 11 (March):4-11.
        Cited in Modern Humanities Research Association Annual
    Bibliography, 1973.

21 LANGBAINE, GERARD. The Lives and Characters of the English
    Dramatic Poets. Edited by Arthur Freeman. New York:
    Garland Press.
        Reprint of 1699.1.

22 MACLEAN, HUGH. "'A More Secret Cause': The Wit of Jonson's
    Poetry." In A Celebration of Ben Jonson. Edited by Wil-
    liam Blissett, Julian Patrick, and R. W. Van Fossen. Toron-
    to: University of Toronto Press, pp. 29-66.
        A detailed definition of Jonson's wit. The nuances of
    the definition are carefully developed setting Maclean's
    concept of Jonson's wit apart from other critics'. "The
    'more secret Cause,' then, presumably refers to the capac-
    ity of the individual (notably the true poet and critic)
    to recognize and express every aspect of the varied order
    that informs nature; and to respond, by a wit at once
    'quick ranging' and decorously restrained, to that larger
    'principal of dynamic unity.'"

23 MORTIMER, ANTHONY. "The Feigned Commonwealth in the Poetry
    of Ben Jonson." SEL 13, no. 1 (Winter):69-79.
        Concentrates on "To Penshurst" and "To Sir Robert Wroth"
    in both of which there is a conflict between virtue within
    the estate and vice from without.

1973

24   PARFITT, G[EORGE] A. E.   "The Nature of Translation in Ben Jon-
      son's Poetry." SEL 13, no. 2 (Spring):344-59.
          Jonson's borrowing of material for his poems from ancient
      writers conformed to the accepted Renaissance practice of
      imitation. However he assimilated these materials with
      greater craftsmanship than other English writers. Moreover,
      he normally borrowed ehtical ideas rather than literary
      devices or allusions.

25   PARTRIDGE, EDWARD [B.].   "Jonson's Epigrammes: The Named and
      Nameless." SLI 6, no. 1 (April):153-98.
          Finds a loose organization in the arrangement of the
      epigrams with a movement from virtue to vice, from the
      nobleman who is identified to the unnamed lecher. This
      movement is not continuous but rather pulsates with the
      throb of life itself.

26   PERRINE, LAURENCE.   "Jonson's Epigrams, XI ('On Something,
      That Walkes Somewhare')." Expl 32, no. 4 (December), item
      30.
          Response to 1972.26. The last five words of the poem
      are not by the courtier but to the courtier spoken by the
      poet. See 1975.4.

27   PETERSON, RICHARD S.   "Virtue Reconciled to Pleasure: Jonson's
      'A Celebration of Charis.'" SLI 6, no. 1 (April):219-68.
          Deals with the moral and ethical qualities of love and
      Jonson's perceptions of the problem of finding a balance
      between pleasure and virtue. Peterson looks at other Ren-
      aissance literary and artistic works finding parallels to
      Jonson's efforts to define a middle ground between neo-
      Platonism and Petrarchanism.

28   QUENNELL, PETER.   "Rare Ben Jonson." In A History of English
      Literature. Springfield, Mass.: G. & C. Merriam, pp.
      70-74.
          Jonson rejected "euphemism and unnecessary word play,
      he employed 'language such as med doe use.'" His impact
      on English literature was momentous.

29   RIBERIO, ALVERA.   "Sir John Roe: Ben Jonson's Friend." RES
      24, no. 94 (May):153-64.
          A biographical sketch of Jonson's friend leading to a
      better understanding of the epigrams both wrote each other.

30   RIVERS, ISABEL.   "Ben Jonson and the Nature of Aristocracy."
      In The Poetry of Conservatism, 1600-1745: A Study of Poets
      and Political Affairs from Jonson to Pope. Cambridge:
      Rivers Press, pp. 21-72.
          Jonson's poems most clearly reveal a "self-centered
      emphasis of Senecan Stoicism." Jonson defines the concept
      of virute and urges his friends to live by it--those
      friends who maintain moral virtue in the face of a
      corrupted world. See also 1970.31.

31 ROLFE, WILLIAM J. <u>A Life of William Shakespeare</u>. New York:
    AMS Press.
        Reprint of 1904.7.

32 ROTH, FREDERIC H., Jr. "'Heaven's Center, Nature's Lap': A
    Study of the English Country-Estate Poem of the Seventeenth
    Century." Ph.D. dissertation, University of Virginia.
        Examines the development of the country-house poem,
    explicates some of those poems including "To Penshurst,"
    and speculates "upon the social, economic, architectural,
    historical, and literary forces that helped shape these
    poems."

33 RUSHTON, WILLIAM LOWES. <u>Shakespeare An Archer</u>. New York:
    Haskell House Publishers.
        Reprint of 1897.8.

34 SHAPIRO, HENRY BERMAN. "Ben Jonson and the Truth of Praise."
    Ph.D. dissertation, Columbia University.
        Inquiry into the rhetorical history of the poetry of
    praise.

35 SIMS, JAMES H. Review of <u>Ben Jonson: Selected Works</u>, edited
    by David McPherson. <u>SCN</u> 31, no. 1 (Spring):13.
        An excellent selection of Jonson's works with helpful
    introductory and critical materials. See 1972.28.

36 WARREN, WILLIAM E. "The Love Elegies of Donne and Jonson:
    A Critical Study." Ph.D. dissertation, Ohio State Univer-
    sity.
        "The principal difference between Donne and Jonson as
    elegists is that Donne conceives of the form as essentially
    dramatic. His speakers reveal themselves from the 'in-
    side'; they do not have omniscience over their situations
    and are often not in control of it. Jonson's speakers
    present well controlled discourses."

*37 WHITE, ROBERT B., Jr. "A Reading of Jonson's 'Epitaph on
    Elizabeth, L. H.'" <u>NDEJ</u> 9, no. 1:9-14.

38 WILLIAMS, FRANKLIN B., Jr. Review of Ben Jonson, by Marie-
    Thérèse Jones-Davies. <u>Moreana</u>, 10, no. 39 (September), 24.
        Briefly traces Jonson's indebtedness to Sir Thomas
    more which Mme. Jones-Davies had failed to do. See 1973.17.

39 WOODHEAD, M. R. "Ben Jonson's Cup-Bearer." <u>N&Q</u> 218, no. 7
    (July):262.
        No new biographical information on Hugh Crompton.

1974

1 ANKLESARIA, SHIRIN SAROSH. "Ben Jonson: The Biographical
Tradition and Its Relation to Critical Appraisal." Ph.D.
dissertation, Cornell University.
    A discussion of Jonson's literary reputation in the
seventeenth, eighteenth, and nineteenth centuries compared
to the biographical treatments he was given during the
same time.

2 ANON. "The Fire in Jonson." TLS, 20 September, p. 1020.
    Review of "Ben Jonson: Public Attitudes and Social
Poetry," by L. C. Knights and "'A More Secret Cause':
The Wit of Jonson's Poetry," by Hugh Maclean. It is in
his poetry that Jonson reveals the positive side of his
personality. In this collection of essays Jonson is treat-
ed "as a serious writer, often an uncomfortable one, and
the epithet 'savage' recurs." See 1973.19, 22.

3 ATTRIDGE, DEREK. Well-weighed Syllables: Elizabethan Verse in
Classical Meters. Cambridge: Cambridge University Press,
pp. 127-29.
    From English Grammar one can see that Jonson recognized
the apparently irreconcilable differences between classical
and native traditions of meter.

4 BARISH, JONAS A. Review of "Jonson's Ode to Sir Lucius Cary
and Sir H. Morison," by Ian Donaldson; "Ben Jonson Full
of Shame and Scorn," by William Kerrigan; "Jonson's
Epigrammes: The Named and the Nameless," by Edward B.
Partridge; and "Virtue Reconciled to Pleasure: Jonson's
'A Celebration of Charis', by Richard S. Peterson. RQ 27,
no. 4 (Winter):596-98.
    Donaldson's essay is "an alert and satisfying reading of
the Cary-Morison Ode." Kerrigan has also revealed a greater degree of complexity in this poem than had been previously noted. See 1973.7, 18, 25, 27.

5 BEAURLINE, L. A. "The Selective Principle in Jonson's Shorter
Poems." In Ben Jonson and the Cavalier Poets. Edited by
Hugh Maclean. Norton Critical Edition. New York: W. W.
Norton & Co., pp. 516-25.
    Revision of 1966.2.

6 BEVINGTON, HELEN. "Three Nice People." Atlantic Monthly 233,
no. 2 (February):55-59.
    Excerpts from Beautiful Lofty People. Brief descrip-
tion of Jonson's visit with Drummond.

7   BLOUNT, Sir THOMAS POPE. De Re Poetica, Part 2, New York:
     Garland Press.
          Reprint of 1694.1.

8   BOWDEN, H. S. The Religion of Shakespeare. New York: AMS
     Press.
          Reprint of 1899.3.

9   BROCK, D. HEYWARD, and WELSH, JAMES M. Ben Jonson: A Quadri-
     centennial Bibliography, 1947-1972. Metuchen, N.J.:
     Scarecrow Press, 165 pp.
          An annotated bibliography of articles, notes, books,
     dissertations, and editions with an introduction, "Ben
     Jonson in the Twentieth Century: Some Critical Trends."

10 CARR, JOAN. Review of Ben Jonson, by Marie-Thérèse Jones-
     Davies. RQ 27, no. 3 (Autumn):366-70.
          "Although she [Mme. Jones-Davies] commendably attempts
     to deal with Jonson as both a lyric poet and a dramatist,
     she draws few connections between the two roles." See
     1973.17.

11 CHATTERJEE, VISVANTH. "Ben Jonson as a Literary Critic."
     Essays and Studies (Jadavpur University, Calcutta), no. 2
     (1973-1974 for 1972):27-44.
          A general survey of Jonson's criticism found in Discov-
     eries concluding "We may say that neo-classicism in Eng-
     lish criticism begins with Jonson."

12 CLARK, J. S., and ODELL, J. P. A Study of English and Amer-
     ican Writers. New York: AMS Press.
          Reprint of 1916.4.

13 DAVIDOW, LAWRENCE LEE. "The English Verse Epistle from Jon-
     son to Burns." Ph.D. dissertation, Princeton University.
          The background and development of the verse epistle
     in the seventeenth and eighteenth centuries. Jonson's
     epistles often have ethical themes speaking to the individ-
     ual's social responsibilities.

14 FIRESTINE, MARTHA W. "The Doctrine of Imitation in the English
     Renaissance: Roger Ascham, Sir Philip Sidney, and Ben
     Jonson." Ph.D. dissertation, Indiana University.
          Imitation can be an enriching pattern of poetic develop-
     ment as was the case with Jonson and other Renaissance poets.

15 FRIEDBERG, HARRIS. "Ben Jonson's Poetry: Pastoral, Georgic
     Epigram." ELR 4, no. 1 (Winter):111-36.

1974

> Jonson is a very realistic poet whose appeal lies in "his ability to reflect the world, its brass as well as its gold, not his ability to transcend it."

16 GARDINER, JUDITH K. Review of "Ben Jonson: Public Attitudes and Social Poetry," by L. C. Knights; and "'A More Secret Cause': The Wit of Jonson's Poetry," by Hugh Maclean. SCN 32, no. 4 (Winter):75-76.
    Short abstracts of essays. See 1973.19, 22.

17 GUNN, THOM., ed. Ben Jonson. Poet to Poet. Harmondsworth: Penguin. 208 pp.

18 KELLY, T. J. "Jonson's 'Celebration of Charis.'" CRI 17:120-26.
    "What I find here--unique to Jonson--is a relaxed wit, a sharpness of intelligence coming with the ease of play, and this with a buoyantly relaxed sensuality--which is in the senses not in the head. I get a firm sense that love and love poetry are for people."

19 MACLEAN, HUGH. "Ben Jonson's Timber, 1046-1115, and Falstaff." PLL 10, no. 2 (Spring):202-6.
    2 Henry IV 3, 2, may be an analogue for lines 1110-15 of Discoveries.

20 MARLBOROUGH, HELEN LOUISE. "Ben Jonson and the Poetry of Praise." Ph.D. dissertation, Brown University.
    Jonson's poetry of praise found its way into the various poetic forms--epigram, verse epistle, and ode--some of which are discussed in this study.

21 McPHERSON, DAVID. "Ben Jonson's Library and Marginalia: An Annotated Catalogue." SP 71, no. 5 (December):3-106, 109-10.
    A full list of the extant books from Jonson's personal library with a description of his marginal annotations.

22 NANIA, ANTHONY J. "Ben Jonson's Epigrammes: The Ripest of Studies." Ph.D. dissertation, University of Notre Dame.
    Based upon an understanding of the epigram we can conclude that Jonson's purpose "is to praise virtuous action and blame vicious action in order to define the good man and the ideal commonwealth."

23 OATES, MARY I. "Jonson's 'The Under-Wood," LXX." Expl 33, no. 1 (September), item 6.
    Notes toward an explication of the poem based on the myths Jonson incorporates.

24   PARFITT, G[EORGE] A. E. "Ethical Thought and Ben Jonson's
       Poetry." In Ben Jonson and the Cavalier Poets. Edited by
       Hugh Maclean. Norton Critical Edition. New York: W. W.
       Norton & Co., pp. 507-16.
            Reprint of 1969.18.

25   PARTRIDGE, EDWARD B. "Jonson's Large and Unique View of Life."
       In The Elizabethan Theatre, IV Toronto: Macmillan, pp.
       143-67.
            A wide ranging essay which attempts to answer the ques-
       tion, "Who is Ben Jonson?" Partridge believes that Jonson
       was a very serious man who "shaped his career and his writ-
       ings with a deliberateness that aroused jibes for its self-
       conscious effort and with a courage that helped him endure
       these jibes as well as unpopularity, poverty, and neglect."

26   PASTER, GAIL K. "Ben Jonson and the Uses of Architecture."
       RenQ 27, no. 2 (Summer):306-22.
            Jonson's use of architectural imagery in his prose and
       poetry. Through poetry Jonson rescues architecture from
       the ravages of time.

27   SARAFINSKI, SISTER DOLORES, O. S. B. "Book Length Studies
       of Ben Jonson Since 1919: A Review." RORD 17:67-83.
            Includes some biographies, apparently all books on
       drama, but no studies of the prose and poetry.

28   SCOTT, GEORGE WALTON. Robert Herrick, 1519-1674. New York:
       St. Martin's Press, pp. 50-54, 109-13.
            Describes Jonson and Herrick's friendship and Jonson's
       influence on the younger poet.

29   SMITH, BRUCE R. "Ben Jonson's Epigrammes: Portrait-Gallery
       Theatre, Commonwealth." SEL 14, no. 1 (Winter):91-109.
            Survey of Jonson's debt to Martial and other epigramaticists
       to indicate how Jonson uses and builds upon an earlier
       tradition to develop his own style in commenting on the
       world. "The person who presides over the closed world of
       Jonson's Epigrammes, who marshals fools and heroes in pro-
       cession before us, is a self-assured legislator and judge."

30   SPENCER, T. J. B. "Ben Jonson on His Beloved, the Author Mr.
       William Shakespeare." In The Elizabethan Theatre, IV.
       Toronto: Macmillan, pp. 22-40.
            An explication of Jonson's poem on Shakespeare which is
       not necessarily of pure praise or the highest praise.
       "It is primarily a literary composition, entertainingly
       making use of literary conventions. It is full of wit and
       clever adaptations of Latinate words and thoughts. It

1974

lacks sobriety, and is all the better for that. It is a
poem and not an affidavit."

31   VAN DEN BERG, SARA. "The Play of Wit and Love: Demetrius'
     On Style and Jonson's 'A Celebration of Charis.'" ELH 41,
     no. 1 (Spring):26-36.
        Jonson was influenced by Demetrius's fourth category of
     style--in this poem. It is marked by "humor, urbanity, and
     evanescent surface." The poem is more than just a satire.

32   WALLER, G. F. Review of "Ben Jonson: Public Attitudes and
     Social Poetry," by L. C. Knights; and "'A More Secret Cause:
     The Wit of Jonson's Poetry," by Hugh Maclean. DalR 54, no.
     3 (Autumn):581-82.
        Remarks on an outstanding collection of essays, but won-
     ders why there need be such a recurrent, consistent affir-
     mation of Jonson's literary art. See 1973.19, 22.

33   WALTON GEOFFREY. "The Tone of Ben Jonson's Poetry." In Ben
     Jonson and the Cavalier Poets. Edited by Hugh Maclean.
     Norton Critical Edition. New York: W. W. Norton & Co.,
     pp. 479-96.
        Reprint of 1955.20; 1962.19.

34   WINDT, JUDITH H. "Not Cast in Other Women's Mold: Strong
     Women Characters in Shakespeare's Henry IV Trilogy, Drayton's
     Englands Heroicall Epistles and Jonson's Poems to Ladies."
     Ph.D. dissertation, Stanford University.
        Analysis of poems by Jonson to women who were his friends.

35   ZITNER, S. P. "The Revenge on Charis." In The Elizabethan
     Theatre, IV. Toronto: Macmillan, pp. 127-42.
        Focuses on the forth poem in "A Celebration of Charis,"
     "Her Triumph," placing it in its dramatic context, and
     attempting to perceive the revenge element more clearly.

1975

1   ARMSTRONG, ALAN RICHARD. "The Love Elegy in the English
     Renaissance." Ph.D. dissertation, Cornell University.
        "Jonson, who turned to the elegy unconventionally late
     in his career, reconciled the light elegy with his Horatian
     persona partly by recreating the Augustan conflict between
     the lover's private world of passion and the larger, pub-
     lic sphere of man's life, but using his elegiac persona
     with reflexive irony to communicate the self-deception of
     the lover and the higher claims of truth and virtue."

2   AYO, NICHOLAS. "Jonson's Greek Ode in Roethke." AN&Q 13, no.
    7 (March):107.
        Roethke may have had Jonson's "To the Immortall Memorie
    and Friendship of that Noble Paire, Sir Lucius Cary, and
    Sir H. Morison" in mind when he wrote "I knew a woman."

3   BABINGTON, B. F. "The Image of Money in Ben Jonson." Master's
    thesis, Oxford University.

4   DANIELS, EDGAR F. "Jonson's Epigrams XI ('On something That
    Walkes Some-where') Expl 33, no. 7 (March), item 58.
        Response to 1972.26 and 1973.26. The change of speakers
    in the last line of the poem from courtier to poet illus-
    strates the central wit of the poem.

*5 DELANEY, J. G. P. "A Study of Ben Jonson's Poetic and Moral
    Ideals, with Particular Reference to the Complementary
    Poems." Ph.D. dissertation, University of Edinburgh.

6   DONALDSON, IAN, ed. Introduction to Ben Jonson Poems. London:
    Oxford University Press, pp. xiii-xix.
        Jonson's poems are public and social. They lead us into
    a complete world of fools, princes, corrupters, and Kings.

7   _____. "Jonson's Epigrams CIII ('To Mary Lady Wroth')." Expl
    33, no. 6 (February), item 46.
        Correction of a comment in 1973.8. Lady Mary Wroth's
    father died in 1626, ten years after this poem was first
    published. He was surely not referred to by Jonson as
    deceased as Fellows suggests.

*8 _____. Review of "Ben Jonson: Public Attitudes and Social
    Poetry," by L. C. Knights; and "'A More Secret Cause':
    The Wit of Jonson's Poetry," by Hugh Maclean. Journal
    of the Australasian University Language and Literature
    Association 44:273-75.
        Cited in Modern Humanities Research Association Annual
    Bibliography, 1975. See 1973.19, 22.

9   EARLEY, ROBERT. "Sir Luckless Woo-all's 'Wast Wife' and the
    OED (Jonson's Epigramme XLVI)." ELN 12, no. 4 (June):265-
    68.
        Decayed may be a better definition of "wast" than "worth-
    less," as the OED suggests.

10 FERRIS, DIANE RUTH ANNE. "Ben Jonson: The Road to 1616."
    Ph.D. dissertation, University of Washington.
        Describes Jonson's literary development up to 1616.

1975

11 FERRY, ANNE. "Jonson." In <u>All in War with Time</u>. Cambridge,
      Mass: Harvard University Press, pp. 127-82.
          Jonson looks to his literary heritage for patterns in
      love poetry and seems to find actual living women that fit
      into those traditions.

12 FETROW, FRED M. "Disclaimers Reclaimed: A Consideration of
      Jonson's Praise of Shakespeare." <u>ELWIU</u> 2, no. 1 (Spring):
      23-31.
          An explication of "To the Memory of My Beloved. . . Mr.
      William Shakespeare" which explains how Jonson praises
      Shakespeare and in so doing answers the question why he
      does so.

13 GARDINER, JUDITH K. <u>Craftmanship in Context: The Develop-
      ment of Ben Jonson's Poetry</u>. Studies in English Litera-
      ture, vol. 110. The Hague: Mouton, 208 pp.
          A full treatment of all Jonson's work, but the emphasis
      is on his poetry. <u>The Epigrammes</u>, <u>The Forrest</u>, and <u>Under-
      wood</u> all receive separate chapter treatments. Points out
      the differences between Jonson's earlier and later verse.
      In the earlier poems "Jonson's uncomplicated moral stance
      . . . is based on a rhetoric of praise and blame." In his
      later poetry he had a more flexible attitude toward his
      subject matter.

14 _____. "Jonson's Friend Colby." <u>N&Q</u> 220, no. 6 (July):306-7.
          Suggests Colby of "An Epistle to a Friend to Persuade
      Him to the Wares," was a friend of Sir John Suckling.
      Both were involved in the Dutch wars in 1629.

15 _____. Review of "Ben Jonson: Public Attitudes and Social
      Poetry," by L. C. Knights; and "'A More Secret Cause':
      The Wit of Jonson's Poetry," by Hugh Maclean. <u>ES</u> 56, no.
      4 (August):381.
          An announcement and description which briefly summarizes
      Knights's and Maclean's essays. See 1973.19, 22.

16 _____. "Syntax and the Platonic Ladder: Jonson's 'Though
      Beauty be the Marke of Praise.'" <u>CP</u> 8, no. 1:35-40.
          Jonson places a love triangle: the ideal lady, the poet,
      and the real lady on the Platonic ladder. "The poem's
      'realism,' that is, its balanced tone and precision in
      defining the moral values of the sides of this triangle,
      is connected with its form, especially its syntax, more
      closely than has previously been recognized."

17 GARRISON, JAMES D. <u>Dryden and the Tradition of Panegyric</u>.
      Berkeley: University of California Press, pp. 83-84, 90-95.

Daniel and Jonson using Latin models provide a trad-
itional basis for the development of the panegyric in
English poetry.

18 _____. "Time and Value in Jonson's 'Epistle to Elizabeth,
Countesse of Rutland.'" CP 8, no. 2:53-58.
Although this poem is often not appreciated by critics
or students, it should be. It is "a classical defense of
poetry for a world who measure is gold."

19 HOGAN, JEROME W. "Two Jonson Allusions." N&Q 220, no. 6
(June):248.
Allusions to Jonson's Epigrammes.

20 KAMHOLTZ, JONATHAN ZACHARY. "Ben Jonson and the Poetry of
Praise." Ph.D. dissertation, Yale University.
Jonson works with the tradition of the poetry of praise
suggesting that it is both an imitation and an alternative
to the world.

*21 KAZNOWSKA, A. "Ben Jonson's Grammar in Theory and Practice."
Ph.D. dissertation, Adam Mickiwicz University, Poznzn,
Poland.

22 KNOLL, ROBERT E. Review of "Ben Jonson: Public Attitude and
Social Poetry," by L. C. Knights; and "'A More Secret
Cause': The Wit of Jonson's Poetry," by Hugh Maclean.
Ren&R 11, no. 1:66-68.
Summary of essays. Maclean extends the meaning of decor-
um. It is this grasp of "decorus expression" which con-
stitutes Jonson's wit. See 1973.19, 22.

23 LeCLERCQ, R. V. "The Reciprocal Harmony of Jonson's 'A Celebration of Charis.'" TSLL 16, no. 4 (Winter):627-50.
A generic study closely reasoned to show the intra-
relationships of the lyrics within the total poem.

24 MARBURY, SILVINE SLINGLUFF. "'Let Me Be Horace': The Influence of Horace on Ben Jonson, John Dryden, and Alexander
Pope." Ph.D. dissertation, City University of New York.
Explores the influence of Horace in the seventeenth and
eighteenth centuries and his emphasis on the poet's moral
and artistic integrity.

25 McCLUNG, WILLIAM A., Jr. "Jonson's 'To Penshurst,' 1-5, 99-
102." Expl 33, no. 9 (May), item 78.
Possible oblique reference to Inigo Jones and the most
ostentatious "lantherne" in Elizabethan England.

1975

26 MEDINE, PETER E. "Object and Intent in Jonson's 'Famous
      Voyage.'" <u>SEL</u> 15, no. 1 (Winter):97-110.
          Although the figures satirized in the poem have or had
      an immediate topical interest, they also are symbolic of
      general and broader problems in England. The satire then
      speaks to every level of society and has implications for
      us even today.

27 OATES, MARY I. "'Jonson's Ode Pindarick' and the Doctrine of
      Imitation." <u>PLL</u> 11, no. 2 (Spring):126-48.
          Jonson did not set out to replicate a Pindaric ode in
      English when he wrote "To the Immortall Memorie, and
      Friendship of that Noble Paire, Sir Lucius Cary and Sir H.
      Morison." Instead he selected those elements of the Greek
      model he wished to imitate and built on them a highly suc-
      cessful and original poem.

*28 PARFENOV, A. T. "Marlo, Sekspir, Dzonson Kak Sovremennike."
      <u>Filologiceski Nauki</u> 17, no. 3:88-96.
          Cited in <u>MLA International Bibliography</u>, 1975.

29 PARFITT, GEORGE [A. E.], ed. Preface to <u>Ben Jonson: The Com-
      plete Poems</u>. Harmondsworth: Penguin, pp. 15-22.
          Discusses textual problems in editing Jonson. Includes
      chronology and selected bibliography.

30 POLLOCK, JOHN J. "A Source for Jonson's Epigram LXXV." <u>AN&Q</u>
      13, no. 6 (February):83-84.
          A gloss on the word "Lippe."

31 PRESTON, MICHAEL JAMES. "A Complete Verse Concordance to the
      Non-Dramatic Poetry of Ben Jonson." Ph.D. dissertation,
      Colorado University.
          Old spelling verse concordance arranged by poetry
      groupings, for example, <u>Epigrammes</u>, <u>The Forrest</u>, <u>Under-
      wood</u>, etc.

32 RIDDELL, JAMES A. "Seventeenth-Century Identification of
      Jonson's Sources in the Classics." <u>RenQ</u> 28, no. 2 (Sum-
      mer):204-18.
          Lists sixty-nine passages in Jonson's <u>Workes</u> 1616 which
      were identified in marginalia in three different hands.

33 ROSENBERG, MARVIN. Review of Ben Jonson, by Marie-Thérèse
      Jones-Davies. <u>ELN</u> 12, no. 4 (June):295-96.
          Tribute to an excellent scholarly book. See 1973.17.

34 RUOFF, JAMES E. "Ben Jonson." In <u>Crowell's Handbook of Eliz-</u>
    <u>abethan & Stuart Literature</u>. New York: Thomas Y. Crowell,
    pp. 231-37.
        Comprehensive article on life and works with a selected
    bibliography. Focuses on Jonson's classical mode in all
    his work including, and perhaps most important, his criti-
    cism.

35 STORHOFF, GARY PALMER. "The Verse Epistles of Donne and Jon-
    son." Ph.D. dissertation, University of Connecticut.
        For Donne and Jonson "the verse epistle was a vehicle
    used to express psychological and moral observations in a
    relaxed, honest, intimate manner." They are excellent
    forms of expression based upon established tradition.

36 THOMPSON, DENYS. <u>What to Read in English Literature</u>. London:
    Heinemann, pp. 75-76.
        Jonson's poems "reveal the conversationalist who could
    listen attentively to talk around him."

37 WADSWORTH, RANDOLPH L., Jr. "Jonson's 'Epistle to Mr. Arthur
    Squib.'" <u>Expl</u> 33, no. 5 (January), item 42.
        How much money did Jonson need?

38 WAYNE, DON EDWARD. "Ben Jonson: The 'Anti-Acquisitive
    Attitude' and the Accumulated Discourse: Contribution
    to a Historical Semiotics." Ph.D dissertation, University
    of California at San Diego.
        A semiotic, Marxist, Freudian approach to Jonson.

39 YOUNG, R. V., Jr. "Style and Structure in Jonson's Epigrams."
    <u>Criticism</u> 17, no. 3 (Summer):201-22.
        That the epigrams are didactic does not make them of any
    less interest. "It still must be conceded that the epigram
    form encourages, if it does not demand, wit and concision
    and hence ironic tension . . . Thus the epigrams demonstrate
    that moral conviction and indignation and experiences to
    the same degree as love, or fear, or doubt, and hence
    equally accessible to the poetic imagination.

<u>1976</u>

1 ANON. "Much to Boast of." Review of <u>Ben Jonson: Public</u>
   <u>Poet and Private Man</u>, by George A. E. Parfitt. Economist
   216 (13 November):142.
       Jonson was so great an observer of society that, "any-
   one interested in the four decades that preceded the civil

1976

war could scarcely do better than read Ben Jonson." Parfitt "makes out an excellent case for the importance of Ben Jonson as a spokesman for his own age who has much worth needing to say to ours." See 1976.9.

2   BAMBOROUGH, J. B. Review of "Ben Jonson: Public Attitudes and Social Poetry," by L. C. Knights; and "'A More Secret Cause': The Wit of Jonson's Poetry," by Hugh Maclean. YES 6:246-47.
    Short critical abstracts of the essays noting that they are not for the general reader. See 1973.19, 22.

3   BROCK, D. HEYWARD. Introduction to The Works of Benjamin Jonson, 1616. London: Scolar Press, n.p.
    A discussion of the publication history of Jonson's Workes 1616 and subsequent major editions.

4   GUIBBORY, ACHSAH. "The Poet as Myth Maker: Ben Jonson's Poetry of Praise." ClioI 5, no. 3 (Spring):315-29.
    One of Jonson's concepts of a poet was that of myth maker. On the basis of historical fact he exaggerated the accomplishments of an individual and immortalized him through his poetry. Jonson did not engage in base flattery but rather was writing in an accepted and established tradition.

5   KRIEGER, MURRAY. Theory of Criticism. Baltimore: Johns Hopkins Press, pp. 234-37.
    Discusses the mythefying elements in "Why I write not of love" in "A Celebration of Charis."

6   LIVINGSTON, MARY L. "Ben Jonson: The Poet to the Painter." TSLL 18, no. 3 (Fall):381-92.
    An explication of "My Answer. The Poet to the Painter" with a tightly reasoned discussion of Jonson's aesthetic philosophy.

7   MAJOR, JOHN M. "A Reading of Jonson's 'Epitaph on Elizabeth, L. H.'" SP 73, no. 1 (January):62-96.
    The identity of Elizabeth L. H. will forever remain hidden, and perhaps it is just as well for the poem is "a sad, unflinching, though beautiful comment on death as extinction, oblivion, nothingness, a poem of universal application, with a title that is nearly superfluous."

8   McPHERSON, DAVID. "Ben Jonson Meets Daniel Heinsius, 1613." ELN 14, no. 2 (December):105-9.
    Provides supporting information for the conjecture that Jonson met Daniel Heisius at Antwerp in 1613.

1976

9 PARFITT, GEORGE [A. E.]. <u>Ben Jonson: Public Poet and Private Man</u>. London: J. M. Dent, 181 pp.
   A search for Jonson through his art and life. A study of his total achievement as poet, playwright, critic, and author of <u>Discoveries</u>. Defends Jonson's view of the role of the poet and his heavy use of classical material. Points out that in his poetry we find revealed the more rounded humanistic side of Jonson's personality.

10 PEBWORTH, TED-LARRY. <u>Owen Feltham</u>. Boston: Twayne Publishers, pp. 90-96.
   A discussion of Feltham's "An answer to the ode of Come leave the loathed Stage & c." Describes Feltham's parodic technique and some responses to it.

11 RANDO, SHARON SANDERS. "'On My First Sonne:' The Aesthetic Radical of Cavalier Poetry." <u>CP</u> 9, no. 1 (Spring): 27-30.
   An explication resting upon the confluence of social and personal elements of Jonson's poetic impetus.

12 REEDY, GERARD, S. J. "A Visit to Penshurst." <u>SCN</u> 34, no. 4 (Winter):91-92.
   Describes the author's personal visit to the Sidneys' home which is now open to the public.

13 REES, CHRISTINE. "'Tom May's Death' and Ben Jonson's Ghost: A Study of Marvell's Satiric Method." <u>MLR</u> 71, no. 3 (July):481-88."
   Jonson's presence in the poem is important because he "lends the necessary weight and authority to the judgment being enforced through this satire."

14 SUNDQUIST, ERIK LINDON. "The Old Way, and the True: A Study of Ben Jonson's <u>Epigrammes</u>." Ph.D. dissertation, Columbia University.
   "The reading is based on the principle that occasional poems in a collection affect readers on three mutually interacting levels: as historical documents, as poetic fictions--symbolic examples of wisdom in action--and as components of a progressive unfolding of the character of the speaker."

15 VAN DEN BERG, SARA. "Jonson's 'Und. 28. An Ode.'" <u>Expl</u> 35, no. 2:24-26.
   This poem is not as somber as had been imagined but combines "moral seriousness and comic pragmatism."

1977

<u>1977</u>

1 BLACKBURN, WILLIAM GEORGE. "Perilous Grace: The Poet as Pro-
tean Magician in the Works of Marlowe, Jonson, and Spenser."
Ph.D. dissertation, Yale University.
 Exploration of the theory of the poet as a kind of Pro-
tean magician in Renaissance literature.

2 DONALDSON, IAN. "Jonson and the Moralists." In <u>Two Renais-</u>
<u>sance Mythmakers: Christopher Marlowe and Ben Jonson.</u>
Baltimore: Johns Hopkins University Press, pp. 146-64.
 Ethics in poetry is not simply a matter of preaching
good thoughts. "What delights us in the poetry of Byron,
of Pope, and (I suggest) of Jonson himself is not primarily
the ethical truths, abstractly considered, that their poetry might be thought to convey. It is rather the poets'
deftness of wit, their warmth, their tolerance, their exas-
peration, their alertness to human absurdity, that in diverse and even at times contradictory ways, assure us of
their fundamental humanity, good humor, and good sense."

3 FRENCH, ROBERTS W. "Reading Jonson: Epigrammes 22 and 45."
<u>CP</u> 10, no. 1 (Spring):5-11.
 Explications of "On My First Daughter," and "On My First
Sonne." Both poems "reveal emotion by trying to restrain
it, and failing; they are poems full of conflict and tension."

4 GRUND, GRAY R. "Ben Jonson, John Hoskyns, and the Anti-Ciceronian Movement." <u>SELit</u> 54, nos. 1 & 2 (December):33-53.
 An analysis of the alterations Jonson makes in Hoskyns
when incorporating his ideas in <u>Discoveries</u> to gain further insight into Jonson's part in the anti-Ciceronian movement.

5 HOBSBAUM, PHILIP. "Ben Jonson in the Seventeenth Century."
<u>MQR</u> 16, no. 4 (Fall):405-23.
 Jonson's influence on mid- and late seventeenth-century
poetry.

6 _____. Reviews of "Jonson's Ode to Sir Francis Cary . . . ,"
by Ian Donaldson; "Ben Jonson Full of Shame and Scorn,"
by William Kerrigan; "Ben Jonson: Public Attitudes and
Social Poetry," by L. C. Knights, "'A More Secret Cause':
The Wit of Jonson's Poetry," by Hugh Maclean; "Jonson's
Epigrammes . . . ," by Edward B. Partridge; "Virtue Reconciled to Pleasure . . . ," by Richard S. Peterson; and
<u>Craftsmanship in Context</u>, by Judith K. Gardiner. <u>RES</u> 28,
no. 109 (February):86-93.

A wide ranging review article with commentary on individual essays as well as complete volumes. Of Miss Gardiner's work notes that she "provides many valuable insights, most strikingly into Jonson's achievement as a love poet in the Charis poems and the elegies. She has learning and sensitivity, and is never self-paradingly ingenious." See 1973.7, 18, 19, 22, 25, 27; 1975.13.

7   JOHNSON, PAULA. "Ben Jonson's Amorous Alternative." CEA 39, no. 2:20-24.
      Jonson rejects traditional love poetry for social truth.

8   LAVINGER, ANN JACOBSON. "The Sylva and Civilizing Form in Ben Jonson's The Forrest and The Under-wood." Ph.D. dissertation, Princeton University.
      Examination and clarification of some of the literary issues raised "when Jonson's poetry is considered as an example of the literary genre of the Sylva."

9   LEMLY, JOHN. "Masks and Self-Portraits in Jonson's Late Poetry." ELH 44, no. 2 (Summer):248-66.
      In his later poetry Jonson turns inward, further removed from his audience, and his poetry benefits greatly for it.

10 McCLUNG, WILLIAM A., Jr. The Country House in English Renaissance Poetry. Berkeley: University of California Press, 192 pp.
      A thorough study of this subgenre in seventeenth- and eighteenth-century poetry. The background and development of the poetry with an illustrated explanation of country-house architecture. "We must abandon, in my opinion, the attractive thesis that Jonson speaks for a preindustrial society and is opposed to one based upon the surplus wealth of capitalism. . . ."

11 NEWTON, RICHARD C. "'Ben./Jonson': The Poet in the Poems." In Two Renaissance Mythmakers: Christopher Marlowe and Ben Jonson. Baltimore: John Hopkins University Press, pp. 165-95.
      Looks at the influence of Sir Francis Bacon and Sir Philip Sidney on Jonson's poetry and personality.

12 PARKER, R. B. Review of Ben Jonson: A Quadricentennial Bibliography, 1497-1972, by D. Heyward Brock and James M. Welsh. MLR 72, no. 2 (April):396-97.
      Notes some omissions and errors in this "very helpful research tool." See 1974.9.

1977

13   RICHMOND, H. M.   Review of "Jonson," by Ann Ferry.   MLR 72,
     no. 2 (April):394-96.
          This book further documents the trend toward profession-
     alism in the study of literature.   "Too often the full text
     of a poem is followed by a long summary, followed in turn
     by a complete requotation in fragments each with its own
     local summary and analysis, with later recapitulations in
     other contexts."   See 1975.11.

14   SADLER, LYNN.   Thomas Carew.   Boston: Twayne Publishers, pp.
     91-93.
          Discussion of Carew's poetic comments on Jonson.

15   WADDINGTON, RAYMOND B.   Review of "Jonson," by Ann Ferry.
     JEGP 76, no. 1 (January):134-36.
          "Jonson has been least-favored with high quality crit-
     icism; and Ferry adds to its body with perceptive discus-
     sion of some poems praising noblewomen as well as the 'aged
     lover' group."   See 1975.11.

16   WALLS, KATHRYN.   "The 'Just Day' in Jonson's "On My First
     Sonne.'"   N&Q 212, no. 2 (April):136.
          Possible allusion to Deuteronomy 15: 1-2.

17   WICKENHEISER, ROBERT J.   "George Herbert and the Epigrammatic
     Tradition."   GHJ 1, no. 1:39-56.
          The relationship of Jonson and Herbert in the development
     of the epigram.   An effort to define the epigram and to
     separate Jonson's epigrams from his short lyrics which he
     called epigrams.

18   WILLIAMS, WILLIAM P.   "Chetwin, Crooke, and the Jonson Folios."
     SB 30:75-95.
          Reexamination and reinterpretation of the confusing
     history of the 1640 Folio edition of Jonson's Works.

19   WILLIAMSON, C. F.   Review of Ben Jonson Poems, by Ian Donald-
     son.   RES 28, no. 111 (August):340-42.
          Welcomes a volume that should bring some well deserved
     recognition to Jonson's nondramatic poetry which "has a
     centrality in the tradition of seventeenth- and eighteenth-
     century poetry that could hardly be claimed for Spenser or
     Donne or even Milton."   See 1975.6.

1978

1   BATES, STEVEN L., and ORR, SIDNEY D., comps.   A Concordance
     to the Poems of Ben Jonson.   Athens: Ohio University Press,
     878 pp.

Computerized concordance based on 1947.5.

2 _____. Review of <u>Ben Jonson Poems</u>, by Ian Donaldson; and
   <u>Ben Jonson: The Complete Poems</u>, by George A. E. Parfitt.
   <u>RQ</u> 31, no. 4 (Winter):672-74.
   Comparison of two complete editions of Jonson's poetry,
   both of which bring a welcomed recognition of Jonson's
   nondramatic work. See 1975.6, 29.

3 BLISSETT, WILLIAM. Review of <u>Ben Jonson: Public Poet and
   Private Man</u>, by George A. E. Parfitt. <u>RQ</u> 31, no. 2 (Summer):256-57.
   Balanced analysis of Parfitt's book which is "plainly
   written and without mystification," but which expects of
   the reader "considerable knowledge of Jonson's life and
   works." See 1976.9.

4 BROCK, D. HEYWARD. "Jonson and Donne: Structural Finger-
   printing and the Attribution of Elegies XXXVIII-XLI."
   <u>PBSA</u> 72:519-27.
   Supports Evelyn Simpson's conclusions in 1939.12 through
   clause-analysis of questionable poems.

5 CHALFANT, FRAN C. <u>Ben Jonson's London: A Jacobean Place
   Name Dictionary</u>. Athens: University of Georgia Press,
   215 pp.
   A glossary of place names of London to which Jonson
   alludes in his plays, poems, and masques. See also 1971.5.

6 CLARK, IRA. "Ben Jonson's Imitation." <u>Criticism</u> 20 no. 2
   (Spring):107-27.
   Jonson's concept of imitation is "a personal and poetic
   re-creation of a model predecessor, a reforming of one's
   self and words according to patterns from the past, which
   might transcend both present and past."

7 DANIELS, EDGAR F. "Jonson's 'To Heaven,' 14." <u>Expl</u> 36, no.
   3:12-13.
   Explains syntax and diction in lines 13-14.

8 DiCESARA, MARIO A., AND FOGEL, EPHIM, comps. <u>A Concordance
   to the Poems of Ben Jonson</u>. Ithaca, N.Y.: Cornell University Press, 881 pp.
   Computerized concordance based upon 1947.5.

9 DRYDEN, JOHN. <u>An Evenings Love, or The Mock Astrologer</u>. In
   <u>The Works of John Dryden</u>. Vol. 10. Edited by John Loftis
   et al. Berkeley: University of California Press.
   Reprint of 1671.1.

1978

10   _____. Of Dramatick Poesie, An Essay. In The Works of John
      Dryden. Vol. 17. Edited by John Loftis et al. Berkeley:
      University of California Press.
           Reprint of 1668.1.

11   _____. The Conquest of Granada: The Second Part. In The
      Works of John Dryden. Vol. 11. Edited by John Loftis et
      al. Berkeley: University of California Press.
           Reprint of 1672.1.

12   INGRAM, R. W. John Marston. Boston: Twayne Publishers, pp.
      43-45.
           Consideration of the roles of Marston and Jonson during
      the poets' war.

13   KOPPEL, CATHERINE CONSTANTINO. "'Of Poets and Poesy': The
      English Verse Epistle, 1595-1640." Ph.D. dissertation,
      University of Rochester.
           Establishes a working definition of the verse epistle;
      discusses the poetic criticism embodied in the epistle
      and the multiple audience to which the author was speaking.

14   KRONENFELD, J. C. "The Father Found: Consolation Achieved
      Through Love in Ben Jonson's 'On My First Sonne.'" SP
      75, no. 1 (January):64-83.
           A tightly reasoned explication based upon a broad under-
      standing of the cultural beliefs surrounding the poem.
      Jonson finds consolation in accepting his son's physical
      death and relying upon the love embodied in his memory.

15   MARSTTI, ARTHUR F. Review of "Jonson and the Moralists,"
      by Ian Donaldson; and "'Ben./Jonson': The Poet in the
      Poems," by Richard C. Newton. RQ 31, no. 4 (Winter):
      656-58.
           Brief critical examination of these "critically percep-
      tive and elegant essays." See 1977.2, 11.

16   PATTERSON, ANNABEL M. Marvell and the Civic Crown. Princeton,
      N.J.: Princeton University Press, pp. 51-55.
           Compares Jonson's "An Epistle to Master John Selden" to
      Marvell's "Epitaph Upon--, an unnamed lady." What dis-
      tinguishes the two "are the tensions which underlie the
      rhetorical act of praise."

17   SQUIER, CHARLES L. Sir John Suckling. New York: Twayne
      Publishers, pp. 107-8.
           Compares Jonson's stanza "Have you seene but a bright
      Lillie grow," from "A Celebration of Charis" with Suckling's
      parody, "Has't thou seen the Doun in th'air."

18 SELDEN, RAMAN. <u>English Verse Satire 1590-1765</u>. London:
     George Allen & Unwin, pp. 74-81.
          Jonson's satire moved back and forth between the Horatian
     and the Juvenalian. However, "his stylistic ideal is always
     expressed in terms of balanced plainness and the avoidance
     of pedantry and extremes."

19 TEAGUE, FRANCIS. "Ben Jonson." <u>LCUT</u> 10:55-57.
          Description and reproduction of William Dobson's por-
     trait of Jonson now in the Iconography Collection of the
     Humanities Research Center, University of Texas at Austin.

20 VAN DEN BERG, SARA. "'The Paths I Meant unto Thy Praise':
     Jonson's Poem for Shakespeare." <u>ShakS</u> 11:207-18.
          Jonson "channels rivalry into praise and finds with
     integrity a perspective that is sympathetic to Shakespeare
     and that simultaneously justifies his own poetic methods
     and principles."

21 WOODS, SUSANNE. "Ben Jonson's Cary-Morison Ode: Some Obser-
     vations on Structure and Form." SEL 18, no. 1 (Winter):57-
     74.
          Although it is helpful to understand the principles of
     the Pindaric ode, Jonson's poem can be appreciated as an
     excellent example of a poet working within a tradition but
     rising above it. "Jonson's Pindaric ode achieves its own
     voice, statement, and power from its fidelity to and tran-
     scendence of its models."

Index